Effective Writing

Effective Writing

A Handbook for Finance People

First Edition

Claire B. May
The Art Institute of Atlanta

Gordon S. May, CPA
University of Georgia

Joseph D. Andrew, Jr.
BIA Consulting, Inc

Prentice Hall, Upper Saddle River, NJ 07458

Executive Editor: Annie Todd
Managing Editor: Diane deCastro
Editorial Assistant: Fran Toepfer
Editor-in-Chief: P. J. Boardman
Executive Marketing Manager: Beth Toland
Production Editor: Susan Rifkin
Managing Editor of Production: Dee Josephson
Manufacturing Buyer: Lisa DiMaulo
Manufacturing Supervisor: Paul Smolenski
Manufacturing Manager: Vincent Scelta
Design Manager: Patricia Smythe
Cover Design: Lorraine Castellano
Cover Illustration: Don Baker
Full Service Composition: Pine Tree Composition, Inc.

Printed in the United States of America

10 9 8 7 6 5 4 3 2 1

Library of Congress Cataloging-in-Publication Data

May, Claire B.
    Effective writing : a handbook for finance people / Claire B. May,
Gordon S. May, Joseph D. Andrew, Jr.—1st ed.
      p.   cm.
    Includes index.
    ISBN 0–13–759408–9 (paper)
    1. English language—Business English. 2. Finance—Authorship–
Problems, exercises, etc. 3. Business writing—Problems,
exercises, etc. I. May, Gordon S. II. Andrew, Joseph D.
III. Title.
PE1479.B87M36   1999
808′.042′024332—dc21   98–36415
                                                          CIP

Prentice-Hall International (UK) Limited, *London*
Prentice-Hall of Australia Pty. Limited, *Sydney*
Prentice-Hall Canada Inc., *Toronto*
Prentice-Hall Hispanoamericana, S.A., *Mexico*
Prentice-Hall of India Private Limited, *New Delhi*
Prentice-Hall of Japan, Inc., *Tokyo*
Simon & Schuster Asia Pte. Ltd., *Singapore*
Editora Prentice-Hall do Brasil, Ltda., *Rio de Janeiro*

Claire B. May, Ph.D.

Claire B. May is on the faculty of The Art Institute of Atlanta. She was for many years a communication specialist at the J.M. Tull School of Accounting at the University of Georgia. She has taught professional writing at the University of Georgia, at the University of South Alabama, and in training programs for major corporations. She frequently speaks to groups of accounting educators and professionals about the integration of writing skills into the accounting curriculum and has co-authored several articles on the subject with Gordon May. The widely used accounting version of this book, which she coauthors with Gordon May, is now in its fifth edition.

Gordon S. May, Ph.D., CPA

Gordon S. May is on the faculty of the J.M. Tull School of Accounting. He has many years of experience in integrating writing skills into accounting courses and has co-authored several articles on the subject with Claire May as well as the accounting version of this book which is now in its fifth edition.

Joseph D. Andrew, Jr.

Joseph Andrew Jr. is a Senior Financial Analyst with BIA Consulting, Inc., a financial consulting firm in Chantilly, Virginia. As an analyst with BIA, Joe performs asset and stock valuations, business plan analyses, industry studies, and litigation support functions for companies in the radio, television, paging, cellular phone, and related industries. Prior to joining BIA Joe served as the chief financial officer for X-Change Software, Inc., a startup software development firm in Oakton, Virginia. In addition to managing corporate finances Joe teaches graduate courses for Webster University of St. Louis, Missouri, dividing his time between the university's Washington, D.C. campus and its international campus in Hamilton, Bermuda. His published works include this book and *Financial Management: Principles and Practice* with Dr. Tim Gallagher of Colorado State University.

The authors' partnership in this book's creation represents a unique opportunity for readers to experience the best of two worlds—the May's development of the principles and techniques of writing and Joe's real world financial orientation. Their combined experience ensures that readers will learn about financial communication in an innovative, up-to-date, and relevant manner.

Brief Contents

Contents

3

The Flow of Thought: Organizing for Coherence   25

4

A Sense of Style: Writing with Conciseness and Clarity   46

5

Standard English: Grammar, Punctuation, and Spelling   74

6

Format for Clarity: Document Design   98

7

Financial Research   111

Part II   BUSINESS DOCUMENTS

Part III   WRITING AND YOUR CAREER

12

Writing for Employment:
Résumés and Letters   211

13

Writing for Publication   223

Part IV   ORAL PRESENTATIONS

14

Oral Presentations   227

Index   251

Preface

Effective Writing: A Handbook for Finance People is designed to help finance students and practitioners improve their communication skills. This handbook can be used as a supplementary text for regular finance courses, as a text in a finance communication course, or as a text in a business communication or technical writing course when these courses include finance students. It is also a useful desk reference or self-study manual for finance professionals.

Effective Writing guides the writer through all the stages of the writing process: planning, including analysis of audience and purpose; generating and organizing ideas; writing the draft; revising it for readable style and correct grammar; and designing the document for effective presentation. In addition to these basic writing principles, the book includes chapters for writing letters, memos (including e-mail), reports, and other formats used by finance professionals in actual practice. Throughout the text, *Effective Writing* stresses coherence, conciseness, and clarity as the most important qualities of the writing done by professionals in finance.

To supplement the instruction on writing effectively, we have included a chapter about oral presentations. Chapter 14 discusses preparation presentations, techniques of effective delivery, and special considerations for financial presentations.

We have also included a special section called "Writing and Your Career." In this section you will find a chapter about writing for professional examinations (including the CFA and CFM exams), a chapter about writing résumés and letters of application, and a chapter about writing for publication.

A special feature of this book is the section about financial research. Here you will find valuable reference material on such topics as

- Where to find financial information (including Internet sites)
- How to write citations of financial sources (including Internet sources)

Exercises and assignments appear throughout *Effective Writing* and reinforce the concepts covered in the text. Some exercises have answers within the text for independent review. The Instructor's Manual contains answers to many other exercises. Most chapters include topics for writing or speaking assignments. The assignments, like the illustrations in the text, focus on finance concepts and situations and thus will seem relevant and familiar to those studying and practicing finance.

Effective Writing can be used in conjunction with traditional finance courses. Instructors can assign cases and topics for research based on the finance concepts being studied in class, or they can use the assignments provided in this handbook. Students can then analyze the finance problem, research the literature if necessary, and prepare answers according to an assigned format such as a letter, technical memo, formal report, or oral presentation. This handbook guides students toward principles of effective writing and speaking. Instructors can then evaluate students' performance based on the criteria discussed in the text and in the Instructor's Manual.

The Instructor's Manual contains suggestions for everyone wishing to improve the communication skills of finance people, whether in a regular finance course or in a course devoted to communication. The manual includes topics such as motivating students to improve their communication skills, designing assignments, and evaluating performance. The manual also contains chapter commentaries and masters for transparencies and handouts.

We hope that this book will help those preparing to enter the profession and those already in practice to achieve greater success through effective communication.

The authors gratefully acknowledge the help of the editors, assistants, reviewers, colleagues, students, friends, relatives, and others without whom the production of this book would not have been possible. In particular we would like to thank Diane deCastro, Managing Editor, Taxation and Accounting at Prentice Hall, for shepherding the work through development and production. Much of the material in this book was drawn from Prentice Hall's *Effective Writing: A Handbook for Accountants, fourth edition,* by Claire and Gordon May, and we are especially grateful to the publishers for permission to use that work.

Claire B. May

Gordon S. May

Joseph D. Andrew Jr.

1

Finance People as Communicators

The ability to communicate effectively, whether through speaking or writing, is essential to success in the finance profession. Unfortunately, some students and financial professionals lack the skills they need to be effective communicators. Time and again, studies show that a major criticism of college graduates is that they do not speak or write well.[1]

Because the ability to communicate effectively plays an important part in a finance person's success on the job, many employers screen prospective financial professionals for skills in oral and written communication. Corporate chief financial officers (CFOs) often view the ability to write and speak effectively as being more important than the ability to use computers or to solve math problems.[2]

Finance people need good communication skills to get a good job and to keep that job after they're hired. Of course, "communication skills" is a broad area. It includes formal and informal oral presentations, interpersonal communication, reading and listening, and many other skills. Because this book is primarily about writing, let's look further at some of the types of documents finance people write on the job.

WHAT DO FINANCE PEOPLE WRITE?

No matter what kind of practice finance people have, writing is an essential part of the job. For example, a financial analyst working for a corporation may write a report for management on how well the company has performed during the past year. People in the finance department may also write letters to the company's customers advising them that payment for credit purchases is due. The quality of writing in this situation may have a direct effect on how promptly the company receives its money. Finance people also write presentations for investors from whom the company is seeking capital. In such a situation, the very survival of the company may depend on how well the finance person states the company's case.

Securities analysts are employed to report on the financial prospects of companies to the investing public. Their work can be seen in such publications as the *Value-Line Investment Survey* and *Standard & Poor's Stock Reports*. The analyst's responsibility to communicate effectively in this capacity is twofold: First, the analyst must accurately report on the situation of the firm under study; second, the analyst must provide investors with the right information upon which to base their investment decision.

Financial planners help individuals with their personal financial affairs. These professionals write out programs for people to follow in order to reach their retirement goals, finance their children's education, and so on. Since the people financial planners deal with are largely untrained in the intricacies of finance, it is particularly important that the planners' programs be written clearly.

No matter what their specialty, all finance people write memos to their supervisors, subordinates, and coworkers to request or provide information. They also write letters to clients, agencies, and a variety of other readers.

To be effective, letters, memos, and reports must be well written. How will clients react if, after reading a letter from their certified financial planner (CFP), they are still confused about what is in their investment portfolio? How will management react to a report that is poorly organized and hard to follow?

HOW WELL DO FINANCE PEOPLE WRITE?

The answer to this question—how well finance people write—has already been suggested by a study in *Financial Practice and Education* reporting that finance students place a relatively low importance on communication skills. At one school, oral and written communication skills were ranked lower in importance than social etiquette.[3] Attitudes such as this are disturbing because unless students believe a skill is important, they're not likely to work toward its mastery.[4]

A letter to *The Wall Street Journal* in 1987 from one of the authors of this book points out the high costs to employers when employees lack adequate writing skills, including the costs of quality control measures to correct faulty writing. In addition, "The expense of hiring and training those who are subsequently fired for [poor writing ability] must surely represent a tremendous waste of resources."[5]

WHAT IS GOOD WRITING?

What is good writing for finance people? The list of tips for writers in Figure 1–1 summarizes many qualities of effective business writing, including writing by finance people. These qualities are stressed throughout this book. Let's examine these tips in a little more detail.

FIGURE 1–1 *Tips for the Effective Writer*

1. *Content:* Be sure that the content is correct and complete. Have you addressed all relevant issues?

2. *Appropriateness for readers:* Write the document with a particular reader in mind. Check that issues are discussed on a level the reader can understand. For most documents, it's better to focus on practical, explicit information and advice related to the case you are discussing, rather than on general financial theory.

3. *Conciseness:* Write as concisely as possible, given the reader's needs and the issues to be addressed.

4. *Clarity:* Develop a style that is clear and readable. Choose words that convey your meaning with precision and clarity.

5. *Coherence:* Structure the document so that it is coherent. The organization should be logical and the train of thought easy to follow. Summarize main ideas near the beginning of the document and begin each paragraph with a topic sentence.

6. *Revision:* Revise the document so that it is polished and professional. It should be free of all spelling errors and typos; grammatical errors should not detract from the message.

The first tip concerns the *content* of the document. You must know what you're talking about, and the information you give should be accurate and relevant.

Writing appropriately for your readers is the second tip for effective writing. The document should be written on a level they understand and find meaningful, and it should anticipate and answer their questions.

The third tip is *conciseness*. Say what needs to be said in as few words as possible. To keep your writing concise, avoid digressions, unnecessary repetition, and wordiness.

Clarity is the next tip. Write as simply as possible, using words and phrases with which the reader is familiar. To improve the clarity of your writing, choose words that mean precisely what you intend so that your sentences convey only one meaning: the meaning you want to convey. Well-structured sentences also contribute to clear writing.

Coherence is the logical, orderly relationship of ideas. Coherent writing is, quite simply, writing that is well organized. The flow of thought is easy to follow and important ideas stand out. To write coherently, you must carefully think through the ideas you wish to convey. The ideas must be arranged logically and then written in a way readers can comprehend. Coherence is the fifth tip for effective writers.

The final tip is to *revise* your writing so that it is polished and professional. Documents should look attractive and be free of grammatical and mechanical errors.

YOU CAN BECOME A GOOD WRITER

With all this talk about the importance of good writing to a successful career in finance, you may feel overwhelmed or discouraged. Many people believe they can never become good writers.

A word of encouragement is in order. Virtually anyone who succeeds in college work has the education and the ability to become at least an adequate writer, and probably even a good one. Problems with writing are often the result of two factors, both of which can be corrected: lack of adequate training in writing skills and lack of self-confidence.

Let's address the latter problem, the poor image some people have of themselves as writers.

One reason to be optimistic about your writing ability is that you've already learned quite a bit about how to write from English courses and other writing classes, as well as from your own experience. Most people are better writers than they realize. They have the potential to become even more effective after they've mastered a few strategies such as the ones we'll cover in this book. As you read this book, note the techniques and principles you already use in your writing. Don't lose sight of your strengths while you work to improve the areas that could be better.

Another reason you should write well as a finance professional is that you will be writing about topics you understand and find interesting. If you have had unpleasant experiences with writing in courses other than finance, the problem may have been that you were writing about topics you weren't particularly interested in or didn't feel qualified to discuss. When we write about subjects we like and understand, it's much easier to write clearly and persuasively.

Finally, you may find it much easier to do the kind of writing recommended in this book because it will be simple, direct writing. Some people believe they must write in long, complicated sentences filled with difficult, "impressive" vocabulary. In fact, just the opposite is true: Effective business writing is written as simply as possible. It is thus easier to do.

WRITING
AND OTHER FORMS
OF COMMUNICATION

Writing is only one of several forms of communication, along with such skills as speaking, reading, listening, and interpersonal communication. In fact, all of these forms of communication work together to determine how well a person gives and receives information. Let's look at how reading, listening, and speaking skills can help you improve your writing.[6]

Reading

Reading affects writing in several ways. Often you will write a memo or letter in response to a written communication from someone else. As a consultant, for example, you may write a letter to clients to answer questions they have posed in a letter to your firm. The ability to read the earlier correspondence carefully is essential to an effective response.

Careful reading is also important when you research finance literature as background for the documents you write. The tax code, government regulations, articles in professional journals, investment publications, and the *The Wall Street Journal* are examples of the material you may have to read to stay informed on finance issues. You will need to understand this material and be able to apply it to particular situations.

You will also read information circulated and stored within your own firm or company, such as client files and memos from colleagues. Reading this material carefully will provide many of the insights and facts you need to deal effectively with situations for which you're responsible.

Listening

Along with reading, the ability to listen carefully determines how well you receive information from others. On the job, you may interact with colleagues, supervisors, subordinates, or clients; at school, you interact with professors and other students. Listening carefully to these people will provide important information you can use as the basis of your writing. It will provide facts about projects you are working on, along with insights into other people's expectations and concerns.

There are many situations in which listening skills contribute to effective writing. Instructions given by the professor in class, interviews with clients, requests from supervisors, and phone conversations with colleagues are a few examples. In all these situations, attentive listening is necessary to hear what people are saying. It's often a good idea to take notes and, when necessary, to ask questions for clarification or additional information.

Speaking

What you write also affects what you say to others. Informally, you may have meetings and conversations to discuss reports or memos you've written. What you write may also be the basis for formal oral presentations before a group. You might make a presentation to a board of directors, senior managers, or members of a professional organization.

WRITING AND DECISION MAKING

Earlier in this chapter, we cited a study showing that many chief financial officers (CFOs) see the need for improved communication skills for those entering the finance profession. These CFOs also identify decision-making skills as essential to successful financial management.

Effective decision-making requires many skills, such as the identification of key issues, research into relevant literature, and the ability to think critically and analytically. At each step of the decision-making process, writing can help you reach sound conclusions.

You can generate ideas on a topic by writing down what you know about that topic, as well as what you have yet to find out. The act of writing about a subject can actually help you clarify your thinking. As one wit has put it, "How do I know what I think until I see what I say?" There's more truth in this quip than might at first be apparent. Research into how people think and learn has shown that writers often generate ideas and improve their insights into a subject as they write down their thoughts.[7]

Writing can help you solve financial problems as well. For example, as you research financial literature, you take notes. You may also write requests to other people for additional information you need in order to solve the problem.

Writing you use to solve problems is writing for yourself. Once the problems have been solved, or at least clearly defined, you can put your insights and conclusions into writing that will help others make financial decisions.

Writing and decision making, then, are often inseparable, interactive processes. Both are essential to the practice of financial management.

In conclusion, remember that finance is a process of analyzing and *communicating* information. Finance people need writing skills for many of their routine professional tasks, whether communicating with investors, management, clients, or fellow professionals. They need to use words effectively and to combine these words into good sentences and paragraphs.

Communication skills pay off in professional advancement. As Zane Robbins of Arthur Andersen & Co. has noted:

> All other things being equal, the professional . . . who can communicate best is likely to progress fastest. Those who are unable to write and communicate effectively often find themselves consigned to the purgatory of technician with little hope for long-term growth.[8]

EXERCISES

Exercise 1–1

Look for examples of effective and ineffective writing in the material you read regularly. Consider letters and memos as well as published professional material such as textbooks, professional articles, and newspaper editorials. Then think about the following questions.

1. What kind of material do you find easiest to read? What are some of the qualities that make this writing readable?
2. Examine closely the writing you find difficult to read. How do you think the writing could be improved?
3. Review the tips for effective writing summarized in Figure 1–1. Do the writing samples you have collected illustrate these qualities of good writing?

Exercise 1–2

Collect samples of your own writing. Analyze your writing, considering the following questions:

1. What kind of response do you usually get from your supervisors, peers, clients, and subordinates? Are readers sometimes uncertain of your meaning?
2. Review the qualities of effective writing summarized in Figure 1–1. Using this list as a benchmark, identify some of the strengths and weaknesses of your own writing.
3. Write a two-paragraph analysis of your writing. The first paragraph should identify the qualities of your writing that make it effective; the second paragraph should discuss what you need to improve. Begin each paragraph with a topic sentence that states the main idea of the paragraph. The first paragraph could begin this way:

My writing is effective in several ways. For example, . . .

Exercise 1–3

If you have the opportunity to talk with financial professionals, ask them about their experiences with writing on the job. Your questions might include these:

- How much writing do they do in a typical day or week?
- What kinds of documents do they write? Who are their readers?
- What kinds of material do they read for their jobs?
- What specific writing skills do they believe are important for finance people?
- What are their pet peeves in the writing done by others?

During your conversations with these finance people, listen carefully to their responses and ask any questions you need for clarification. Later, write notes based on your conversations. Share your notes with your classmates during class discussions.

Exercise 1–4

Assume you are a financial analyst in a major corporation. The CFO, Elaine Peters, has complimented you on the memos you have written. However, Ms. Peters has noticed that some of the firm's other financial analysts do not write very good memos, nor do they believe that effective writing is important.

Write a memo to the other financial analysts in your firm. Discuss why well-written memos are important and suggest some qualities that make the writing effective. Be sure that your own memo illustrates those qualities. You will find suggestions on how to write a memo in chapter 9.

NOTES

1. Lyman W. Porter and Lawrence E. McKibben, *Management Education and Development: Draft or Thrust into the 21st Century?* (New York: McGraw-Hill, 1988). Cited by Julie R. Dahlquist in "Writing Assignments in Finance: Development and Education," *Financial Practice and Education* 5, No. 1 (spring/summer 1995): 107.
2. Graham & Krueger, "What Does a Graduate Need?," *Financial Practice and Education* 6, No. 2 (fall/winter 1996): 60.
3. Graham & Krueger, page 66.
4. Michael B. Paulson and James A. Gentry, "Motivation, Learning Strategies, and Academic Performance: A Study of the College Finance Classroom," *Financial Practice and Education* 5, No. 1 (Spring/Summer 1995): 78–79.
5. Gordon S. May, "No Accounting for Poor Writers," *The Wall Street Journal* (Letter to the editor, May 29, 1987): 27.

6. See Elizabeth E. Orem and Jane O. Burns, "The Problems and Challenges of Teaching Accounting Students to Communicate," *Georgia Journal of Accounting* (Spring 1988): 9–24.

7. Lee Odell, "The Process of Writing and the Process of Learning," *College Composition and Communication* (February 1980): 41–50.

8. H. Zane Robbins, "How to Develop Basic Writing Skills," *The Chronicle* 40, no. 1 (1981): 9.

2

The Writing Process: An Overview

Effective writing, like financial analysis, is a *process*. Like any process, it contains steps that must be followed to achieve the desired result. In financial analysis, the steps include defining the problem or issue to be solved, obtaining data relevant to the issue, and then applying the appropriate financial analysis techniques to arrive at a conclusion. In effective writing, following the proper steps is just as important.

Figure 2–1 summarizes the steps of the writing process. In this chapter, we will discuss the process from beginning to end and show you how to apply the process to overcome much of the anxiety you may feel about writing, including the problem of writer's block. Throughout the chapter, we also discuss how computers, especially word processors, can help you at every stage of the writing process.

GETTING STARTED: IDENTIFYING PURPOSE

The first stage in the writing process—analyzing the purpose of the document—is easy to overlook. When you think about purpose, you decide what you want to accomplish with your letter, memo, or other document. Do you want to provide your readers with information about some topic,

FIGURE 2–1   *The Writing Process*

> *Plan*
>
> - Read the assignment carefully.
> - Analyze the purposes of the document.
> - Identify the financial issues.
> - Analyze the reader's interests, needs, and expectations.
> - Gather and organize material.
>
> *Draft*
>
> - Put the ideas down on paper.
> - Don't stop to edit.
> - Write the parts of the paper in whatever order you wish.
>
> *Revise*
>
> - Revise the document so that it is clear, coherent, and concise.
> - Proofread for grammatical, mechanical, and typographical errors.

answer their questions, recommend a course of action, persuade them to do something, or agree with you on some point?

These are just a few of the purposes a document can have. What is important is to think carefully about the purpose *before* beginning to write. It might be helpful to think of purpose in terms of three categories: to give information about something, to propose a course of action, or to solve a problem. For example, suppose you are the controller for the Hamilton Art Supply Company. Hamilton is considering a purchase of stock from Colors Galore, one of Hamilton's major suppliers of crayons. A report on this possible purchase could have any of the following purposes:

- *To give information:* to inform management of the advantages (or disadvantages) of such a purchase
- *To propose a course of action:* to recommend that Hamilton purchase (or not purchase) the stock
- *To solve a problem:* to suggest a way to finance the purchase

The purpose of the report, or of any writing, determines what material it should contain. If, for example, your purpose is to inform management of the advantages and disadvantages of purchasing Colors Galore stock, your report will most likely contain a discussion of the advantages and disadvantages of the purchase. On the other hand, if your purpose is to suggest a way to finance the purchase, your report would probably contain a list of financing alternatives. That is why defining the purpose of your writing is so important—it determines the content of the document to be created.

Once you have analyzed your purposes carefully, it's a good idea to write them down. Be as specific as possible and try to define the purpose in one sentence. This sentence may later become part of the introduction of the letter, memo, or report.

Two final words about purpose: *be specific.* Remember that you are writing to particular individuals in a particular situation. Relate the purpose of your writing to these people and their concerns. That is, state the purpose in the context of the specific situation rather than in broad, general terms. In the Hamilton Art Supply example you would limit your discussion to the financing alternatives available to Hamilton and those practical for it to consider.

ANALYZING THE READERS

Another important consideration in the planning of a writing task is the identity of the readers. A memo on a highly technical topic would be written one way for a colleague in finance, but another way for a client or manager with only limited knowledge of financial concepts and terminology.

Effective writers analyze the needs and expectations of their readers before they begin to write. In writing a letter or memo, you will probably be writing to a limited number of people, perhaps to only one person. You also know, or can find out, important information about the readers. Again, you must ask certain questions. How much knowledge do the readers have of the subject being discussed? The answer to this question suggests the terms that should be defined, the procedures that should be explained, or the background information that should be provided.

Financial professionals dealing with the public should be particularly careful in analyzing the needs of their readers. A personal investment advisor, for example, might have clients with widely varying experience and knowledge of stocks and bonds. A corporate executive would probably understand such concepts as compound interest and yield to maturity, but a small shopkeeper might not be familiar with them. Business letters to these two clients, even on the same topic, would be written quite differently.

Other factors to consider are the readers' attitudes and biases. Are the readers likely to be neutral to your recommendations, or will they need to be convinced? Remember to write with the readers' interests, needs, and concerns in mind. Ask yourself how the readers will benefit, directly or indirectly, from what you propose. Then ask yourself how you can present your arguments to overcome readers' objections and biases. To answer this last question, you must anticipate readers' questions, research the issues, and then organize your arguments into a convincing sequence.

Two easily overlooked considerations when analyzing readers are tone and style. Some readers react well to an informal, friendly style of writing, but other readers believe that professional writing should be more formal. Whoever your readers are, remember always to be courteous. Whether you write in a technical or simplified style, all readers appreciate (and deserve!) consideration, tact, and respect.

Word choices also contribute to an effective writing style. Many readers might find this sentence troubling:

> An efficient chief financial officer dictates letters to his secretary; she then prepares the letters for his signature.

Some readers might argue that the choice of pronouns (chief financial officer/he, secretary/she) implies a gender bias. Use plural nouns and pronouns to avoid gender bias:

> Efficient chief financial officers dictate letters to their secretaries, who then prepare the letters for their supervisors' signatures.

Sometimes your readers will have additional expectations about your documents. In a classroom situation, the instructor will usually give directions for your papers, such as length, format, and due date. The instructor expects you to follow these directions. How well you do so usually affects your grade.

Readers' expectations are also important when you write on the job. Managers in some firms expect in-house memos and reports to follow certain conventions of format, organization, and style. If you work for such a firm, your memos and reports will seem more professional—and be more effective—if they are consistent with these conventions.

Tone and style conventions may actually be a matter of company or firm policy. Policies may govern how certain documents are written or the procedures they must go through for approval. Many corporations will not let new staff send letters to customers or suppliers unless they are first approved by a manager. If you were a new staff member in such a firm, you might draft the letter, but a manager would review it and possibly ask you to make revisions. Moreover, for certain documents, such as collection letters or financial status reports, the actual language used in the letter might be determined by firm policy. The manager will expect you to follow these policies with great care.

In the situation above, there are actually two readers: the manager who reviews and approves the letter, and the customer or supplier who receives it. Such letters should be written on a technical level that is appropriate for the customer or supplier, but it should also meet the expec-

FIGURE 2–2   *Questions to Ask Yourself When Planning Your Writing*

Consider these questions as you plan the documents you write:

1. Answer after you read and analyze the assignment:

   - What are the finance issues in this case?
   - What literature will I research to resolve these issues?
   - Who are the readers of this document?
   - What are the readers' concerns?
   - What are the purposes of this document?

2. Answer after you research and analyze the case:

   - What are the main points (conclusions) I need to make in this document?
   - What material should I conclude to make these conclusions clear and meaningful to the readers?

tations of the manager. Analyzing readers' needs, interests, and expectations is obviously more complex when there are several readers. Think carefully about the different readers and use your best judgment to meet the expectations of them all.

Analyzing readers' needs and expectations is an important part of the preparation for writing. Planning, which considers both your audience and your purpose, is the first guideline for effective writing:

1. **Analyze the purpose of the writing and the needs and expectations of the readers.**

Figure 2–2 summarizes questions you can ask yourself to help you plan your writing.

GETTING YOUR IDEAS TOGETHER

Once you have evaluated the purpose of the writing and the needs of the readers, you are ready for the second stage in the writing process: gathering information and organizing the ideas you want to present. This step may be quick and simple. For a short letter you can write without further research, organizing your ideas may involve only a short list of the main topics you wish to include in the letter, perhaps one topic for each paragraph.

For much of the writing you do, gathering information and organizing may be a more complicated process, one involving a great deal of thought, and perhaps some research as well. Let's look at some techniques you can use.

Gathering Information

Before you begin to write the document, be sure you have all the information you need and that this information is accurate. Two useful ways to gather this information are to check the work that has already been done and to find out new information.

For many projects, there may already be some information available. If you're working on a stock research report, for example, there may be information available from the financial press as well as from previous reports. Explore these sources of information fully: review the files carefully and, when possible, talk with the people who have already worked on the project.

Sometimes you may need to do additional research. This may involve background reading on a technical topic or a careful review of financial information contained in a company's annual report. As you read this material, take notes carefully and be alert for information that will help you when you write.

This research may also require you to interview people who will be affected by the project you're working on. Suppose you're writing a report to propose a new time-accounting system for your company. You can gain important insights into topics your report should cover by talking with the people who would be affected by the proposed system. You can learn what they want the system to accomplish or what their questions about it are.

Generating Ideas

Once you have gathered the information you need, you're ready to begin the next phase of the writing process: deciding exactly what to say.

If you have not already written your statement of purpose, now is the time to do so. Try to break up the purpose into several subtopics. Suppose the purpose of a company memo you are planning is to recommend that the company update its computerized accounting system. The statement of purpose for this memo could specify the different accounting jobs for which the expanded system would be useful, or outline its major advantages.

Another useful technique for generating ideas is brainstorming. With this technique, you think about your topic and write down all the ideas that come to you, in whatever order they come. Don't worry about organizing the ideas or evaluating them. Just write them down. Later you can consider how these ideas fit into the skeletal outline that you developed when you analyzed the purposes of the document you are writing.

You may find brainstorming easier to do at the computer using a word processor. As you type in the key words and phrases that occur to you, it's possible that the phrases will start to become sentences and the sentences will flow together to become paragraphs. Most people can type faster than they can write with a pencil or pen. You may find that the faster you record your ideas, the more freely the ideas flow. Thus, a word processor can be a valuable tool for generating ideas.

Arranging Ideas: Organization

Once you've decided what you want to say, consider how best to arrange these ideas so that the readers will find them easy to follow. In other words, think about how the document will be organized.

Much of the work you've already done will help you decide on the best pattern of organization. You may be able to use your statement of purpose as the basis of your organization, or your paper may be structured so that the reader's major concerns will be your principle of organization—that is, each concern might be a major division of your paper. Some documents can be organized according to the financial issues they address.

When considering all these approaches to organization, and possibly deciding among them, remember this principle: The document's organization should be determined by the needs and interests of your readers. Arrange your ideas in the order that they will find most helpful and easiest to follow.

There are a few other principles of organization to consider. First, nearly all writing has the same basic structure:

- *Introduction*: identifies the subject of the document and tells why it was written. Sometimes the introduction also provides background information about the topic or stresses its importance. You may also use the introduction to build rapport with your reader, perhaps by mentioning a common interest or concern or referring to previous communication on the topic.
- *Concise statement of the main ideas*: summarizes explicitly main ideas, conclusions, or recommendations. This part of a document may be part of the introduction or a separate section. It can be as short as a one-sentence statement of purpose or as long as a three-page executive summary.
- *Development of the main ideas*: includes explanations, examples, analyses, steps, reasons, factual details. This part of an outline or paper is often called the body.
- *Conclusion*: brings the paper to an effective close. The conclusion may restate the main idea in a fresh way, suggest further work, or summarize recommendations, but an effective conclusion avoids unnecessary repetition.

Later chapters of this handbook will discuss more fully this basic structure as it is used for particular kinds of writing.

Another principle of effective organization is to arrange ideas in a logical order, perhaps simply according to their importance.

One final word about organization. Once you've decided how to arrange your ideas, it's a good idea to actually write an outline, if you haven't already done so. Having an outline before you as you draft your paper will help you keep the paper on track. You'll be sure to include all the information you had planned and avoid getting off the subject.

The guidelines for effective writing can now be expanded:

1. **Analyze the purpose of the writing and the needs and expectations of the readers.**
2. **Organize your ideas so that readers will find them easy to follow.**

WRITING THE DRAFT

The next major step in the writing process is writing the draft. The purpose of this step is to get the ideas down on paper (or on a disk). Spelling, punctuation, and style are not important in the draft. What is important is to write the ideas down so that later you can polish and correct what you have written.

If you did your brainstorming at the computer, you may already have parts of your draft if the list of ideas you began with evolved into sentences or paragraphs as you typed.

An excellent way to start composing your draft is to use the outline you prepared during the planning step. (You did prepare an outline, didn't you? If not, be sure to do so before beginning your draft.) The outline will guide you as you write. However, you may decide to change the outline as you go, omitting some parts that no longer seem to fit or adding other ideas that now seem necessary. Changing the outline is fine, because when you revise the draft later you can make sure your thoughts are still well organized.

Although you will use your outline as a guide to the ideas you want to include in your draft, you may find it easier to write the various parts of the document in a different order from the one in the outline. Some people find introductions hard to write, so they leave them until last. You may also choose to write the easiest sections of your draft first, or you may start writing some parts of the draft while you are still getting the material together for other parts. If you're composing at a computer, rearranging the parts of your paper is particularly easy because word processing programs enable you to move blocks of text.

One final word of advice about the draft stage: Don't allow yourself to get stuck while you search for the perfect word, phrase, or sentence. Leave a blank space or write something that is more or less what you mean. You'll probably be able to find the right words later.

REVISING THE DRAFT

The third stage in the writing process is the revision of the draft. In this step, you check your grammar, polish your style, and make a final check to see that the ideas are effectively and completely presented. As you revise, read the document from the reader's point of view.

You'll need to revise most of your writing more than once—perhaps even three or four times. The key to revising is to let the writing get cold between revisions; a time lapse between readings enables you to read the draft more objectively and to see what you have actually said, instead of what you meant to say. Ideally, revisions should be at least a day apart.

Another technique is to have a colleague review the draft for both the content and the effectiveness of the writing. Choose a reviewer who is a good writer and evaluate the reviewer's suggestions with an open mind.

If you've put your draft on a word processor, you might check the text with an editing program, grammar checker, or spelling checker. These programs identify certain errors in style, such as sentences that are too long and paragraphs that use the same word too often. Programs are also available that identify some mistakes in punctuation and grammar as well as most misspelled words. However, a word of caution is in order about these style analyzers, grammar checkers, and spelling checkers: they're not infallible. They can't catch all the weaknesses in your text, and sometimes they flag problems that aren't really there. If you use these programs to analyze your writing, you still have to use your own judgment about what changes to make. Figure 2–3 illustrates this point admirably.

FIGURE 2–3 *Spelling Checkers Don't Catch Everything!*

A Tribute to Spelling Checkers

I have a spelling checker, it came with my PC
It plane lee marks four my revue miss steaks aye can knot sea.
Eye ran this poem threw it. Your sure reel glad two no
Its vary polished in it's weigh. My checker tolled me sew.
A checker is a bless sing. It freeze yew lodes of thyme.
It helps me right awl stiles two reed, and aides me when aye rime.
Each frays come posed up on my screen eye trussed too bee a joule.
The checker pours o'er every word, to cheque sum spelling rule.
Be fore a veiling checkers, hour spelling mite decline.
And if were lacks or have a laps, we wood be maid to wine.
Butt now bee cause my spelling is checked with such grate flare
Their are know faults with in my cite. Of non eye am a wear.
Now spelling does not phase me. It does not bring a tier.
My pay purrs awl due glad den with wrapped words fare as hear.
To rite with care is quite a feet of witch won should be proud.
And wee mussed dew the best wee can sew flaws are knot aloud.
Sow eye can sea why aye dew prays such soft ware four pea seas
And why I brake in two averse by righting want too pleas.

(Written by Jerrold H. Zar, Dean of the Graduate School, Northern Illinois University. Reprinted with permission from the Journal of Irreproducible Results.)

Another revision technique that works with a word-processed text is to print the document and edit the hard copy by hand. Then make the revisions on your disk the next time you work at the computer. Some writers find that they revise more effectively if they work with a hard copy rather than text on a screen.

In sum, if you've put the draft on a word processor, the revision will be much easier and quicker than if you have to revise by hand and then retype the entire manuscript. With a few commands to the computer, you can add text, delete it, or rearrange it. You can insert sentences, change wording, and move paragraphs around. You can make both minor and major changes to your draft, all the time preserving the remainder of your draft without retyping.

The next four chapters of the handbook discuss what to look for when putting your writing in final form.

THE FINAL DRAFT

After you have polished the style and organization of the paper, it is ready to be put into its final form. With this step, you consider questions of document design, such as the use of headings, white space, and other elements of the paper's appearance.

Proofreading is also important at this stage. Here are some suggestions for effective proofreading:

1. Proofreading is usually easier if you leave some time between typing and looking for errors. You will see the paper more clearly if you have been away from it for a while.

2. If you've drafted your paper on a word processor, use a spelling checker program to eliminate spelling and typographical errors. Remember that such a program will not find errors of word choice; for example, it will not distinguish between homonyms such as *their* and *there* or *affect* and *effect*.

3. If you don't have access to a word processor, use a dictionary to look up any word that could possibly be misspelled. If you are a poor speller, have someone else read the paper for spelling errors.

4. If you know you tend to make a certain type of error, read through your paper at least once to check for that error. For example, if you have problems with subject-verb agreement, check every sentence in your paper to be sure the verbs are correct.

5. Read your paper backwards, sentence by sentence, as a final proofreading step. This technique will isolate each sentence and should make it easier to spot errors you may have overlooked in previous readings.

We can now summarize the writing process in three steps:

1. **Analyze the purpose of the writing and the needs and expectations of the readers.**

2. **Organize your ideas so that readers will find them easy to follow.**

3. **Write the draft and then revise it to make the writing polished and correct.**

These steps complete the summary of the writing process as described in Figure 2–1. Now let's turn to some issues that affect the application of the writing process.

DEALING WITH WRITER'S BLOCK

Writer's block is a problem all of us face at some time or another. This problem occurs when we stare at blank paper or at a blank screen with no idea of how to get started. The ideas and the words just don't come.

Many of the techniques already discussed in this chapter will help you overcome writer's block. Thinking of writing as a process, rather than a completed product that appears suddenly in its final form, should help make the job less formidable. Any difficult task seems easier if you break it down into manageable steps.

The discussions of the steps in the writing process, especially the section on writing the draft, have included suggestions that will help you overcome writer's block. Here is a summary of these techniques:

1. Plan before you write so that you know what you need to say.

2. Write with an outline in view, but write the paper in any order you wish. You can rearrange it later.

3. Don't strive for perfection in the draft stage. Leave problems of grammar, spelling, style, and so forth to the revision stage.

4. Begin with the easiest sections to write.

5. Don't get stuck on difficult places. Skip over them and go on to something else. You may find that when you come back to the rough spots later they will not be as hard to write as you had thought at first.

WRITING UNDER PRESSURE

Throughout this chapter, we've seen how writing is easier if you break the project down into steps. It's easy to manage these steps when you have plenty of time to plan, research, draft, revise, and polish.

But what about situations where you don't have the luxury of time? What about writing essay questions on an exam, or on-the-job writing tasks where you have only a little while to produce a letter or memo?

The truth is that any writing project, no matter how hurriedly it must be done, will go more smoothly if you stick with the three basic steps of the writing process: plan, draft, and revise. Even if you have only a few minutes to work on a document, allow yourself some of that time to think about who you're writing to, what you need to say, and the best way to organize that material. Then draft the paper.

Allow yourself some time to revise as well. If you have access to a word processor, revision will be much quicker and easier to do. Using a spelling checker program, which takes only a few seconds for a short memo or letter, can help eliminate embarrassing spelling and typographical errors.

WRITING AT THE COMPUTER

This chapter has discussed ways a computer, especially a word processor, can help you write. We've mentioned spelling checkers, and there are other types of computerized writing aids you may want to investigate. Some writers find these supplementary programs helpful; others find that a good word processor with a spelling checker program is the only computer help they need.

If you don't have ready access to a computer, you can still write effectively (people wrote well for centuries before computers were ever invented), but writing by hand will take you longer, especially when you revise and polish your draft.

It is beyond the scope of this book to discuss particular word processing programs or other computerized aids to writing. Whether you're still at school or already on the job, find out what computer programs are available and learn the features of the programs that will help you to write well. Time spent learning these programs will pay off as you begin to write more effectively and quickly.

EXERCISES

Exercise 2–1

Among your business correspondents are the following people:

1. A senior financial analyst in a large corporation.
2. A marketing manager in a large corporation (educated and experienced in business, but not trained in finance).
3. The owner/president of a recently opened small business (little business education or experience).
4. A bookkeeper under your supervision.

For each correspondent, which of the following terms or procedures would you *probably* need to explain?

GAAP
opportunity cost
net present value
retained earnings
double-entry bookkeeping
capital leases vs. operating leases

Exercise 2–2

One of the universities in your area is offering a continuing professional education seminar titled "Effective Writing." You want your firm to give time off with pay to attend the seminar and you would like to have your expenses, including the $100 registration fee, paid. Your supervisor, Karen Schuman, is unfamiliar with the seminar; you need to convince her that your attendance would benefit the firm by making you a more effective employee. Write a memo to Ms. Schuman explaining your request.

1. What ideas and information should you include in the memo?
2. How could you arrange this information in an effective order? Write an outline that includes all relevant details about the seminar and an adequate justification for your request.
3. Write the memo.

(Note: Study chapter 9 for suggestions on memo organization and format.)

Exercise 2–3

What computer equipment and software packages are available on your campus? How can you use these tools to help you with your writing?

Write a memo to your classmates to tell them what computers and programs are available. Consider what information your classmates need and questions they may ask. If you describe computer labs on campus, readers will want to know the hours of the lab, the number and types of computers and software packages available, and whether lab assistants are available for help. If you're describing a word processing or editing package, readers may want to know how these programs can make their writing easier and more effective.

Chapter 9 provides advice on how to write a memo.

Exercise 2–4

Analyze the letter in Figure 2–4. How would you react if you received this letter?

Wright and Wrongh,Investment Counselorss
123 Anystreet
Anytown, US 12345

Corner Dress Shop
123 Anyother Street
Anytown, US 12345

Gentlemen
We are in receipt of your correspondence and beg to thank you.

After extensive research we have found what we hope will be a satisfactory response to your questions, we hope you will find our work satisfactory.

There were two possibilities for the resolution of this issue that we considered after a careful analysis of the factors applicable to your situation. If the first possibility proved relevant, then your portfolio would experience a loss of $5500, plus sales commissions. If the other possibility was the best solution, then you would receive a $4400 capital gain because of profits from the sale of the two companies in question.

As you no doubt know, SEC regulation 45 Sec.341(6)a [paras.5-9] stipulate the regulations we must follow. Thus, to be in compliance with the rules and regs. you must follow the provisions of the pertinent sections.

As your investment counselorss, we are most concerned that we be in compliance with all standards of professional ethics, and we always keep this in mind when we advise you on your questions.

After extensive research, we advise you to sell your holdings in Nile Water Importers and Babble Interpreters immediately because the second possibility enumerated in the above paragraph proves to be the correct solution to you problem.

Thanking you in advance, we remain

Yours with highest regards,

M. Ostley Wrongh

M. Ostley Wrongh
Wright and Wrongh, Investment Counselors

FIGURE 2–4   *Letter for Exercise 2–4: What Is Wrong with This Letter?*

1. Think about and then discuss with your classmates these questions:
   - What are the weaknesses of the letter? (Hint: The letter has many typos and spelling errors. Can you find them all? In addition to these problems, the letter has a number of less obvious weaknesses. What are they?)
   - What are the strengths of this letter? (It does have some strengths!)
2. Revise the letter so that it is more effective. Invent any details you need for your revision.

(Note: chapter 8 provides information on letter writing.)

3

The Flow
of Thought: Organizing
for Coherence

Coherence is one of the six tips for effective business writing discussed in chapter 1 (see Figure 1–1). Coherent writing is organized so that important ideas stand out. The flow of thought is logical and easy to follow.

Chapter 2 introduced several techniques to help you make your writing more coherent: analyzing your purpose and the reader's needs, then planning and outlining before you begin to write. This chapter discusses additional ways to ensure that your writing is coherent. It explores how to write with unity, use summary sentences and transitions, and structure effective paragraphs and essays.

WRITING WITH UNITY

The key to unified writing is to establish the main idea of each document. An office memo may contain only one paragraph, but that paragraph has a central idea. A report may run to many pages, but it still has a central idea or purpose, and probably secondary purposes as well. It's important to decide on your main ideas before you begin writing, preferably before beginning your outline. Deciding on the main idea of a document is similar to analyzing its purpose, as discussed in chapter 2.

You should be able to summarize a main idea in one sentence. In a paragraph, this sentence is called the topic sentence. In longer documents involving more than two or three paragraphs, this sentence may be called the thesis statement or statement of purpose.

The main idea is the key to the entire document. Every other sentence should be related to it, either directly or indirectly. The central idea is like the hub of a wheel or the trunk of a tree. All other ideas branch off from the central idea—they explain it, analyze it, illustrate it, or prove it. Any sentences or details that are unrelated to the main idea, either directly or indirectly, are irrelevant and should be omitted. In longer documents, entire paragraphs may be irrelevant to the main purpose. These irrelevant paragraphs are called digressions.

When you remove digressions and irrelevant sentences, your writing becomes unified: Every sentence is related, directly or indirectly, to the main idea.

The paragraph below is not unified. Which sentences are irrelevant to the topic sentence?

> (1) Incorporation offers many advantages for a business and its owners. (2) For example, the owners are not responsible for the business's debts. (3) Investors hope to make money when they buy stock in a corporation. (4) Incorporation also enables a business to obtain professional management skills. (5) Corporations are subject to more government regulation than are other forms of organization.

Sentence 1, the topic sentence, identifies the main idea of the paragraph: the advantages of incorporation. Sentences 3 and 5 are off the subject.

Writing with unity is an important way to make your writing coherent.

USING SUMMARY SENTENCES

In coherent writing, the main ideas stand out. You can emphasize your main ideas by placing them in the document where they will get the reader's attention.

First, as chapter 2 suggested, it's usually a good idea to summarize your main ideas at the beginning of the document. A long document, especially a report, should have a separate summary section at or near the beginning of the paper. This formal summary may be called an abstract, an executive summary, or simply a summary.

When writing these summary sections, be specific and remember the reader's interests and needs. Let's say you are writing a memo to the managers at Winston Sales Company to explain the advantages of using the net present value (NPV) method to evaluate investment proposals. Summarize those advantages specifically and relate them to Winston Sales. One of these advantages might be "By using the NPV method, you can estimate how much the value of your company would increase as a result of adopting a proposal."

The summary at the beginning of a document may be several sentences or even pages long, depending on the length of the document and the complexity of the main ideas or recommendations. Here is an example:

> The following procedures will ensure a smooth transition to the new computerized system:
>
> - Management should designate a representative from each department to attend the three-week workshop at company headquarters.
> - Each department should plan a training session for its employees to emphasize the department's use of the system.
> - A two-month transition period should be allowed for converting from the old system.
> - Troubleshooters should be available to all departments to solve any problems that occur.

Summary sentences are important in other places besides at the beginning of a document. They are also important at the beginning of each section of the paper and as part of the conclusion.

Any paper that is longer than three or four paragraphs probably has more than one main idea or recommendation; each of these ideas is suggested in the introduction or in a separate summary section. Often, the logical way to organize the remainder of the document is to use a separate section of the paper to discuss each idea further. Each section begins with a summary statement to identify the main idea, or the topic, of that section. The reader will then have a clear idea of what that section is about. It's a good idea to use somewhat different wording from that used in the beginning of the paper.

The principle we've been discussing sounds simple: Begin with your conclusion and then give your support. However, many writers have trouble putting this advice into practice. The difficulty may occur because this order of ideas is the reverse of the process writers go through to reach their conclusions. The typical research process is to gather information first and then to arrive at the conclusions. A writer may try to take the reader through the same investigative steps as those he or she used to solve the problem or answer the question.

Think about your readers' needs. They're mainly interested in the findings of your research, not in the process you went through to get there. They may very well want to read about the facts you considered as well as your analytical reasoning; in fact, some readers will carefully evaluate the soundness of your data and methodology. However, their first concern is with the conclusions themselves.

When a paper is organized in the way recommended here, we say that it has a deductive structure: It begins with the conclusion and then gives the proofs. The opposite of deductive organization is an inductive structure, which gives the data and then presents the conclusions. Research is usually done inductively, but most readers prefer that the results be presented in a deductive organization.

Conclusions may be presented again in a concluding section, especially if the document is very long. Once again, you may need to remind the reader of your main ideas, but be careful not to sound repetitive. The length and complexity of the document determine how much detail to include in your conclusion.

TRANSITIONS

Transitions, which are another element of coherent writing, link ideas together. They can be used between sentences, paragraphs, and major divisions of the document. Their purpose is to show the relationship between two ideas: how the second idea flows logically from the first, and how both are related to the main idea of the entire document.

As an example of how transitions work, consider this paragraph. The topic sentence (main idea) is the first sentence; the transitional expressions are in italics:

> (1) Financial statements are important to a variety of users. (2) *First*, investors and potential investors use the statements to determine whether a company is a good investment risk. (3) These users look at such factors as net income, the debt-to-equity ratio, and retained earnings. (4) *Second*, creditors use financial statements to determine whether a firm is a good credit risk. (5) Creditors want to know whether a firm has a large enough cash flow to pay its debts. (6) *Third*, government agencies analyze financial statements for a variety of purposes. (7) *For example*, the Internal Revenue Service wants to know whether the company has paid the required amount of taxes on its income. (8) These examples of financial statement users show how diverse their interests can be.

The sentences beginning *first* (2), *second* (4), and *third* (6) give three examples of the paragraph's main idea: the variety of financial statement users. These three sentences relate to one another in a logical, sequential way, which the transitions make clear. These sentences also relate directly to the topic sentence; they illustrate it with specific examples. Sentence 7, which begins with *for example*, relates only indirectly to the main idea of the paragraph, but it relates directly to sentence 6. Sentence 7 identifies one reason why government agencies need access to financial statements.

Transitions can express a number of relationships between ideas. In the sample paragraph, the transitions indicate an enumerated list (2, 4, and 6) and a specific illustration of a general statement (7). Transitions can also imply other relationships between ideas—conclusions, additional information, or contrasts, for example.

To see the importance of transitions within a paragraph, look at the following example, which lacks transitions:

> Incorporation offers several advantages to businesses and their owners. Ownership is easy to transfer. The business is able to maintain a continuous existence even when the original owners are no longer involved. The stockholders of a corporation are not held responsible for the business's debts. If the Dallas Corporation defaults on a $1,000,000 loan, its investors will not be held responsible for paying that liability. Incorporation enables a business to obtain professional managers with centralized authority and responsibility. The business can be run more efficiently. Incorporation gives a business certain legal rights. It can enter into contracts, own property, and borrow money.

Now see how much easier it is to read the paragraph when it has appropriate transitions:

> Incorporation offers several advantages to businesses and their owners. *For one thing*, ownership is easy to transfer, and the business is able to maintain a continuous existence even when the original owners are no longer involved. *In addition*, the stockholders of a corporation are not held responsible for the business's bad debts. If the Dallas Corporation defaults on a $1,000,000 loan, *for example*, its investors will not be held responsible for paying that liability. Incorporation *also* enables a business to obtain professional managers with centralized authority and responsibility; *therefore*, the business can be run more efficiently. *Finally*, incorporation gives a business certain legal rights. *For example*, it can enter into contracts, own property, and borrow money.

Transitional Words and Phrases

Here is a list of commonly used transitional expressions, their meanings, and example sentences showing how some of them work.

ADDING A POINT OR PIECE OF INFORMATION: *and, also, in addition, moreover, furthermore, first/second/third, finally*

> Finance is a demanding profession. It can also be financially rewarding.

MAKING AN EXCEPTION OR CONTRASTING POINT: *but, however, nevertheless, on the other hand, yet, still, on the contrary, in spite of . . ., nonetheless*

> The use of the payback period evaluation method has many drawbacks. Nevertheless, it is still very popular in the business community.

GIVING SPECIFIC EXAMPLES OR ILLUSTRATIONS: *for example, for instance, as an illustration, in particular, to illustrate*

> Financial statements serve a variety of users. For example, investors use them to evaluate potential investments. Other users include . . .

CLARIFYING A POINT: *that is, in other words, in effect, put simply, stated briefly*

> The basic accounting equation is assets equal liabilities plus owners' equity. That is, A = L + OE.

CONCEDING A POINT TO THE OPPOSITE SIDE: *granted that, it may be true that, even though, although*

> Although generally accepted accounting principles are not perfect, their use may offer considerable assurance that financial statements are presented fairly.

INDICATING PLACE, TIME, OR IMPORTANCE:

Place: *above, beside, beyond, to the right, below, around*

Time: *formerly, hitherto, earlier, in the past, before, at present, now, today, these days, tomorrow, in the future, next, later on, later*

Importance: *foremost, most importantly, especially, of less importance, of least importance*

> In earlier centuries there was no need for finance people. However, the size and complexities of today's businesses make modern finance a complicated process indeed.

INDICATING THE STAGES IN AN ARGUMENT OR PROCESS, OR THE ITEMS IN A SERIES: *initially, at the outset, to begin with, first, first of all, up to now, so far, second, thus far, next, after, finally, last*

> The financial analysis process works in stages. First, accounting information must be analyzed.

GIVING A RESULT: *as a result, consequently, accordingly, as a consequence, therefore, thus, hence, then, for that reason*

> Portfolio management techniques allow flexibility in their application. Therefore, investment advisors are able to meet the changing needs of the business world.

SUMMING UP OR RESTATING THE CENTRAL POINT: *in sum, to sum up, to summarize, in summary, to conclude, in brief, in short, as one can see, in conclusion*

> In conclusion, transitions often make writing much easier to read.

Repetition of Key Words and Phrases

Another way to add coherence to your writing is to repeat key words and phrases. This repetition may be particularly useful in connecting paragraphs and major divisions of the document. These repetitions are typically located at the beginning of a new paragraph or section.

The following outline of a student's essay shows the structure of a discussion on alternatives to the historical basis of cost accounting. Notice how the combination of transitional expressions and repeated key phrases holds the report together. These techniques also tie the parts of the report to the main idea of the paper, which is summarized in the thesis statement. Notice also how summary sentences appear throughout the outline.

THE MONETARY UNIT ASSUMPTION

I.   Introductory paragraph
    A.   Introductory sentences
        One of the basic assumptions financial researchers made in the past was that money was an effective common denominator by which business enterprises could be measured and analyzed. Implicit in this assumption was the acceptance of the stable and unchanging nature of monetary units. Recently, however, the validity of this assumption has been questioned not only by academicians and theorists, but by practitioners as well.
    B.   Thesis statement (main idea of entire paper)
        Several solutions have been proposed by researchers to correct for the changing value of the monetary unit.

II.   Body
    A.   Nature of the problem
        The unadjusted monetary unit system has been criticized because it distorts financial statements during periods of inflation.
    B.   First solution to the problem
        1.   One solution to overstating profits solely because of inflation is to adjust figures for changes in the general purchasing power of the monetary unit. (This paragraph describes the solution and its advantages.)
        2.   However, the general purchasing power approach has been criticized for several reasons. (The paragraph describes the disadvantages of this approach.)
    C.   Second solution to the problem
        1.   Instead of the general purchasing power procedure, some favor adjusting for changes in replacement cost. (Paragraph describes this solution.)
        2.   One of the major advantages of the replacement cost approach . . . (Paragraph discusses several advantages.)
        3.   One authority has summarized the criticisms of replacement cost accounting: "Most of the criticisms . . ." (Paragraph discusses the disadvantages of this approach.)

III. Concluding paragraph
    Adjusting for changes in the general purchasing power and adjusting for changes in replacement cost represent attempts to correct the problems of the stable monetary unit assumption in times of inflation.

Pronouns Used
to Achieve Coherence

Another tool you can use to achieve coherent writing is the pronoun. A pronoun stands for a noun or a noun phrase that has previously been identified. The noun that the pronoun refers to is called its *antecedent*. Consider this sentence:

Firms usually issue their financial statements at least once a year.

In this sentence, the pronoun *their* refers to the noun *firms*. Put another way, *firms* is the antecedent of *their*.

Because pronouns refer to nouns that the writer has already used, pronouns help connect the thoughts of a paragraph. Look at how the pronouns work in this paragraph:

The research staff reviewed the financial statements of Toppo Industries to determine whether the firm represented a safe investment for our pension plan funds. *We* found two problems that may require *us* to withhold a positive recommendation. First, Toppo has not been consistent in *its* payment of dividends. Second, *we* identified several financial ratios that were not within allowable limits. *We* suggest a meeting with Toppo's management to discuss these issues.

Pronouns require a word of warning, however. Unless a writer is careful, the reader may not be sure what noun the pronoun refers to. Look at the problem in this sentence:

The managers told the people in the finance department that they did not understand company policy.

Who doesn't understand company policy—the managers or the people in the finance department? This sentence illustrates the problem of ambiguous pronoun reference. Chapter 5 discusses this problem further.

Problems with Transitions

A few problems can occur with transitions other than the failure to use them when they are needed. One problem occurs when a writer uses transitional expressions too often. These expressions are necessary to make the relationship of ideas clear when there might be some confusion. Often this logical relationship is clear without the use of transitional expressions. Consider this paragraph:

Investment analysts never finish their education. They work hard for their college degrees, but after college they must continue studying to stay current on the latest developments in the profession. They must be thoroughly familiar with changing financial markets and new securities offerings. To improve their professional competence, they participate in a variety of continuing education programs sponsored by such organizations as the Association for Investment Management and Research and the Financial Management Association. Indeed, well-qualified investment analysts are lifetime students, always seeking better ways to serve their clients and the public.

Notice how easy this paragraph is to follow, even though it doesn't use a single transitional expression.

Another problem with transitions occurs when the writer uses the wrong expression, suggesting an illogical connection of ideas. Consider these examples:

FAULTY TRANSITION:	Professional requirements for financial planners are not established by federal law. For instance, organizations such as the CFP Board of Standards issue these requirements, and the CFP Board is not part of the federal government.
REVISED:	Professional requirements for financial planners are not established by federal law. Rather, organizations that are not part of the federal government, such as the CFP Board of Standards, issue these requirements.
FAULTY TRANSITION:	If financial planners do not meet the CFP requirements, they may lose their CFP designation. Therefore, they must meet CFP requirements to conform to their code of professional ethics.
REVISED:	If financial planners do not meet the CFP requirements, they may lose their CFP designation. They must also meet CFP requirements to conform to their code of professional ethics.

Transitions, when used correctly, are a valuable tool for clarifying the relationship between ideas. If you use transitions carefully along with summary sentences and a logical organization, your writing will be easy to follow.

The next sections of this chapter show how to use these techniques to write coherent paragraphs, discussion questions, essays, and other longer forms of writing.

PARAGRAPHS

This section of the chapter is devoted to techniques of paragraphing: how to plan length, structure, and development so that your paragraphs are coherent.

Length

You may not be sure how long paragraphs should be. Are one-sentence paragraphs acceptable? What about paragraphs that run on for nearly an entire typed page?

One rule is that a paragraph should be limited to the development of one idea. Thus, the length of most paragraphs is somewhere between one sentence and an entire page. However, an occasional short paragraph, even of only one sentence, may be effective to emphasize an idea or to provide a transition between two major divisions of the writing.

Be wary of long paragraphs, which look intimidating and are often hard to follow. You may need to divide a long paragraph into two or more shorter ones. Appropriate transitions can tie the new paragraphs together and maintain a smooth flow of thought.

A good rule is to limit most of your paragraphs to four or five sentences.

Structure

Another feature of well-written paragraphs is an appropriate structure. We have already suggested that a strong topic sentence can contribute to a unified, coherent paragraph. A topic sentence states the main idea of the paragraph. It is usually the first sentence in the paragraph, and sometimes it contains a transition tying the new paragraph to the previous one. All other sentences in the paragraph should develop the idea expressed in the topic sentence.

Two patterns of paragraph organization are useful for finance people's writing tasks; the simple deductive paragraph and the complex deductive paragraph. The simple deductive arrangement states the main idea in the first sentence (topic sentence); all other sentences *directly* develop that idea by adding details. A concluding sentence is sometimes helpful. Look again at this paragraph, which illustrates a simple deductive organization:

> (1) Investment analysts never finish their education. (2) They work hard for their college degrees, but after college they must continue studying to stay current on the latest developments in the profession. (3) They must be thoroughly familiar with changing financial markets and new securities offerings. (4) To improve their professional competence, they participate in a variety of continuing education programs sponsored by such organizations as the Association for Investment Management and Research and the Financial Management Association. (5) Indeed, well-qualified investment analysts are lifetime students, always seeking better ways to serve their clients and the public.

In this paragraph, sentence 1 is the topic sentence, sentences 2–4 develop the main idea, and sentence 5 is the conclusion. A simple deductive paragraph has a simple structural diagram such as this one:

  (1) Topic sentence—main idea
      (2) Supporting sentence
      (3) Supporting sentence

(4) Supporting sentence

(5) Concluding sentence (optional)

A complex deductive paragraph has a more elaborate structure. This paragraph is complex deductive:

(1) Financial statements are important to a variety of users. (2) First, investors and potential investors use the statements to determine whether a company is a good investment risk. (3) These users look at such factors as net income, the debt-to-equity ratio, and retained earnings. (4) Second, creditors use financial statements to determine whether a firm is a good credit risk. (5) Creditors want to know whether a firm has a large enough cash flow to pay its debts. (6) Third, government agencies analyze financial statements for a variety of purposes. (7) For example, the Internal Revenue Service wants to know whether the company has paid the required amount of taxes on its income. (8) These examples of financial statement users show how diverse their interests can be.

In this paragraph, sentence 1 (the topic sentence) states the main idea. Sentence 2 directly supports the main idea by giving an example of it, but sentence 3 explains sentence 2. Thus sentence 3 directly supports sentence 2, but only indirectly supports sentence 1. Complex deductive paragraphs have a structural diagram similar to this one:

(1) Topic sentence—main idea

  (2) Direct support

    (3) Indirect support

  (4) Direct support

    (5) Indirect support

  (6) Direct support

    (7) Indirect support

(8) Conclusion (optional)

Complex deductive paragraphs can have numerous variations. The number of direct supporting sentences can vary, as can the number of indirect supports. Sometimes direct supports may not require any indirect supports.

Consider another example of a complex deductive paragraph:

(1) Two of the most popular inventory flow assumptions used by businesses today are FIFO (first-in, first-out) and LIFO (last-in, first-out). (2) FIFO assumes that the first goods purchased for inventory are the first goods sold. (3) Therefore, ending inventory under FIFO consists of the most recent purchases. (4) Because older, usually lower costs are matched with sales revenues, FIFO results in a higher net income and thus higher income tax liabilities. (5) The LIFO flow assumption, on the other hand, assumes that the most recent purchases are the first goods sold. (6) Cost of goods sold, however, is based on more recent, higher prices. (7) Thus, LIFO usually results

in lower net income and lower income tax liabilities. (8) This advantage makes LIFO very popular with many businesses.

This paragraph can be outlined to reveal the following structure:

I.   Topic sentence (1): Two popular inventory flow assumptions
    A.   FIFO (2B4)
        1.   Description (2)
        2.   Effect on inventory (3)
        3.   Effect on net income and taxes (4)
    B.   LIFO (5B8)
        1.   Description (5)
        2.   Effect on inventory (6)
        3.   Effect on net income and taxes (7)
        4.   Popularity (8)

The descriptions of FIFO and LIFO in this paragraph are very condensed, probably too condensed for most purposes. Moreover, the paragraph is really too long. It would probably be better to divide it between sentences 4 and 5. The result would be two shorter but closely related paragraphs. Both would have simple deductive structures. However, the first paragraph would be a modified version of a simple deductive structure because the main idea of this paragraph would be the second sentence.

The important idea about both simple and complex deductive paragraphs is their unity: All sentences, either directly or indirectly, develop the main idea of the paragraph as expressed in the topic sentence.

Some writers may wonder about a third type of paragraph organization: paragraphs with an inductive structure. Inductive paragraphs put the main idea last. Supporting sentences lead up to the topic sentence, which is the last sentence in the paragraph.

For most business writing, inductive paragraphs are not as effective as simple or complex deductive paragraphs. Business readers like to identify main ideas from the start. They don't like to be kept in suspense, wondering "What's all this leading up to? What's the point?" Thus, it's a good idea to stick with deductive organization for most, if not all, of your paragraphs.

Paragraph Development

An effective paragraph is not only well organized; it is also well developed. That is, the idea expressed in the topic sentence is adequately explained and illustrated so that the reader has a clear understanding of what the writer wishes to say.

Several techniques are useful for paragraph development: descriptive and factual details, illustrations or examples, definitions, and appeals to authority.

Descriptive and factual details give a more thorough, concrete explanation of the idea expressed in a general way in the topic sentence. Factual details give measurable, observable, or historical information that can be objectively verified. Descriptive details are similar to factual details. They give specific characteristics of the subject being discussed.

When you use details with which your readers are familiar, they can better understand your observations and conclusions. In the following paragraph, the main idea is stated in the first sentence. The paragraph is then developed with factual details:

> Our net income for next year should increase because we've signed a contract with an important new customer. Flip's Frog Ponds, Inc., which last year had over $4 billion in revenue, has ordered a million lily pads from our horticultural division. This new business should increase our revenues by at least 15 percent.

Another useful technique of paragraph development is illustrations or examples—typical cases or specific instances of the idea being discussed. Illustrations can take a variety of forms. A paragraph may combine several brief examples, or it may use one long, extended illustration. The examples may be factually true, or they may be hypothetical, invented for the purpose of illustration.

Definitions are useful to explain concepts or terms that might be unfamiliar to the reader. A definition can be formal, such as the meaning given in a dictionary or an accounting standard, or it can be a more informal explanation of a term. Often, a definition is more effective when combined with an illustration.

Here is a paragraph developed by definition and illustration:

> Every day you make decisions based on *forecasts*. When you go shopping, for example, you decide how much money to spend based on your forecast of how much money you need for other reasons. When you plan trips, you decide how much money to take along based on your forecast of the trip's expenses. You choose what to wear in the morning based on the weather forecaster's prediction of the good or bad weather.[1]

Finally, some paragraphs are developed by appeals to authority—facts, illustrations, or ideas obtained from a reputable source such as a book, article, interview, or official pronouncement. Appeals to authority may be paraphrases—someone else's idea expressed in your own words—or direct quotations from the source being used. The paragraph above is a direct quotation from a finance textbook to highlight the need for forecasting. Chapter 7 gives more information on the correct use of quotations and paraphrases.

By using a variety of techniques, you can develop fully the ideas expressed in the topic sentences of your paragraphs. Factual and descriptive detail, illustration, definition, and authority all give the reader a clear understanding of what you wish to explain.

However you decide to develop your paragraphs, remember the importance of your reader's interests and needs. It's better to select supporting details and examples with which the reader is already familiar.

DISCUSSION QUESTIONS AND ESSAYS

A section about discussion questions and essays might seem too academic for a writing handbook for finance practitioners, but many finance students take exams with discussion questions, and essay questions are an important part of some professional certifications exams. In addition, many of the principles of organizing and developing an essay are applicable to memos, reports, and other types of writing used by financial professionals in practice.

Discussion Questions

The key to answering a short discussion question (one to three paragraphs) is well-organized paragraphs with strong topic sentences. Usually the question itself will suggest the topic sentence. Consider this question:

Discuss who the users of financial statements are.

The answer to this question might begin with the following sentence:

The users of an organization's financial statements are mainly external to the organization.

The first paragraph of the answer would discuss external users, such as investors, creditors, and government agencies. A second, shorter paragraph might then discuss internal users of financial statements, such as management and employees. The second topic sentence might be as follows:

People within an organization are also interested in its financial statements.

Short paragraphs with strong topic sentences will help the exam grader identify your main ideas, and thus give you credit for what you know.

Essays

Before you read this section, review the discussion of paragraph development on pages 36–38. Pay particular attention to the complex deductive pattern of organization.

Complex deductive paragraphs have a main idea (topic sentence) supported by major and minor supports.

Essays—discussions of four or more paragraphs—are organized the same way, except that the main idea (thesis statement) has as its major supports paragraphs rather than sentences. In addition, the thesis statement may come at the end of the first paragraph, in which case it may be preceded by sentences that give background on the topic or otherwise interest the reader in what is being discussed. Here is the outline of a five-paragraph essay:

I.   Introduction—first paragraph
      A.   Attention-getting sentences (optional)
      B.   Thesis statement—main idea of the essay, usually expressed in one sentence
II.   Body of the essay—develops the thesis through analysis, explanation, examples, proofs, or steps
      A.   Major support—second paragraph
          1.⎫ Minor supports—sentences that develop the
          2.⎬ paragraph in a simple or complex
          3.⎭ deductive organization
      B.   Major support—third paragraph
          1.⎫
          2.⎬ minor supports
          3.⎭
      C.   Major support—fourth paragraph
          1.⎫
          2.⎬ minor supports
          3.⎭
III.   Conclusion—fifth paragraph
      A.   Repeats the essay's main idea (a variation of the thesis statement) or otherwise provides closure
      B.   Forceful ending (optional)

Some of the parts of this outline need more discussion.

ATTENTION-GETTING SENTENCES Some essays begin with attention-getting sentences, which are used to get the reader interested in the subject. Several techniques can be used:

- Give background information about the topic. Why is the topic of current interest?
- Pose a problem or raise a question (to be answered in the essay).
- Define key terms, perhaps the topic itself.
- Show the relevance of the topic to the reader.
- Begin with an interesting direct quotation.
- Relate a brief anecdote relevant to the topic.
- Relate the specific topic to a wider area of interest.

The following essay introduction uses two of these techniques. It poses a question and then suggests the relevance of the topic to the reader (assuming that the essay was written for finance people). The final sentence of the paragraph is the thesis statement.

> Do finance people need to be good writers? Some people would answer "No" to this question. They believe a financial analyst's job is limited to arithmetical calculations with very little need to use words or sentences. But this picture of an analyst's responsibilities is a misconception. In fact, good writing skills are essential to the successful practice of finance.

Sometimes you may choose not to use attention-getting sentences, but decide instead to begin your essay with the thesis statement. This is a particularly good strategy to use for exam questions.

THESIS STATEMENT   The thesis statement summarizes the main idea of the essay, usually in one sentence. It may be a simple thesis statement, such as the one in the preceding example. Alternatively, the thesis statement may be expanded. That is, it may summarize the main supports of the discussion. Here is an example of an expanded thesis statement:

> In fact, successful finance people must have good writing skills to communicate with clients, managers, agencies, and colleagues.

Sometimes, to avoid a long or awkward sentence, you may want to use two sentences for the thesis statement:

> In fact, good writing skills are essential to the successful practice of finance. For example, during a typical business day, a finance professional may write to clients, managers, agencies, or colleagues.

CONCLUSION   The conclusion should provide the reader with a sense of closure—a feeling that the essay is complete, that the train of thought has come to a logical end. Sometimes you can give your essays closure by repeating the main idea, usually in some variation of the thesis statement. You may also want to end with a forceful statement that will stay in the reader's mind, thus giving the discussion a more lasting impact. For a strong ending, you can use several techniques, many of which resemble those used in the introduction:

- Show a broad application of the ideas suggested in the discussion.
- End with an authoritative direct quotation that reinforces your position.
- Challenge the reader.
- Echo the attention-getting sentences. For example, if you began by posing a question in the introduction, you can answer it explicitly in the conclusion.

If you're writing an essay on an exam, a concluding paragraph may not be necessary, but it's important that the essay seem finished. It will probably seem complete if you've developed your thesis statement fully.

Applying Essay Techniques to Other Kinds of Writing

If you are answering an essay question on an exam, you can use the techniques just discussed to organize and develop an effective discussion. Chapter 11, which discusses essay exams more fully, provides additional suggestions. But how do the techniques you use for essays work with the writing formats more typically used by finance people (letters, memos, and reports)?

Everything you write should have a main idea. In an essay this idea is called the thesis statement; in a memo or report the main idea might be included in the statement of purpose or recommendations. Whatever you're writing, it's a good idea to identify the main idea before you even begin your outline. Unless this idea is clear in your mind—or clearly written in your notes—your writing may be rambling and confusing. Your reader might then wonder, "What's this person trying to say? What's the point?"

Whatever you write should be organized around a central idea, just as an essay is organized. Letters, reports, and memos share other features of an essay as well: a basic three-part structure (introduction, body, conclusion), complex deductive organization, and the need for adequate transitions and concrete support.

If you understand the principles discussed in this chapter, you will find it easier to plan and organize the writing tasks that are part of your professional responsibilities.

Sample Essay

The following is an actual assignment for an essay in an advanced finance class. Figure 3–1 shows an essay answer that illustrates some of the principles of good organization and development.

Assignment.[2] When asked what the objective of a firm's managers should be, many people reply "to maximize profits." If you agree with that objective, so state and justify your opinion. If you do not agree, so state and explain why you think maximizing profits is incorrect. Then describe what you think the objective of a firm's managers should be and justify your opinion.

For a response to this question, see the essay in Figure 3–1.

This chapter has added four guidelines to our list of ways to make your writing more effective. We now have seven guidelines:

1. **Analyze the purpose of the writing and the needs and expectations of the readers.**

FIGURE 3–1   *Sample Essay*

PROFIT MAXIMIZATION VS. WEALTH MAXIMIZATION

Blindly striving to increase profits is not a proper objective of a firm's managers. Instead, the objective of a firm's managers should be to maximize the wealth of the shareholders.

Concentrating on profits may produce the appearance of wealth in the short run, but the ability of the firm to remain competitive in the long run may suffer. Profits rise when expenses are reduced and sales are increased. High-pressure sales techniques and aggressive cost-cutting policies may result in short-term profit increases, but such methods can hurt the credibility of the firm and limit its ability to do business in the future. For example, misleading advertising may cause sales to increase until customers become aware of the true situation. Likewise, laying off employees, cutting back on training, and foregoing maintenance on company equipment may reduce expenses this year, but they can ultimately harm the firm as productivity drops.

Shareholder wealth is maximized when the market price of the company's stock is maximized. Market price is maximized when the present value of expected dividends and capital gains from the company are at their highest possible values. Investors' perceptions drive these values up or down according to investors' views about the future of the firm. For example, if investors observe that the company is not developing new products to meet market needs, they will value the stock of the company less highly than otherwise. If investors believe that layoffs and training and maintenance cutbacks jeopardize the ability of the firm to remain competitive, they may actively try to sell their stock, thus driving the price down. In both cases, shareholders lose wealth.

In summary, maximizing profits is important in maximizing wealth, but alone it does not accomplish the task. Good marketing programs, research and development, quality products and services, and strategic planning are necessary to build up wealth for the long term.

---

2. **Organize your ideas so that readers will find them easy to follow.**
3. **Write the draft and then revise it to make the writing polished and correct.**
4. **Make the writing unified. All sentences should relate to the main idea, either directly or indirectly. Eliminate digressions and irrelevant detail.**
5. **Use summary sentences and transitions to make your writing coherent.**
6. **Write in short paragraphs that begin with clear topic sentences.**
7. **Develop paragraphs by illustration, definition, detail, and appeals to authority.**

TEST YOURSELF

Is this paragraph coherent? If not, revise it to improve its organization, using some of these techniques:

- Write a strong topic sentence stating the paragraph's main idea.
- Use transitional devices to show the relation between sentences.
- Eliminate sentences that don't fit.
- Divide long, disunified paragraphs into shorter, unified ones.
- Rearrange sentences by grouping ideas together (add sentences if necessary).

Government financial experts help national, state, and local governments control spending and budgeting. Government spending could run rampant. Governmental finance is similar to industrial finance in many of its functions. Government financial experts help prevent the government from wasting taxpayers' money.

TEST YOURSELF: ANSWERS

This paragraph needs revision. Here is one possibility:

Government financial experts help national, state, and local governments control spending and budgeting. Without controls, government spending could run rampant. Thus, one function of government financial experts is to help prevent the government from wasting taxpayers' money.

EXERCISES

Exercise 3–1

Homer Baer is a junior financial analyst for a medium-sized manufacturing firm in Mobile, Alabama. The Chief financial officer (CFO) has asked him to investigate two computer systems for possible purchase by the firm. The CFO has also asked him to recommend the system the firm should buy. Homer has drafted the following outline for his report and asked for your critique.

I.   Introduction
II.   The history of computer technology
III. Simple Sam Computer Model B-13
    A.   General description of features
    B.   Nearest service center in Atlanta, Georgia
    C.   Can handle much of the firm's computer work
    D.   Limited capacity for future expansion
    E.   Takes up only a small amount of office space
IV.   Whiz Kid Computer Model 1004

A. Easily adaptable in the future to new programs and functions
B. Slightly larger than the Simple Sam Model
C. Service center in Mobile
D. Can handle all the firm's current computer work
E. General description of features
V.   The need for employees to have more training in computer science
VI. The role of computers in the future of manufacturing
VII. Conclusion

1. What is the purpose of Homer's report?
2. What do you think is the main idea of the report?
3. What material included in Homer's outline is irrelevant to his purpose?
4. What necessary information has he forgotten to include?
5. Are the ideas in the outline arranged logically? If not, rearrange the ideas into a more effective outline. Include only relevant material.
6. What kinds of transitional devices could Homer use when he writes his report? Rewrite the outline in sentence form and include transitional devices.

Exercise 3–2

Are the following paragraphs effectively organized, or do they lack unity or coherence? Analyze the paragraphs to determine whether they need revision. Then revise the faulty paragraphs, using some of these techniques:

- Write a strong topic sentence stating the paragraph's main idea.
- Use transitional devices to show the relation between sentences.
- Eliminate sentences that don't fit.
- Divide long, disunified paragraphs into shorter, unified ones.
- Rearrange sentences by grouping relevant ideas together (add sentences if necessary).

1. One service that certified financial planners perform is retirement planning. Financial planners help clients define their goals and needs for retirement. Certification gives credibility to financial planners. Financial planners offer portfolio management consulting services. Portfolio management consultants suggest ways people can improve yield and reduce risk in their investments. Taxes are an increasingly complex area. Financial planners advise clients how to incur the smallest tax liability with their investments.

2. Although the purchase of our supplier's stock may offer us several advantages, there are also some potential problems we should consider. For one thing, we may not always need the supplier's raw material, because we may not always manufacture the product that requires this material. And even if we continue to manufacture that product, our research and development staff may develop a cheaper, synthetic raw material. Finally, if we do purchase the stock but later need to resell it, we cannot be assured that the stock will be marketable at that time.

Exercise 3-3

Discuss the following topics in well-organized and well-developed paragraphs or essays.

1. Opportunity cost
2. Internal rate of return (IRR)
3. Retained earnings
4. Capital structure
5. Depreciation
6. Market value versus book value
7. Statement of cash flows

Exercise 3-4

Discuss the topics defined below, using the techniques covered in this and earlier chapters. Your answers might range from one to five paragraphs or more, depending on the topic.

1. Contrast the net present value (NPV) and internal rate of return (IRR) investment evaluation techniques.
2. Discuss the advantages and disadvantages of the payback period evaluation technique.
3. Discuss the liquidity/profitability tradeoff in working capital management.
4. Explain why the presence of debt in a firm's capital structure increases the risk borne by stockholders.
5. Discuss the role of investment bankers in the financial system.

NOTES

1. Timothy J. Gallagher and Joseph D. Andrew, Jr., *Financial Management: Principles and Practice* (Upper Saddle River, N.J.: Prentice Hall, 1996):113.
2. Joseph D., Jr. Andrew, Essay question from mid-term exam, Financial Planning class, Webster University, 1992.

4

A Sense of Style: Writing with Conciseness and Clarity

So far we've looked at writing mainly as an organizational task: planning the structure and contents of the paper so that it achieves its purpose in a way readers will find meaningful. We have stressed the quality of coherence: writing that is easy to follow, with main ideas that stand out. Chapters 2 and 3 looked at writing in terms of large units. They discussed the structure of the paper as a whole and the organization of sections and paragraphs.

We turn now to a more detailed level of effective writing. This chapter looks at word choices and sentence structures that contribute to a vigorous, readable writing style. In this discussion of style, we emphasize two other important qualities of effective writing: conciseness and clarity, which are two of the tips for writing in Figure 1–1.

CONCISENESS

Chapter 3 suggested several ways to make your writing more concise by eliminating digressions and irrelevant detail. In general, we can define concise writing as writing that contains no unnecessary elements—no extra words, phrases, sentences, or paragraphs.

Be concise—make every word count.

Unnecessary Words

The easiest way to make every word count is to see how many words you can cross out of your writing, often with only a simple revision of the sentence. Beware of dead words (words that fill up space without adding meaning). Here are some examples of sentences littered with dead words:

WORDY: To stay informed on the latest information, analysts must read a great number of published materials about finance. [18 words]

CONCISE: To stay current, analysts must read many finance publications. [9 words]

WORDY: This report has the capacity of providing important information to creditors and investors. [13 words]

CONCISE: This report can provide important information to creditors and investors. [10 words]

WORDY: For the sake of our cost reduction goals, we changed the way we ordered the equipment. [16 words]

CONCISE: To reduce costs, we changed the way we ordered equipment. [10 words]

WORDY: There is one organization that has been very influential in improving the profession of finance—the FMA. [17 words]

CONCISE: The FMA has improved the finance profession significantly. [8 words]

WORDY: We hope the entire staff will assist us in our efforts to improve sales. [14 words]

CONCISE: We hope the entire staff will help us improve sales. [10 words]

WORDY: The estimates range all the way from $100 to $350. [10 words]

CONCISE: The estimates range from $100 to $350. [7 words]

Watch out for *there is* and *there are*. They can usually be eliminated. *The fact that, which is,* and *which are* can sometimes be left out:

WORDY: There are several planning strategies that we can use to reduce our income taxes. [14 words]

CONCISE: We can reduce our income taxes by using planning strategies. [10 words]

WORDY: I would like to call your attention to the fact that our earnings last month were down 50 percent. [19 words]

CONCISE: Remember that our earnings were down 50 percent last month. [10 words]
or (even better)
Our earnings dropped 50 percent last month. [7 words]

WORDY: In spite of the fact that our costs rose by 10 percent, we still were able to keep our prices stable. [21 words]

CONCISE: Although costs rose by 10 percent, our prices remained stable. [10 words]

WORDY: His partner, who is an engineer, . . . [6 words]

CONCISE: His partner, an engineer, . . . [4 words]

Simplicity

Another way to make your writing concise is to write as simply as possible. Sometimes writers get into the habit of using big words and long, complicated sentences. Such writing is hard to read. Look at the following sentence:

An increase in an employee's rate of pay will not become effective prior to the date on which the employee has completed a minimum of 13 weeks' actual work at his regular occupational classification.

If we simplify this sentence, it becomes easier to understand:

An employee must work at least 13 weeks at his regular job before he can receive an increase in pay.[1]

Sometimes words and sentences get so complicated that their meaning is completely lost:

Ultimate consumer means a person or group of persons, generally constituting a domestic household, who purchase eggs generally at the individual stores of retailers or purchase and receive deliveries of eggs at the place of abode of the individual or domestic household from producers or retail route sellers and who use such eggs for their consumption as food.

Translation:

Ultimate consumers are people who buy eggs to eat them.[2]

Therefore, another technique for effective writing style is simplicity.

Keep it simple—simple vocabulary and short sentences.

Good writers use short, everyday words as much as possible. For example, they usually write *use* instead of *utilize*, *help* instead of *assistance*. Short, familiar words are easier to read and make writing more forceful.

Table 4–1 shows two columns of words. Column B lists short, familiar words; Column A lists longer, more difficult words that are often substituted for the everyday words in Column B. The table also shows how single words (*because*) can often replace phrases (*for the reason that*). As a general rule, use the words and phrases in Column B rather than those in Column A. Some of the terms in Column A can be omitted (such as *it should be noted that*).

Another way to achieve a simple, readable style is to use short sentences. Short sentences are particularly important when you are explaining complicated ideas. The average sentence should be about 15 words long.

Note that 15 words is an *average*. Some sentences are longer, some shorter. In fact, it's a good idea to vary sentence lengths so the writing

TABLE 4–1 Simplifying Word Choices

As a rule, use the words and phrases in column B rather than those in column A.

COLUMN A	COLUMN B
above-mentioned firms	these firms
absolutely essential	essential
activate	begin
advise	tell
aggregate	total
anticipate	expect
along the lines of	like
as per your request	as you requested
assist	help
at all times	always
at this point in time	now
at this time	now
attempt	try
communicate	write, tell
commence	begin
completely eliminated	eliminated
comprise	include
consider	think
constitute	are, is
discontinue	stop
disutility	uselessness
due to the fact that	because
during the time that	while
earliest convenience	promptly, soon
effort	work
enclosed herewith	enclosed
enclosed please find	enclosed is
endeavor	try
exercise care	be careful
facilitate	ease, simplify
failed to	didn't
few in number	few
for the purpose of	for
for the reason that	because
from the point of view that	for
furnish	send, give
i.e.	that is
implement	carry out
in advance of	before
in all cases	always
in many cases	often

TABLE 4–1   Simplifying Word Choices (*continued*)

COLUMN A	COLUMN B
in most cases	usually
in behalf of	for
in connection with	about
in terms of	in
in the amount of	of, for
in the case of	if
in the event that (of)	if
in the nature of	like
in the neighborhood of	about
in this case	here
inasmuch as	because
in view of the fact that	because
indicate	show, point out
initiate	begin
investigate	study
it has come to my attention	Ms. Jones has just told me; I have just learned
it is felt	I feel; we feel
it is our understanding that	we understand that
it should be noted that	(omit)
maintain	keep
maintain cost control	control cost
make a purchase	buy
make application to	apply
make contact with	see, meet
maximum	most, largest
minimum	least, smallest
modification	change
obtain	get
on the order of	about
on the part of	by
optimum	best
past history	history
per annum	annually, per year
period of time	time, period
pertaining to	about, for
philosophy	plan, idea
please be advised that	(omit)
please don't hesitate to call on us	please write us
prepare an analysis	analyze
presently	soon
prior to	before
procure	get, buy

TABLE 4–1   Simplifying Word Choices (*continued*)

COLUMN A	COLUMN B
provide	give
provide continuous indication	indicate continuously
pursuant to your inquiry	as you requested
range all the way from	range from
regarding	about
relative to	about
represent	be, is, are
require	need
so as to	to
subsequent to	after, later
substantial	large, big
sufficient	enough
terminate	end, stop
the major part of	most of
the manner in which	how
the undersigned; the writer	I, me
thereon, thereof, thereto, therefrom	(omit)
this is to acknowledge	thank you for, I have received
this is to inform you that we shall send	we'll send
through the use of	by, with
transpire	happen
true facts	facts
under separate cover	by June 1, tomorrow, separately, by parcel post
until such time as	until
utilize	use
vital	important
with a view to	to
with reference to	about
with regard to	about
with respect to	on, for, of, about
with the object to	to
with the result that	so that

doesn't become monotonous. Sentence variation will be discussed again later in this chapter.

Verbs and Nouns

Another technique to make writing more concise is to use active verbs and descriptive nouns, rather than lots of adverbs and adjectives.

Write with active verbs and descriptive nouns.

See how this sentence can be improved:

WORDY: There are some serious, unfortunate results of forecasting future performance based on historical performance during times of unusual price fluctuations of the stock in question. [25 words]

CONCISE: Using past results to forecast results creates problems during volatile periods. [11 words]

One common cause of wordy writing is hidden verbs. For example,

came to a conclusion that instead of *concluded*

causes a misstatement of instead of *misstates*

provides a matching of instead of *matches*

makes an analysis of instead of *analyzes*

will serve as an explanation of instead of *will explain*

What are the hidden verbs in these sentences?

Johnson made reference to the price-earnings ratio to support his recommendation.

The company's history of marginal performance over the past several years may be an indication of future solvency problems.

In the first sentence, the hidden verb is *refer;* in the second sentence, it is *indicate*. The revised sentences are a little less wordy, a little more forceful:

Johnson referred to the price-earnings ratio to support his recommendation.

The company's history of marginal performance over the past several years may indicate future solvency problems.

Here are some other sentences with hidden verbs, followed by revisions to make them more concise:

HIDDEN VERB: We made an analysis of ways to cut costs. [9 words]
REVISED: We analyzed ways to cut costs. [6 words]

HIDDEN VERB: I will make a recommendation concerning the best way to word this report. [13 words]
REVISED: I will recommend the best way to word this report. [10 words]

HIDDEN VERB: I have come to the conclusion that we should update our equipment. [12 words]
REVISED: I have concluded that we should update our equipment. [9 words]

HIDDEN VERB:	This method will result in a distribution of the costs between the holding company and the subsidiaries. [17 words]
REVISED:	This method will distribute the costs between the holding company and the subsidiaries. [13 words]
HIDDEN VERB:	We are able to make the determination of the cost of an asset due to the fact that we have records of its purchase. [24 words]
REVISED:	We can determine an asset's cost because we have records of its purchase. [13 words]

Finally, avoid sentence introductions that weaken the sentence idea. Don't apologize for or hedge about what you're saying:

WORDY:	Enclosed please find our invoice for $400. [7 words]
CONCISE:	Our invoice for $400 is enclosed. [6 words]
WORDY:	It has come to my attention that our department has overrun its budget for supplies. [15 words]
CONCISE:	Our department has overrun its budget for supplies. [8 words]
WORDY:	This report is an attempt to explain the conditions under which our company utilizes derivatives. [15 words]
CONCISE:	This report explains our use of derivatives. [7 words]
WORDY:	This is to acknowledge receipt of your letter of June 1. [11 words]
CONCISE:	Thank you for your letter of June 1. [8 words]
WORDY:	This is to inform you that we are sending a check in the amount of $798.14. [16 words]
CONCISE:	We're sending a check for $798.14. [6 words]

In summary, clear, readable writing contains no unnecessary or dead words. Be concise—your writing will be more forceful.

CLARITY

Concise writing is clearer because important ideas are not buried in unnecessary words and details. Writing as simply as possible will also help you achieve clarity because you'll be using words the reader knows and feels comfortable with.

Other techniques for improving the clarity of your writing include the careful use of jargon and precise, concrete word choices.

Jargon

Jargon is the "specialized or technical language of a . . . profession."[3] We all know what finance jargon is. It's words and phrases such as *amortization, capitalization, debt restructuring, systematic risk*, and *modified IRR*.

One kind of jargon is acronyms: words composed of the first letter of a group of words, such as *IRR, CAPM, MACRS,* and *LIFO.* To introduce an acronym, write out the words of the acronym, with the acronym in parentheses:

> One of the most prominent models relating return with degree of risk is the capital asset pricing model (CAPM).

After you have identified the acronym fully, you can use the acronym alone throughout the rest of the document. If you're sure that the readers will be familiar with an acronym, and if you're writing an informal document, it's usually acceptable to use the acronym without writing it out.

Unless you use acronyms and other forms of jargon carefully, they will detract from the clarity of your writing. Two guidelines can help you decide when to use jargon and when to look for other words. The first is to remember the readers' needs and to use language they will understand. Another finance person will probably understand what you mean by *net present value,* but managers or clients who have not studied finance may be unfamiliar with the term. Be careful when using jargon even with your finance colleagues. Would everyone with a degree in finance know what you mean by a *leveraged buyout?*

The second guideline for the use of jargon is to keep your word choices as simple as possible. Avoid jargon when ordinary language will say what you mean. For example, why say "the bottom line" if you mean net income or loss?

Of course, jargon is often unavoidable when you need to communicate technical information as efficiently as possible, but remember the needs of your readers. Define or explain technical terminology with which they may not be familiar.

> **Use jargon only when your readers understand it.**
> **Define technical terms when necessary.**

Precise Meaning

One of the most important elements of clear writing is precision. Word choices must be accurate and sentences constructed so that their meaning is clear. Precision is particularly important in finance people's writing because finance people are often dealing with large sums of money. Moreover, the technical nature of finance makes precise writing a necessity. Thus, one rule for an effective writing style is precision.

> **Be precise—avoid ambiguous and unclear writing.**

WORD CHOICES Imprecise writing can result from several causes. One culprit is poor diction, or the inaccurate use of words:

The major *setback* of the current method is that it is inefficient. [Poor diction: the writer meant *drawback*.]

The advantage of measurements in terms of market values is that the amounts reflect *what the item is worth*. [What is the precise meaning of the italicized phrase? *Worth* is vague.]

In these examples the diction problems are italicized:

POOR DICTION:	The users of our financial statements may see the decline in our revenues and become *worrisome*.
REVISED:	The users of our financial statements may see the decline in our revenues and become worried.
POOR DICTION:	Our advertising expense, which is 1 percent of total sales, is a *negligent* amount.
REVISED:	Our advertising expense, which is 1 percent of total sales, is a negligible amount.
POOR DICTION:	The reason for this purchase was to help from incurring rental charges.
REVISED:	The reason for this purchase was to prevent rental charges.
POOR DICTION:	This memo will discuss how to account for the theft of the filling station. [This sentence says that the filling station itself was carried off.]
REVISED:	This memo will discuss how to account for the robbery at the filling station.

Unclear, awkward writing can also result from the misuse of words ending in *-ing*:

AWKWARD AND UNCLEAR:	The lease does not meet the 90 percent test, therefore, classifying the lease as an operating lease.
REVISED:	The lease does not meet the 90 percent test, so it must be classified as an operating lease.
AWKWARD AND UNCLEAR:	By using the net present value method, the chances of accepting a poor investment are reduced.
REVISED:	Use of the net present value method reduces the chances of accepting a poor investment. [Note: This revision also changes the sentence from passive to active voice—see pages 60–63.]
AWKWARD AND UNCLEAR:	In finding out this information, we will have to be thorough in our asking questions of the concerned parties.
REVISED:	To find out this information, we must thoroughly question the concerned parties.

FAULTY MODIFIERS   Another type of imprecise writing is misplaced and dangling modifiers. A misplaced modifier is a modifying word or phrase that is not placed next to the sentence element it modifies. The result is a confusing sentence:

> Discounted cash flow techniques are often used by businesses that sell high-priced products, *such as defense contractors and automobile manufacturers.* [The italicized phrase appears to modify *products*, but it really modifies *businesses.*]

> Discounted cash flow techniques are often used by such businesses as defense contractors and automobile manufacturers, which sell high-priced products.

Consider another sentence with a misplaced modifier:

> This technique identifies computer models for review with a high probability of error.

Revised:

> This technique identifies, for review, computer models with a high probability of error.

Dangling modifiers, which usually come at the beginning of a sentence, do not actually modify any word in the sentence. Usually the word modified is implied rather than stated directly. Look at this sentence:

> After buying the bonds, the market price will fluctuate.

The writer probably meant something like this:

> After we buy the bonds, the market price will fluctuate.

Here's another example:

> As a successful company, disclosure of quarterly profits will attract investors.

One possible revision:

> Because we are a successful company, disclosure of our quarterly profits will attract investors.

PRONOUN REFERENCE   Faulty pronoun reference can also cause writing to be ambiguous and confusing:

> Capitalization of interest is adding interest to the cost of an asset under construction which increases its book value.

The meaning of this sentence is unclear. What increases book value? *Which* and *its* are confusing; their references are vague. Here is one possible revision:

Capitalization of interest is adding interest to the cost of an asset under construction. The added interest increases the asset's book value.

Faulty pronoun reference can be labeled *vague, ambiguous,* or *broad.* These terms all mean that the writer doesn't make clear what the pronoun refers to. The pronoun *this* is particularly troublesome:

FAULTY REFERENCE:	Last year Excelsor Company modified its products to one-size-fits-all and built a central distributing facility. Because of this, the company decided to reduce inventories.
REVISED:	Last year Excelsor Company modified its products to one-size-fits-all and built a central distributing facility. Because of this change, the company decided to reduce inventories.
FAULTY REFERENCE:	The use of standardized financial statements does not always show the true financial position of a company. This is a problem for investors.
REVISED:	The use of standardized financial statements does not always show the true financial position of a company. The weakness of these statements is a problem for investors.

A good rule is never to use *this* by itself. Add a noun or phrase to define what *this* is.

Another pronoun that can cause reference problems is *it*:

FAULTY REFERENCE:	Many people prefer to itemize the deductions for their income tax to decrease their tax liability, but it is not always done.
REVISED:	Many people prefer to itemize the deductions for their income tax, but not everyone chooses to itemize.

Misplaced and dangling modifiers and faulty pronoun reference are grammatical errors; they are discussed further in chapter 5. However, writing can be grammatically correct and still be imprecise. Consider this sentence:

The major drawback of using current market prices to value assets is verifiability.

Revised:

The major drawback of using current market prices to value assets is *the lack of* verifiability.

The revision makes quite a difference in meaning!

Often, the ability to write precisely is a function of precise reading—and thinking. A finance professor assigned his Finance 588 students two papers for the quarter. He then wrote the following statement on the board:

> A Finance 588 student who completes the course requirements will write a total of two papers this quarter. True or false?

The precise thinkers in the class realized that the statement might not be true. The students could write papers for other classes as well. Thus, some students could write *more than* two papers for the quarter.

Learn to analyze carefully what you read. Then you will be able to perfect your own writing so that your meanings are clear and precise.

Here are some other examples of sentences revised to improve their clarity:

UNCLEAR:	This bond is not considered risky because it sells at only 70 percent of its maturity.
REVISED:	The selling price of this bond, which is 70 percent of its maturity value, does not necessarily indicate that the bond is risky.
UNCLEAR:	When purchasing bonds at a discount, the investment cost is less than the face value of the investment.
REVISED:	When bonds sell at a discount, the investment cost is less than the face value of the investment.
UNCLEAR:	When reviewing the prior analyst's work papers, no recognition of a possible cash management problem was found.
REVISED:	When we reviewed the prior analyst's work papers, we found no recognition of a possible cash management problem.
UNCLEAR:	The IRR method has several problems that do not consider different project sizes and investing cash flows at different rates.
REVISED:	The IRR method causes several problems because it does not take into account differences in project size or the reinvestment of cash flows at a rate other than the IRR.

Concrete, Specific Wording

Chapter 3 discussed the use of concrete facts, details, and examples as a way to develop paragraphs. Concrete, specific writing adds clarity to your documents and makes them much more interesting.

We can explain concrete writing by defining its opposite—abstract writing. Abstract writing is vague, general, or theoretical. It's hard to understand because it's not illustrated by particular, material objects. Concrete writing, on the other hand, is vivid and specific; it brings a picture into the mind of the reader.

Illustrations of abstract and concrete writing styles make them easier to understand.

ABSTRACT

Historical cost is important in finance. It is easy for financial analysts to understand, and it is often seen in the financial statements. Historical cost has some disadvantages, but it has its good points, too.

CONCRETE

Historical cost is the amount of money paid for an object when it was purchased. For example, if a truck was purchased in 1998 for $30,000, then $30,000 is the truck's historical cost. Many financial analysts favor historical cost accounting because the values of assets are easy to determine from invoices and other records of the original purchase.

However, in times of inflation the historical cost of an asset may not indicate its true value. For example, an acre of land bought in 1950 for $5,000 might be worth several times that amount today, but it would still be recorded in the owner's books—and on the balance sheet—at its historical cost. Therefore, one disadvantage of historical cost accounting is that it often undervalues assets.

By giving more detailed information and specific, concrete examples of historical cost, the second example makes this concept easier to understand and more interesting to read.

In the following examples, vague, abstract sentences are replaced by more concrete writing:

VAGUE: Finance people should write well.

REVISED: Finance people need to write clear, concise letters to their clients and other business associates. [This sentence replaces the vague *well* with two characteristics of effective writing: *clear* and *concise*. The revision also gives an example of one type of writing done by finance people: letters to clients and associates.]

VAGUE: Action on today's stock market was interesting.

REVISED: The Dow Industrial Average dropped 200 points today.

The example just given illustrates a particularly effective technique you can use to make your writing concrete: illustrate your ideas with specific details about the situation you're discussing. That is, if you're writing about action on the stock market, as in the above example, add relevant details about what happened to clarify what you mean.

By adding specific, concrete details, you will avoid vague sentences like this one:

I believe we should adjust for this year's stock split because of comparability.

If we revise the sentence to be more specific and concrete, the meaning becomes much clearer:

> I believe we should adjust the number of shares outstanding for prior years so that this year's financial statements, which reflect this year's stock split, will be comparable to those of prior years.

See how specific wording improves the clarity of this sentence:

VAGUE: This liability should not appear on the balance sheet because of materiality.

CLEAR: This liability should not appear on the balance sheet because the amount is not material.

Finally, remember the readers' interests when you select the details to include in your writing; choose the details they will find meaningful and relevant. Which of the following two sentences would you prefer to read in a letter from your financial advisor?

> Your portfolio this year poses some interesting possibilities.

> If interest rates decline one percentage point this year, the bonds in your portfolio may increase in value by nine percent.

> ***Be concrete and specific. Use facts, details, and examples.***

READABLE WRITING

If your writing is interesting to read, it will almost always be clear. Lively, natural sentences hold readers' attention and keep them involved in what you are saying, so they have an easier time understanding your ideas.

This section of the chapter is devoted to several techniques that will make your sentences readable and clear: the use of active voice, writing with variety and rhythm, and using the appropriate tone.

Passive and Active Voice

This technique for achieving a good writing style may seem technical, but it will become clear after a few definitions and examples.

> ***Use active voice for most sentences.***

In the active voice, the subject of the sentence performs the action described by the verb.

ACTIVE: Most corporations issue financial statements at least once a year.

Passive voice, on the other hand, describes action done to somebody or something by another agent. The agent is not always named in the sentence.

PASSIVE: Financial statements are issued (by most corporations) at least once a year.

This formula will help you identify passive voice verbs:

Passive voice =

a form of the verb *to be*	+	the past participle of another verb (usually ending in *-ed*

forms of the verb *to be*	typical past participles
is, are, were, was, been,	accrued, received, used,
being, be, am	computed, given, kept

Sometimes passive verb phrases also contain a form of *to have* (has, have, had, having) or an *auxiliary* (will, should, would, must, etc.), but passive voice always contains a *to be* form plus a past participle.

Active voice sentences are often clearer than passive voice sentences. Consider these examples:

PASSIVE: Taxes were increased by 50 percent. [In this example, most readers would want to know who raised taxes.]
ACTIVE: The Labor Party increased taxes by 50 percent.

PASSIVE: It was decided that employees would be required to work on Saturday.
ACTIVE: The company president decided to require employees to work on Saturday.

PASSIVE: Deliberate understatement of assets and stockholders' equity with the intention of misleading interested parties is prohibited.
ACTIVE: SEC regulations prohibit deliberate misstatement of assets and stockholders' equity if the intention is to mislead interested parties.

Unfortunately, writers of "officialese," especially in government, business, and research, have so badly overused passive voice that we tend to accept it as standard style. Passive voice is seldom effective—it lacks the forcefulness and clarity of active voice. Compare the following pairs of sentences:

PASSIVE: This letter hasn't been signed.
ACTIVE: You haven't signed the letter.

PASSIVE: A determination has been made that the statements do not reflect current earnings.

ACTIVE:	The accountants have determined that the statements do not reflect current earnings.
PASSIVE:	Further research should be conducted before a report can be issued.
ACTIVE:	The analysts should conduct further research before they issue a report.
PASSIVE:	In many college finance courses, effective writing skills are emphasized.
ACTIVE:	Many college finance courses emphasize effective writing skills.
PASSIVE:	In SEC regulations it is required that prospectuses be sent to potential investors.
ACTIVE:	SEC regulations require companies to send prospectuses to potential investors.

Good writers avoid using passive voice in most situations. They ask themselves two questions: What is the action (verb)? Who or what is doing it (subject)?

One word of warning: Avoid substituting a weak active verb for passive voice. Be particularly careful of colorless verbs such as *to exist* and *to occur*. The following sentences are written in active voice, but the sentences are weak:

Capitalization of option costs on land subsequently purchased should occur.

FIFO bases itself on the assumption that the first inventory acquired is the first inventory sold.

Use descriptive, vigorous verbs to substitute for weak verbs, or reword the sentence.

We must capitalize option costs on land subsequently purchased.

The assumption that underlies FIFO is that the first inventory acquired is the first inventory sold.

WHEN TO USE PASSIVE VOICE   Although it is usually better to write in active voice, passive voice is sometimes preferable. For example, the two sentences in the preceding example could be effectively written in passive voice:

Option costs on land subsequently purchased should be capitalized.

FIFO is based on the assumption that the first inventory acquired is the first inventory sold.

Passive voice may also be necessary to avoid an awkward repetition of sentence subjects, especially in paragraphs where the same agent is performing all the action or the agent is obvious or irrelevant:

The property was appraised in 1998 at $100,000.

In this sentence, it would probably not be necessary to identify who did the appraisal.

Another consideration about active and passive voice is that sometimes you may want to emphasize the passive subject. For example, you would say

The Corner Grocery Store was robbed.

rather than

Some person or persons unknown robbed the Corner Grocery Store.

Finally, passive voice may enable you to be tactful when you must write bad news or some sort of criticism:

These figures were not calculated correctly.

This sentence doesn't say who is at fault for the erroneous calculation; here, passive voice may be the most diplomatic way to identify the problem without assigning blame.

We talk more about writing tactfully later in the chapter.

Variety and Rhythm

Another way to make your writing natural and more readable is to add variety.

> *Vary vocabulary, sentence lengths, and sentence structures.*
> *Read the writing aloud to hear how it sounds.*

The purpose of sentence variety is to avoid monotony—a sing-song, awkward repetition of the same sentence rhythms or the overuse of a word or phrase. Read the following paragraph aloud:

Financial analysts use ratios to analyze financial statements. Ratios show a company's liquidity. The current ratio shows the ratio of current assets to current liabilities. Ratios also show a company's solvency. The equity ratio is an example of a solvency ratio. It shows the ratio of owners' equity to total assets. Ratios also show profitability. The return-on-investment ratio is an example. It shows the ratio of net earnings to owners' equity.

This paragraph does not sound pleasing. In fact, it could easily lull the reader to sleep. The sentences are too similar in length and structure and the word *ratio* is repeated too often. Let's try again:

Ratios based on financial statements can reveal valuable information about a company to investors, creditors, and other interested parties. Liquidity ratios show whether a company can pay its debts. The quick ratio, for example, is a good indication of debt-paying ability for companies with slow inventory turnover. Ratios can also indicate a company's solvency; the equity ratio, for instance, shows the percentage of owners' equity to total assets.

Investors in bonds use this figure to evaluate the safety of a potential investment. Finally, ratios can give a measure of a company's profitability, which
is of special interest to potential investors. The earnings-per-share ratio is
probably the most popular of the profitability ratios.

Another cause of monotonous sentences is too many prepositional
phrases, particularly when they are linked together to form a chain. Look
again at the following sentence. Prepositions are in bold; the rest of the
phrase is underlined:

There are some serious, unfortunate results **of** <u>forecasting stock prices</u>
based **on** <u>past performance</u> **during** <u>times</u> **of** <u>market volatility</u>.

This sentence contains a chain of prepositional phrases four links
(phrases) long. A good rule is to avoid more than two prepositional
phrases in a row.

If you are not sure what prepositions are, here is a partial list:

across, after, as, at, because of, before, between, by, for, from, in, in front of,
in regard to, like, near, of, on, over, through, to, together with, under, until,
up, with

Variety is an important element of readable writing because it gives
sentences and paragraphs a pleasing rhythm. Read your paragraphs
aloud. If you notice a word or phrase repeated too often, look for a syn-
onym. If the sentences sound choppy and monotonous, vary their structures and lengths. Often a change in the way sentences begin will improve
the rhythm of the paragraph. Add an occasional short sentence and an
occasional longer one (but be sure longer sentences are still easy to understand). Avoid using too many prepositional phrases. You don't want
to bore your readers, and varied sentences are one way to keep your writing lively.

Tone

The tone of a document is the way it makes the reader feel, or the
impression it makes. A letter can have a formal or informal tone, be personal or impersonal. It can be apologetic, cold, humorous, threatening, ar-
rogant, respectful, or friendly.

Vary your tone according to the reader. If you are writing to a colleague who is also a good friend, you can be much more informal than if
you are writing to someone you know only slightly. Be particularly careful
to show respect to those who are much older than you or in higher positions of authority.

One way to decide on the proper tone of a document you are writing
is to imagine that you are in a conversation with your reader. How formal
would you be? How would you show that you were interested in your
reader's point of view and concerns? No matter how formal (or casual)
you decide to make your tone, always be courteous. Treat your corre-

spondent with tact, politeness, and respect. Avoid abruptness, condescension, and stuffiness, or any other form of rudeness. Here are some examples of poor tone:

Financial planning is a complicated subject, so I have tried to simplify it for you. [This sentence is condescending; it implies that the reader is not very bright.]

I acknowledge receipt of your letter and beg to thank you. [Too formal and artificial—stuffy, in fact.]

Send me that report immediately. I can't understand why it has taken you so long to prepare it. [In certain situations you might think this way, but you'll get better results if you write with tact and courtesy.]

For all but the most formal documents, such as some contracts, the use of personal pronouns (*you, I, we*) can contribute to a warm, personal tone. Keep the first person singular pronouns (*I, me, my*) to a minimum; focus instead on the reader with second person (*you, your*) or, in some cases, first person plural (*we, us, our*).

A personal tone, including personal pronouns, is especially effective when the message you are conveying is good news or neutral information. When you must write bad news or criticize someone, it's better to be impersonal in order to be tactful. Passive voice can also make a sentence more tactful:

TACTLESS: You failed to sign your income tax return.
BETTER: Your return wasn't signed.

Another guideline for an effective tone is to stress the positive. Emphasize what can be done rather than what cannot:

NEGATIVE: Because you were late in sending us your invoice, we cannot make payment within 30 days.
POSITIVE: Now that we have your invoice, we can process it for payment. We will issue a check by next Thursday.

Finally, be honest and sincere; avoid exaggeration and flattery.

In the final analysis, the guidelines for an effective writing tone are the same as those for good relationships. Learn to view a situation from the other person's point of view and communicate in a way that shows empathy and respect.

Here, then, is another guideline for an effective writing style.

Write from the reader's point of view.
Use tone to show courtesy and respect.

EDITING FOR STYLE
AT THE COMPUTER

The section on revision in chapter 2 mentioned software programs that some writers use to help them edit for style. These programs analyze text and give such information as the average sentence and word length. They may also identify passive voice constructions, clichés, and pretentious word choices. Some programs also tell you how difficult your writing is to read—that is, they use a formula to determine the readability level.

Keep in mind that these programs are not completely reliable. They don't identify all the weaknesses in your writing, and some of the passages they flag are not really errors. For example, we've seen in this chapter that passive voice is sometimes preferable to active voice, yet a style analyzer may identify all passive verbs as potential problems. It takes the writer's own judgment to decide when to change the passive voice and when to let it stand.

On the other hand, some of the information given by a style analyzer can truly be helpful. For example, if the analyzer tells you that your average sentence length is twenty-five words long, you know you have a problem.

In sum, style analyzers do not automatically ensure that you write effectively, but they may point out potential problems you should consider.

Whatever techniques you use to revise your text, take time to ensure that your prose is readable, clear, and concise. Your readers will be grateful.

This chapter on style has added 9 guidelines for effective writing, making a total of 16.

1. **Analyze the purpose of the writing and the needs and expectations of the readers.**
2. **Organize your ideas so that readers will find them easy to follow.**
3. **Write the draft and then revise it to make the writing polished and correct.**
4. **Make the writing unified. All sentences should relate to the main idea, either directly or indirectly. Eliminate digressions and irrelevant detail.**
5. **Use summary sentences and transitions to make your writing coherent.**
6. **Write in short paragraphs that begin with clear topic sentences.**
7. **Develop paragraphs by illustration, definition, detail, and appeals to authority.**
8. **Be concise—make every word count.**
9. **Keep it simple—use simple vocabulary and short sentences.**
10. **Write with active verbs and descriptive nouns.**
11. **Use jargon only when your readers understand it. Define technical terms when necessary.**
12. **Be precise—avoid ambiguous and unclear writing.**

13. **Be concrete and specific. Use facts, details, and examples.**

14. **Use active voice for most sentences.**

15. **Vary vocabulary, sentence lengths, and sentence structures. Read the writing aloud to hear how it sounds.**

16. **Write from the reader's point of view. Use tone to show courtesy and respect.**

TEST YOURSELF

Revise the following sentences, using the techniques covered in this chapter. Answers are provided on pages 68–69.

a. Can you revise these sentences so that they are simpler and more concise? Watch for hidden verbs.

1. To determine what information to include in our report for 1997, we will make an analysis of the investors' needs.
2. The history of United Teacup's performance, which is marginal at best, may be an indication of solvency problems that will occur in the future.
3. A number of problems revealed in our report have come to light that may make it necessary for us to issue a "sell" recommendation.
4. I have attempted to explain the three proposed alternatives for selecting the machinery.
5. It is our recommendation that Hamilton Corporation offer to purchase the property at $95,000.

b. The meaning of these sentences is not clear. Revise them so that they are unambiguous and precise.

1. After reading the following discussion, a recommendation will suggest a way we can save on our machinery purchase.
2. Each method has its rational for use.
3. The SEC has not officially written a policy for this kind of disclosure.
4. Proponents claimed that the proposed legislation would provide changes from the old method of depreciation that would increase deductions and simplify computations.
5. The letter discussed the alternative ways to finance the purchase of the new equipment. Its purpose was . . .

c. Identify the passive verbs in these sentences and revise them so they are in active voice. If necessary, invent a subject for the verb.

1. Management wanted complete information on the new project that had been proposed by the engineers.
2. The accounts receivable report is distorted by uncollectible accounts.
3. Inventory should be monitored by a system of internal controls.

4. This recommendation can easily be implemented by our clients.

5. This information was prepared by our research department.

d. Identify the prepositional phrases in these sentences. Where too many are linked together, revise the sentence.

1. Now that the choice of sites has been made and the expiration of options is occurring, this transaction must be recorded by the accounting department promptly.

2. We have designed a forecasting model for use in future spreadsheets of Hudson's Pest Control Company.

3. A statement of cash flows reports a more accurate picture of the operations of the current business period of the company.

4. The important issue to address in this company's situation is that of the expression of an opinion of increasing growth.

5. The main problem of this company is to minimize the amount of taxes for 1997.

TEST YOURSELF: ANSWERS

(Note: Some of the errors in the above sentences can be corrected in more than one way, but this key will show only one possible correction. If you recognize the error, you probably understand how to correct it.)

a.

1. To determine what to include in our 1995 report, we will analyze the investors' needs.

2. United Teacup's history of marginal performance may indicate future solvency problems.

3. We have found several problems that may require us to recommend selling the stock.

4. I have explained the three proposals for selecting the machinery.

5. We recommend that Hamilton Corporation offer to purchase the property at $95,000.

b.

1. The following discussion will conclude with a recommendation of how we can save on our machinery purchase.

2. Each method has its rationale for use.

3. The SEC has not written an official policy for this kind of disclosure.

4. Proponents claimed that the proposed legislation would provide changes from the old method of depreciation; these changes would increase deductions and simplify computations.

5. The letter discussed the alternative ways to finance the purchase of the new equipment. The purpose of the letter was . . .

c.

1. Management wanted complete information on the new project proposed by the engineers.

2. Uncollectible accounts distort the accounts receivable report.

3. An internal control system is necessary to monitor inventory. [Note: This sentence as it was originally written would be fine in most situations, even though the original sentence is in passive voice.]

4. Our clients can easily implement this recommendation.

5. Our research department prepared this information.

d.

1. Now that the choice **of** <u>sites</u> has been made and the expirations **of** <u>options</u> is occurring, this transaction must be recorded **by** <u>the accounting department</u> promptly.

   Now that we have chosen the site and the options have expired, the accounting department must record the transaction promptly.

2. We have designed a forecasting model **for** <u>use</u> **in** <u>future spreadsheets</u> **of** <u>Hudson's Pest Control Company</u>.

   We have designed a forecasting model for future spreadsheets of Hudson's Pest Control Company.

3. An statement **of** <u>cash flows</u> reports a more accurate picture **of** <u>the operations</u> **of** <u>the current business period</u> **of** <u>the company</u>.

   Cash flow statements report a more accurate picture of the company's current operations.

4. The important issue to address **in** <u>this company's situation</u> is that **of** <u>the expression</u> **of** <u>an opinion</u> **of** <u>increasing growth</u>.

   Before we can issue our opinion, we must determine whether this company's growth rate is increasing.

   [Note: *to address* is an infinitive (a verb), not a prepositional phrase. However, too many infinitive phrases can also make a sentence awkward.]

5. The main problem **of** <u>this company</u> is to minimize the amount **of** <u>taxes</u> **for** <u>1997</u>.

   This company's main problem is to minimize taxes for 1997.

EXERCISES

Exercise 4–1

Revise the following sentences so that they are written as simply and concisely as possible. Be alert for hidden verbs.

1. We should make reference to the work done by the analysts during the previous year's study.
2. The benefits of this educational program will avail themselves to the corporation via language and letters that are fresh, accurate, and clear.
3. I hope this letter will provide for an increased understanding of the best way to reduce your income taxes to a minimum.
4. Wordiness is the problem that makes my writing ineffective.
5. As you are no doubt aware, in the economic environment of today, having these services available from a firm with experience is indispensable and quite valuable.
6. I am in need of improved writing skills.
7. In conclusion, I would like to state that I feel our relationship will provide all of us, both you and us, with many opportunities to work together for our mutual benefit.
8. There are several benefits that can come from attending the seminar.
9. Enclosed please find our analysis of the best way to reduce costs in the departments under your supervision.
10. This method provides proper matching of asset maturities to liability maturities.

Exercise 4–2

Review the lists of simplified word choices in Table 4–1 of this chapter (pages 49–51). Then write a shorter or simpler version of the following words and phrases.

1. advise	16. vital
2. enclosed please find	17. with the result that
3. for the purpose of	18. this is to inform you that we shall send
4. indicate	19. failed to
5. pertaining to	20. anticipate
6. terminate	21. commence
7. true facts	22. above-mentioned firms
8. this is to acknowledge	23. aggregate
9. make a decision	24. pursuant to your inquiry
10. earliest convenience	25. transpire
11. in the amount of	26. at this point in time
12. due to the fact that	27. in advance of
13. at all times	28. optimum
14. the writer	29. exercise care
15. with regard to	30. pertaining to

Exercise 4–3

Identify the jargon in the following sentences.

1. The long bond is yielding 8 percent.
2. Our recommendation is based on thorough research into the regs and rules.
3. The AIMR and the ICFP, as well as the FMA, are organizations that concern the profession of finance.
4. Negative cash flows may affect our position with our creditors.
5. Reject the proposal, as the NPV is negative.
6. While the coupon interest rate remains fixed, the YTM may vary.
7. My CFO advised me to use our company's Beta in the CAPM.
8. Because of her superior performance, she achieves positive alphas.
9. The IRR contains a reinvestment assumption.
10. Short-term bonds were up three basis points this week.

Exercise 4–4

The meaning of the following sentences is not clear. Revise the sentences so that they are unambiguous and precise.

1. The value of the option is to buy land at a stated price.
2. The return of an investment in bonds is based on the number of years to maturity and the current market rate of interest.
3. Abigail's Energy Company has a unique way of doing business; very few other companies operate in the same way.
4. The HB Transportation Company's deficit position is due to increasing fuel prices and the company's response in increasing prices.
5. All companies incur expenses that do not provide future benefits to keep their business going to produce revenue.
6. Capitalization states that once a cost expires, we should capitalize expense.
7. Calculating the present value of the bonds' principal and future cash flows will determine our risk.
8. The riskiness of these bonds does not depend on their selling price.
9. Under LIFO the lower costs are assigned to inventory, which causes the cost of inventory to increase.
10. The most recent acquisitions upset two of our trading rules.

Exercise 4–5

The following sentences are abstract or vague. Revise them, using facts, details, or examples to make them more concrete. You may need to replace one vague sentence with several concrete sentences, or even a short paragraph. Alternatively, you could introduce a short paragraph with an abstraction and then develop the idea with more concrete, specific sentences. Feel free to invent details that will make the ideas more specific.

1. Accurate record keeping is important.
2. Sometimes firms keep two sets of records.

3. We must record this asset at its true value. [Hint: What is "true value"?]
4. The financial statements disturbed the investors.
5. The firm sold the asset for its value. [Hint: what value?]
6. Managing pensions is tricky.
7. The nature of this asset requires us to capitalize it.
8. The manager in the inventory department is not doing his job.
9. These mutual funds look like a good buy.
10. Financial analysts must use good judgment.

Exercise 4–6

Identify the passive construction in the following sentences and revise them to active voice. Be careful not to substitute weak active verbs for passive voice. For some sentences, you may need to invent a subject for the active verb. For other sentences, you may decide that passive voice is acceptable.

EXAMPLE

PASSIVE: That alternative could have been followed.
ACTIVE: We [or the firm, our client, McDonough Corporation, etc.] could have followed that alternative.

1. Our income statement was distorted by these incorrect figures.
2. All of our files were destroyed in the fire.
3. No follow-up work was performed on receivables by our firm.
4. Most letters sent to clients are reviewed by a manager.
5. The recommendations to be issued on the 1997 portfolio must be deferred by our firm.
6. Although our computer was purchased last year, it is already obsolete.
7. Each month our company's profits are consumed by operating expenses.
8. At the seminar, the provisions of the new pension plan will be explained.
9. The structure of the 1998 financial statements must be changed.
10. The bonds will be recalled as stock is issued during the restructuring.

Exercise 4–7

Identify the prepositional phrases in the following sentences. Where too many phrases are linked together, revise the sentence.

EXAMPLE

The problem of Sam Enterprises will be solved through the selection of one of the candidate CFOs presented.

Prepositional phrases identified

The problem **of** <u>Sam Enterprises</u> will be solved **through** <u>the selection</u> **of** <u>one</u> **of** <u>the candidate CFOs presented</u>.

REVISED

One of these candidate CFOs should solve Sam Enterprises' problem.

1. The effect on the balance sheet of the sale of the division is twofold.
2. The calculation of the present values of the principal of the bonds and their cash flows will reveal our risk.
3. The amortization of the discount of the bond results in the recognition of the cash flows of the bond at an even rate throughout the life of the bond.
4. The determination of the accounts receivable collection status will pose no problem for the analysts in our department.
5. An increase in advertising will make potential customers more aware of the products of the company.
6. The controller of the company called a meeting at 3:00 P.M. to discuss the annual report for this year.
7. The income tax return for Cindy Baer was filed on Friday.
8. Personnel of the corporation were pleased to learn of the increase in their salaries this year.
9. Representatives from the division in South Alabama met for a meeting in the morning.
10. Clients of our firm are concerned about the new regulations for capital gains on stock trades.

Exercise 4–8

Read this paragraph aloud and notice how monotonous it sounds. Then revise it so that sentence lengths and structures are more varied. Note also when a word or phrase is repeated too often.

Howard's Air Taxi runs scheduled flights between several local communities. Howard also provides charter service for several local businesses. Howard's financial statements reveal marginal profits for the past several years. Last year, Howard was forced to raise prices to compensate for increased maintenance expenses. These price increases and several economic downturns caused passenger volume to decline drastically. Thus 1997 was a disastrous year for Howard's Air Taxi. The preliminary information showed that 1997 losses were in excess of $2,000,000. This will force Howard into a deficit position. The 1996 balance sheet showed a net worth of $2,000,000 with total assets of $10,000,000.

NOTES

1. George deMare, *How to Write and Speak Effectively* (New York: Price Waterhouse, 1958): 9.
2. Ibid.: 11.
3. William Morris, ed., *The American Heritage Dictionary of the English Language,* New College Edition (Boston: Houghton Mifflin, 1979): 701.

5

Standard English: Grammar, Punctuation, and Spelling

One way to improve the clarity of your writing is to use standard English. Standard English (as opposed to nonstandard English) is the variety of the language that is characterized by standard, accepted forms of spelling, grammar, capitalization, and word usage. It is the language of business, industry, government, education, and the professions.

In addition to improving the clarity of what you write, the use of standard English will help you produce professional and polished documents, which is the final tip for writers given in Figure 1–1. A mastery of standard English tells the reader much about you as a person and as a professional. Your use of correct grammar says that you are an educated person who understands and appreciates the proper use of our shared language.

A grammatically correct document, free of mechanical and typographical errors, also shows that you know the importance of detail and are willing to spend the time necessary to prepare an accurate, precise document.

This chapter presents some of the most common errors in grammar, punctuation, and spelling. Because only a few principles can be covered in this short space, you should consult an English handbook for more complete coverage. The discussion here focuses on areas that give finance people the most trouble.

MAJOR SENTENCE ERRORS

Major sentence errors include three kinds of problems: fragments, comma splices, and fused sentences. These errors are very distracting to readers and often interfere seriously with their ability to understand the meaning of the sentence.

Fragments

A sentence fragment is just what its name suggests: part of a sentence. Recall that every sentence needs two essential elements: a subject and a verb. In sentence fragments, one of these elements is left out. Here are some examples:

To measure the yield correctly.

For example, all the employees who are eligible for retirement.

The reason being that we must find ways to cut overhead. [*Being* is a present participle;* it cannot be substituted for a complete verb such as *is* or *was*.]

Although our new computer system makes billing much faster. [This dependent clause has a subject and verb, but it cannot stand alone as a sentence because it is introduced by a subordinate conjunction, *although*.]

Comma Splices

The second major sentence error is comma splices, which occur when independent clauses are linked by a comma alone.

An independent clause is a group of words with a subject and a verb; it can stand alone as a sentence. Here are two independent clauses punctuated as separate sentences:

In general, increases in asset accounts from one time period to the next represent uses of funds. Decreases represent sources of funds.

Sometimes writers want to combine two independent clauses into one sentence. This can be done correctly in several ways:

1. Put a semicolon (;) between the clauses.

   In general, increases in asset accounts from one time period to the next represent uses of funds; decreases represent sources of funds.

2. Combine the clauses with a coordinating conjunction (*and, but, for, or, nor, yet, so*).

   In general, increases in assets from one time period to the next represent uses of funds, and decreases represent sources of funds.

---

*Consult a grammar handbook for explanations of technical grammatical terms such as this.

3. Combine the clauses with a semicolon, a conjunctive adverb, and a comma. (Conjunction adverbs include *however, therefore, thus, consequently, that is, for example, nevertheless, also, furthermore, indeed, instead, still.*)

In general, increases in asset accounts from one time period to the next represent uses of funds; however, decreases represent sources of funds.

Study the following comma splices. The independent clauses are joined by a comma alone:

COMMA SPLICE: We have been able to reduce the costs of manufacturing these machines, therefore we can lower our prices.

REVISED: We have been able to reduce the costs of manufacturing these machines; therefore, we can lower our prices.

COMMA SPLICE: Finance people write many letters as part of their professional responsibilities, for example, they may write letters to potential investors.

REVISED: Finance people write many letters as part of their professional responsibilities. For example, they may write letters to potential investors.

COMMA SPLICE: These orders were not processed correctly, they were not assigned control numbers.

REVISED: These orders were not processed correctly; they were not assigned control numbers.

or

(to make the sentence more concise)   These orders were not assigned control numbers.

Fused Sentences

Fused sentences, which are also called run-on sentences, occur when two independent clauses are joined without any punctuation at all:

FUSED SENTENCE: Discounted cash flow techniques are not used by all companies however, they are popular in large corporations.

REVISED: Discounted cash flow techniques are not used by all companies. However, they are popular in large corporations.

FUSED SENTENCE: The controller sent a memo to all the new employees she wanted them to have complete information about their pension benefits.

REVISED: The controller sent a memo to all the new employees; she wanted them to have complete information about their pension benefits.

or

The controller sent a memo to the new employees about their pension benefits.

PROBLEMS
WITH VERBS

The correct use of verbs is a complicated matter in any language, as you will appreciate if you have ever studied a foreign language. Fortunately, because English is the native language for most of us, we usually use verbs correctly without having to think about them. We just know what sounds right.

A few kinds of verb problems do occur, however, even in the writing of educated people. We will now look briefly at some of those problems.

Tense and Mood

The *tense* of a verb reflects the time of the action described by the verb:

PAST TENSE:	Mr. Roberts signed the contract.
PRESENT TENSE:	Mr. Roberts is signing the contract.
or	
	Should Mr. Roberts *sign* the contract now?
or	
	Everyone *signs* the contract.
FUTURE TENSE:	Ms. Jameson *will sign* after she has consulted her attorney.

Usually the choice of tense is logical and gives writers few problems.

The *mood* of a verb, however, is a little more confusing than its tense. Three moods are possible: indicative (states a fact or asks a question), imperative (a command or request), and subjunctive (a condition contrary to fact). The subjunctive mood causes the most trouble, although we often use it without realizing it:

If I *were* you, I would double-check those vouchers. [condition contrary to fact]

The most common use of the subjunctive is to follow certain verbs such as *recommend, suggest,* and *require:*

I recommend that the company *depreciate* the dump truck over five years.

I suggest that he *meet* with the sales representative next week to discuss the lost orders.

The IRS requires that our company *include* that income in this year's return.

One common problem is an unnecessary shift in tense or mood:

TENSE SHIFT:	Sales *dropped* by 20 percent last year. That drop *is* the result of increased competition. [Shift from past to present tense.]
REVISED:	Sales dropped by 20 percent last year. That drop was the result of increased competition.
MOOD SHIFT:	We *must compute* the return on the investment. Then, *accept* or *reject* it. [Shift from indicative to imperative mood.]
REVISED:	We must compute the return on the investment and then accept or reject it.
MOOD SHIFT:	If we *increase* inventory, we *would* service orders more quickly. [Shift from indicative to subjunctive.]
REVISED:	If we increase inventory, we will service orders more quickly.
or	
	If we increased inventory, we would service orders more quickly.
MOOD SHIFT:	If we *changed* our credit policy, we *will attract* more customers. (Shift from subjunctive to indicative.)
REVISED:	If we changed our credit policy, we would attract more customers.
or	
	If we change our credit policy, we will attract more customers.

Subject-Verb Agreement

Another major problem with verbs is subject-verb agreement. A verb should agree with its subject in number. That is, singular subjects take singular verbs; plural subjects take plural verbs. Note that singular verbs in the present tense usually end in *s*:

That [one] *analyst works* hard.

Those [two] *analysts work* hard.

Some irregular verbs (*to be, to have*, etc.) look different, but you will probably recognize singular and plural forms:

That *stock is* a good investment.

These *stocks are* risky.

The Drastic Measures *Corporation has* five frantic analysts on its staff.

Some *corporations have* enough analysts to handle the workload efficiently.

There are a few difficulties with this rule. First, some singular subjects are often thought of as plural. *Each, every, either, neither, one, everybody*, and *anyone* take singular verbs:

Each of the divisions *is* responsible for maintaining financial records.

Second, sometimes phrases coming between the subject and the verb make agreement tricky:

The *procedure* used today by most large companies breaking into international markets *is explained* in this article.

Finally, two or more subjects joined by *and* take a plural verb. When subjects are joined by *or*, the verb agrees with the subject closest to it:

Either *Company A or Company B is planning* to issue new stocks.

Either the *controller or the managers have called* this meeting.

PROBLEMS WITH PRONOUNS

Two common problems with pronouns are agreement and reference. Understanding agreement is easy: A pronoun must agree with its antecedent (the word it stands for). Thus, singular antecedents take singular pronouns and plural antecedents take plural pronouns:

Mr. Jones took *his* check to the bank.

Each *department* keeps *its* own records of transfer costs.

This rule usually gives trouble only with particular words. Note that *company, corporation, firm, management*, and *board* are singular; therefore, they take singular pronouns.

The *company* increased its net income by 20 percent. [Not *company . . . their*]

The *board* of directors discussed acquiring a subsidiary in *its* latest meeting. [Not *board . . . their*]

Management issued *its* quarterly report. [But: The *managers* issued *their* report.]

The second problem with pronouns is vague, ambiguous, or broad reference. The pronouns that give the most trouble are *that, which,* and *it.* This problem was discussed chapter 4, but here are some additional examples:

FAULTY REFERENCE:	Sales are often made on credit, and expenses may be accrued. This illustrates that reported net income is not always the same as cash income.
REVISED (one possibility):	Since sales are often made on credit and expenses may be accrued, reported net income is not always the same as cash income.
FAULTY REFERENCE:	We add new stocks to the portfolio periodically and conduct formal evaluations. *This* is a very important step.
REVISED:	Before we add new stocks to the portfolio, we evaluate them. These evaluations are a very important step.

Although agreement and reference cause writers the most problems with pronouns, occasionally other questions arise.

One of these questions is the use of first and second person, which some people have been taught to avoid. In the discussion of tone in chapter 4 we saw how the use of these personal pronouns can contribute to an effective writing style for many documents. Personal pronouns are not usually appropriate, however, in formal documents such as some reports and contracts.

There are a few other cautions about the use of personal pronouns. First, use first person singular pronouns (*I, me, my,* and *mine*) sparingly to avoid writing that sounds self-centered. The second problem to avoid is using *you* in a broad sense to mean people in general, or as a substitute for another pronoun:

| INCORRECT: | I don't want to file my income tax return late because the IRS will fine *you.* |
| REVISED: | I don't want to file my income tax return late because the IRS will fine me. |

Pronouns and Gender

In English, there are no singular personal pronouns that refer to an antecedent that could be either masculine or feminine. Until about a generation ago, the masculine pronouns (*he, him, his*) were understood to stand for either gender:

Each *taxpayer* must file *his* tax forms by April 15.

Sentences like this one were common even though the pronoun's antecedent (in this case, *taxpayer*) could be either male or female.

Most people today believe that this older pronoun usage is no longer appropriate. They prefer the use of language that doesn't indicate gender, including pronouns that are gender-neutral, unless, of course, the antecedent is clearly male or female:

The *controller* of Marvelous Corporation was pleased with *his* company's financial statements. [The controller is a man.]

or

The *controller* of Marvelous Corporation was pleased with *her* company's financial statements. [The controller is a woman.]

When the pronoun's antecedent is not clearly male or female, many people write sentences like these:

Each *taxpayer* must file *his or her* tax forms by April 15.

Each *taxpayer* must file *his/her* tax forms by April 15.

Unfortunately, the *he or she* and *he/she* constructions can be awkward, especially if several occur in the same sentence:

Each *taxpayer* must file *his or her* tax forms by April 15 unless *he or she* has filed for an extension.

What is the solution? The best approach for most sentences is to use plural nouns and pronouns:

Taxpayers must file *their* tax forms by April 15 unless *they* have filed for a extension.

For some sentences, though, you won't be able to use plurals. In these situations, some writers use gendered pronouns arbitrarily and switch often; sometimes they use a feminine pronoun and sometimes a masculine one. Whatever approach you use to avoid gender bias in your use of pronouns, keep these guidelines in mind:

- Most of today's business publications use language that avoids a gender bias, including a careful use of pronouns. If you use the older style, your writing will seem outdated.
- Some of your readers will be annoyed by a choice of pronouns that seems to be gender-biased.
- Perhaps the most important guideline is to write what your readers expect.

PROBLEMS WITH MODIFIERS

Chapter 4 discussed the two main problems that can occur with modifiers: misplaced modifiers, which occur when the modifier is not placed next to the word it describes, and dangling modifiers, which do not modify any word in the sentence:

MISPLACED MODIFIER:	We only sold five new cars last week. [*Only* is misplaced. It should be next to the word or phrase it modifies.]
REVISED:	We sold only five new cars last week.

DANGLING MODIFIER: When issuing checks, the proper procedure must be adhered to.

REVISED: When issuing checks, we must adhere to the proper procedures.

The best guideline for using modifiers correctly is to place them next to the word or phrase they describe. For a further discussion of problems with modifiers and additional examples, see chapter 4.

PARALLEL STRUCTURE

Parallel sentence elements are those that are grammatically equal (nouns, phrases, clauses, etc.). When these items appear in a list or a compound structure, they should be balanced, or parallel. Nouns should not be matched with clauses, for example, nor should sentences be matched with phrases:

STRUCTURE NOT PARALLEL: This report will discuss the computer's features, how much it costs, and its disadvantages. [This sentence combines a noun, a dependent clause, and another noun.]

REVISED: This report will discuss the computer's features, cost, and disadvantages.

STRUCTURE NOT PARALLEL: We recommend the following procedures:

- Hire a consultant to help us determine our needs. [verb phrase]

- Investigate alternative makes and models of equipment. [verb phrase]

- We should then set up a pilot program to assess retraining needs for employees who will use the new equipment. [sentence]

REVISED: We recommend the following procedures:

- Hire a consultant to help us determine our needs. [verb phrase]

- Investigate alternative makes and models of equipment. [verb phrase]

- Set up a pilot program to assess retraining needs for employees who will use the new equipment. [verb phrase]

APOSTROPHES
AND PLURALS

The rules for apostrophes and plurals are quite simple, but many people get them confused.

Most plurals are formed by adding either *s* or *es* to the end of the word. If you are unsure of a plural spelling, consult a dictionary.

With one exception, apostrophes are never used to form plurals. Apostrophes are used to replace letters in contractions (*can't, isn't*) or to show possession. For possessive singular words, the form is *'s*. For possessive plural words, the apostrophe comes after the *s*:

singular	plural
client's file	clients' files
statement's format	users' needs
business's budget	businesses' budgets

A common mistake is *stockholder's* equity. When stockholder(s) is plural (it usually is), the apostrophe comes after the *s*: *stockholders' equity*.

There is one exception to the plural-apostrophe rule. The plurals of letters can be formed with *'s*:

Cross your *t*'s and dot your *i*'s.

Often a phrase requiring an apostrophe can be rewritten using *of* or its equivalent:

the company's statements [the statements of the company]

the month's income [the income of the month]

a week's work [the work of a week]

the year's total [the total for the year]

Either of these possessive forms is correct, but remember the caution given in Chapter 4 about using too many prepositional phrases in a sentence. The result can be awkward or wordy.

Finally, note these possessive plurals:

two companies' earnings

five months' income

three weeks' work

prior years' earnings

ten years' total

Ten years' total might also be written *ten-year total*, but analyze the difference in meaning between *ten-year total* and *ten years' totals*.

Finally, some writers confuse *it's* with *its*. *It's* is a contraction of *it is*; *its* is the possessive pronoun:

> It's important to make careful forecasting estimates.

> The company recalled its bonds.

COMMAS

Commas are important because they can make sentences easier to understand. Lack of a comma makes the meaning of this sentence ambiguous:

> I wouldn't worry because you appear to have a thriving business.

Adding a comma clears up the confusion:

> I wouldn't worry, because you appear to have a thriving business.

Comma Guide sheet

USE COMMAS:

1. before *and, but, or, not, for, so,* and *yet* when these words come between independent clauses.

   > We sent our customer an invoice for the product, and they mailed a check the next day.

   > Our competitors increased their advertising, but our customers remained loyal.

2. following an introductory adverbial clause.

   > When investors consider buying stock in a corporation, they are especially interested in the company's cash flows.

   > Because production costs are up, we will be forced to raise our price.

   > Although we worked all night, we didn't finish the report.

3. following transitional expressions and long introductory phrases.

   > In the prospectus for the initial public offering, the company described its research and development costs.

   > To improve the service to our Atlanta customers, we are adding three new sales representatives. However, we still need four more representatives.

4. to separate items in a series (including coordinate adjectives).

   Finance people must be intelligent, dedicated, and conscientious.

   The controller, the senior bookkeeper, and the manager of the parts department formulated a new policy.

5. to set off nonrestrictive clauses and phrases (compare rule 4 under *DO NOT USE COMMAS*).

   The SEC, which is an agency of the federal government, is concerned with proper presentation of financial statements.

   The annual report, which was issued in March, contained shocking news for investors.

   The main office, located in Boston, employs 350 people.

6. to set off contrasted elements.

   Treasury stock is a capital account, not an asset.

   We want to lower our prices, not raise them.

7. to set off parenthetical elements.

   Changes in accounting methods, however, must be disclosed in financial statements.

   "Our goal," he said, "is to dominate the market."

DO NOT USE COMMAS:

1. to separate the subject from the verb or the verb from its complement.

   Incorrect:

   Some emerging growth companies, have impressive net income.

   Correct:

   Some emerging growth companies have impressive net income.

2. to separate compound verbs or objects.

   Incorrect:

   She wrote angry letters to the company president, and to her attorney.

   Correct:

   She wrote angry letters to the company president and to her attorney.

3. to set off words and short phrases that are not parenthetical.

   Incorrect:

Cash receipts are deposited, each day, in the company checking account.

Correct:

Cash receipts are deposited each day in the company checking account.

4. to set off restrictive clauses, phrases, or appositives (compare rule 5 under *USE COMMAS*).

   Incorrect:

   A problem, that concerns many financial analysts, is the measurement of risk.

   Correct:

   A problem that concerns many financial analysts is the measurement of risk.

5. before the first item or after the last item of a series (including coordinate adjectives).

   Incorrect:

   Some assets are long-term, such as, land, buildings, and equipment.

   [The faulty comma is the one before *land*.]

   Correct:

   Some assets are long-term, such as land, buildings, and equipment.

COLONS
AND SEMICOLONS

The rules for colons (:) are few and easy to master, although sometimes writers use them incorrectly. Used correctly—and sparingly—colons can be effective because they draw the readers' attention to the material that follows.

Colons can be used in the following situations:

1. to introduce a series.

   Three new investment banking firms have located in this area recently: Smith and Harrison, Thomas R. Becker and Associates; and Johnson & Baker.

2. to introduce a direct quotation, especially a long quotation that is set off from the main body of the text.

   The chief financial officer issued the following instruction: "All work papers should include concise, well-organized memos summarizing any problem revealed by the analysis."

3. to emphasize a summary or explanation.

Our study of Sebastian Enterprises has revealed one primary problem: Unless management hires new researchers to develop technical innovations, Sebastian will lose its position of market dominance.

4. following the salutation in a business letter.

Dear Mr. Evans:

When a colon introduces a series, an explanation, or a summary, the clause that precedes the colon should be a complete statement:

We have sent reminder letters to the following clients: B and B Conglomerates, Abigail's Catnip Boutique, and Sharkey's Aquarium Supplies.

not

We have sent reminder letters to: B and B Conglomerates, Abigail's Catnip Boutique, and Sharkey's Aquarium Supplies.

Semicolons (;) are used for only two situations: between independent clauses (see page 75) and between items in a series, if the items themselves have internal commas:

The proposal was signed by Joan Underwood, President; Alice Barret, Vice-President; and Sam Barnes, Treasurer.

DIRECT QUOTATIONS

The punctuation of direct quotations depends on their length. Short quotations (fewer than five typed lines) are usually run in with the text and enclosed with quotation marks. Longer quotations are set off from the text—indented five spaces from the left margin—with no quotation marks. Direct quotations should be formally introduced; a colon may separate the introduction from the quoted material. Study the following examples:

Gallagher and Andrew define commercial paper as "a type of short-term promissory note ... issued by large corporations with strong credit ratings."[1]

Gallagher and Andrew give the following definition of commercial paper:

Commercial Paper Commercial paper is a type of short-term promissory note—similar to an IOU—issued by large corporations with strong credit ratings. Commercial paper is *unsecured*, meaning that the issuing corporation does not provide any property as collateral that the lender (the one who buys the commercial paper note) can take instead of a payment if the issuing corporation defaults on the note.[2]

A direct quotation requires a citation identifying its source. It's also better to identify briefly the source of a quotation within the text itself, as the preceding examples illustrate. If a quotation comes from an individual, use his or her complete name the first time you quote from this person. You may also need to give the title or position of the person you are quoting, or otherwise explain that person's credentials. Study the following examples:

According to Richard Smith, an executive officer of the Fairways Corporation, "The industry faces an exciting challenge in meeting foreign competition."

Elaine Howard, who supervised the market research for the new product, provided this assessment of its sales potential: "Within five months from the product's introduction into the market we expect sales to approach 500,000 units."

Notice the placement of punctuation in relation to quotation marks:

Inside quotation marks:

period	*quotation."*
comma	*quotation,"*

Outside quotation marks:

colon	*quotation":*
semicolon	*quotation";*

Inside or outside quotation marks:

question mark	?" or "?

—depending on whether the question mark is part of the original quotation:

Mr. Misel asked, "Where is the file of our new client?"

Did Mr. Misel say, "I have lost the file of our new client"?

One final remark. Sometimes writers depend too heavily on direct quotation. It's usually better to paraphrase—to express someone else's ideas in your own words—unless precise quotation would be an advantage. As a rule, no more than 10 percent of a paper should be direct quotation. To be most effective, quotations should be used sparingly, and then only for authoritative support or dramatic effect.

Chapter 7, which discusses research papers, gives more information on the use of sources, including direct quotations and paraphrases.

SPELLING

Finished, revised writing should be entirely free of misspelled words. When you work at a word processor, use a spell-check program to catch misspelled words and typographical errors. Note that a spell-check program will not distinguish between homonyms such as *affect* and *effect* or *their* and *there*. If you are writing without a word processor, keep a dictionary on your desk and use it if you have any doubt about a word's spelling.

Spelling: Always check every word!

The following short list contains words commonly misspelled or misused by finance people:

accrual, accrued

advise/advice

affect/effect

cost/costs, consist/consists, risk/risks

led, misled

occurred, occurring, occurrence

principal/principle

receivable, receive

separate, separately

The italicized words in the following sentences are often confused:

Please *advise* us about the best way to pay for this purchase. [*Advise* is a verb.]

We appreciate your *advice*. [*Advice* is a noun.]

This change in accounting policy will not *affect* the financial statements. [*Affect* is usually a verb, but in the social and cognitive sciences, it can be used as a noun meaning *emotion* or *mood*.]

This change in accounting policy will have no *effect* on the financial statements. [*Effect* is usually a noun. Rarely, *effect* is a verb meaning to cause to happen.]

The *cost* of the truck fleet is more than we expected. [*Cost* is singular.]

The *costs* to manufacture this part stem from two sources. [*Costs* is plural, but when you say the word aloud, you can't hear the final *s*.]

The ambiguous mission statement may *mislead* investors. [*Mislead* is present or future tense.]

This ambiguous mission statement *misled* investors. [*Misled* is past tense.]

How should we compute the *principal* to be paid on this bond investment?

This procedure does not make use of discounted cash flow *principles*.

HELP FROM THE COMPUTER

Some writers check their text for grammatical errors by using grammar-check software. These programs can help you identify some problems with grammar, including errors with verbs, pronouns, and punctuation. Like programs that analyze writing style, these computer aids may not catch all your grammatical errors, and they may flag as an error a usage that is indeed correct. Thus, the decision to use grammar checkers to review your text is a matter of personal experience and preference: Some excellent writers praise them highly, but others find them of limited use.

A word processor with a good spell-check program is another matter. As we've pointed out many times, it is much easier to make corrections when you use a word processor. Spell-check programs are also a tremendous help in correcting spelling and typographical errors.

A final word: Be sure to proofread the final *hard copy* of your document for errors you may have missed earlier, whether you or someone else does the actual keyboarding. Computers aren't foolproof; sometimes what appears on the screen doesn't look the same on a printed page. Any errors, including those caused by the computer or printer, make work look sloppy and the writer seem careless. Effective writing should look professional: correct, neat, and polished.

In summary, standard English—including correct grammar, punctuation, and spelling—is essential for polished, professional writing. Don't just guess about the correct usage. Resolve your uncertainties with a grammar handbook, dictionary, spelling checker, or grammar-check computer program. Remember the needs of your readers. The use of standard English is necessary for smooth, clear reading.

This chapter has given us another guideline for effective writing; we now have 17.

1. **Analyze the purpose of the writing and the needs and expectations of the readers.**
2. **Organize your ideas so that readers will find them easy to follow.**
3. **Write the draft and then revise it to make the writing polished and correct.**
4. **Make the writing unified. All sentences should relate to the main idea, either directly or indirectly. Eliminate digressions and irrelevant detail.**
5. **Use summary sentences and transitions to make your writing coherent.**
6. **Write in short paragraphs that begin with clear topic sentences.**

7. Develop paragraphs by illustration, definition, detail, and appeals to authority.

8. Be concise—make every word count.

9. Keep it simple—use simple vocabulary and short sentences.

10. Write with active verbs and descriptive nouns.

11. Use jargon only when your readers understand it. Define technical terms when necessary.

12. Be precise—avoid ambiguous and unclear writing.

13. Be concrete and specific. Use facts, details, and examples.

14. Use active voice for most sentences.

15. Vary vocabulary, sentence lengths, and sentence structures. Read the writing aloud to hear how it sounds.

16. Write from the reader's point of view. Use tone to show courtesy and respect.

17. Proofread for grammar, punctuation, spelling, and typographical errors.

TEST YOURSELF

Identify and correct the errors in the following exercises using the guidelines discussed in this chapter. Answers are provided on pages 92–94.

a. Identify and correct fragments, comma splices, or fused sentences. Some sentences are correct.

1. Ms. Ellison, the chief financial officer, argued that these expenses were necessary, thus, she approved them.

2. Honeybees Honey Supplies Corporation must not only improve its internal control system it must also review its procedures for accounts receivable.

3. Many types of users rely on financial statement information, for example, investors may use the information to decide whether to purchase stock in the company.

4. Physical volume is one factor that affects cost behavior; other factors include efficiency, changes in technology, and unit prices of inputs.

5. In spite of the uncertain outlook for the economy, however, we project that our sales will increase this year by at least 50 percent.

b. Some of these sentences have verb errors (subject-verb agreement or shifts in tense or mood). Identify these errors and correct the sentences.

1. In times of inflation, changes in the general purchasing power of the dollar forces analysts to deal with an unstable monetary unit.

2. If we change our marketing strategy, we would attract more customers.

3. Neither the president nor the supervisors understand the new tax laws.

4. One problem we found in our reviews of the records were that dividends were not always paid in the year declared.

5. A prospectus containing past performance charts provide additional information to investors.

c. Correct any pronoun errors you find in the following sentences.

1. When an investor or creditor wishes to compare two companies, they cannot always rely on the information in annual reports for the comparison.
2. We should alert the company that they may be required to pay additional taxes.
3. The Fed attempts to influence interest rates during their Open Market Committee meetings.
4. Management is interested in improving the revenue figures for their report to the stockholders.
5. Each analyst is required to keep detailed records of their work on the project.

d. Revise the following sentence for parallel structure.

We recommend the following improvements in our system of internal controls:

- the controls over cash should be strengthened.
- a finance manual to ensure that transactions are handled uniformly.
- improved documentation of financial procedures.

e. Punctuate the following sentences correctly.

1. When the financial statements were issued in March the company showed a net loss of $5,000,000.
2. To increase the revenues from its new muffin products the Muffet Muffin Company introduced an advertising campaign in New York Chicago and Los Angeles.
3. The biggest problem in our firm however is obsolete inventories.
4. We currently value our inventories according to LIFO not FIFO.
5. We might suggest to the portfolio manager that he consider the current value of the bonds which is over $10 million.

TEST YOURSELF: ANSWERS

(Note: Some of the errors can be corrected in more than one way. For most sentences, this key will show only one possible correction. If you recognize the error, you probably understand how to correct it.)

a.

1. Ms. Ellison, the chief financial officer, argued that these expenses were necessary; thus, she approved them.

   or

Ms. Ellison, the chief financial officer, argued that these expenses were necessary. Thus, she approved them.

2. Fused sentence. Correction:

   Honeybees Honey Supplies Corporation must not only improve its internal control system; it must also review its procedures for accounts receivable.

3. Comma splice. Correction:

   Many types of users rely on financial statement information; for example, investors may use the information to decide whether to purchase stock in the company.

4. Correct.

5. Correct. [*However* doesn't come between two independent clauses in this sentence.]

b.

1. Subject-verb agreement. In times of inflation, changes in the general purchasing power of the dollar force analysts to deal with an unstable monetary unit. [The verb should agree with the subject *changes*.]

2. Mood shift. If we changed our marketing strategy, we would attract more customers.

   or

   If we change our marketing strategy, we will attract more customers. [The original sentence contained a shift in mood from indicative to subjunctive. Either mood is correct here; the key is to be consistent.]

3. Correct.

4. Subject-verb agreement. One problem we found in our reviews of the records was that dividends were not always paid in the year declared. [The verb should agree with *problem*.]

5. Subject-verb agreement. A prospectus containing past performance charts provides additional information to investors. [The verb should agree with *prospectus*.]

c.

1. When investors or creditors wish to compare two companies, they cannot always rely on the information in annual reports for the comparison. [Alternative: an *investor or a creditor/. . . he or she cannot . . .*]

2. We should alert the company that it may be required to pay additional taxes.

3. The Fed attempts to control interest rates during its open market committee meetings.

4. Management is interested in improving the revenue figures for its report to the stockholders.

5. The analysts are required to keep detailed records of their work on the project. [Alternative: *Each analyst is . . . his or her work . . .*]

d.

We recommend the following improvements in your system of internal controls:
- stronger controls over cash
- a finance manual to ensure that transactions are handled uniformly
- improved documentation of financial procedures

e.

1. When the financial statements were issued in March, the company showed a net loss of $5,000,000.
2. To increase the revenues from its new muffin products, the Muffet Muffin Company introduced an advertising campaign in New York, Chicago, and Los Angeles.
3. The biggest problem in our firm, however, is obsolete inventories.
4. We currently value our inventories according to LIFO, not FIFO.
5. We might suggest to the portfolio manager that he consider the current value of the bonds, which is over $10 million.

EXERCISES

Exercise 5–1

Join these independent clauses together in three ways.

we should file our federal income taxes with the IRS by April 15

for our state taxes we can request an extension

Exercise 5–2

Identify and correct fragments, comma splices, or fused sentences. Some sentences are correct.

1. The finance department had added several new employees, thus, we had a training session.
2. To increase employee satisfaction; therefore, we tried a new system of promotion.
3. However, not all committee members agreed with the president.
4. Tax season is our busiest time of the year everyone works long hours.
5. Because everyone worked extra hours, we were able to finish on time.
6. Although, the new equipment has improved our rate of production.
7. The reason for our low inventory turnover being that this is our slow season.
8. Accountants do not depreciate land, therefore, land's book value remains the same year after year.
9. Beta represents nondiversifiable risk and therefore provides the relevant measure of risk in the portfolio.

10. Although the consultant reviewed the recommendations at some length, five staff members still didn't understand what would be involved.

Exercise 5–3

Some of these sentences have verb errors (subject-verb agreement or shifts in tense or mood). Identify these errors and correct the sentences.

1. If we hired a systems specialist, we will be able to design a new system.
2. Either the analysts or the treasurer is responsible for this report.
3. One of our biggest successes during recent years are the number of models we offer.
4. The physical flow of goods generally follow the FIFO pattern.
5. Each of these statements is prepared monthly.
6. Neither John nor Elena is participating in this project.
7. We will depreciate this asset over ten years. First, however, determine its salvage value.
8. The future benefits provided by the bond is partly due to its high interest rate.
9. Selling some of the stocks results in realized holding gains and losses.
10. We review the client's system of internal control. Then we will recommend ways to improve it.

Exercise 5–4

Correct any faulty pronouns you find in the following sentences.

1. According to the IRS, each taxpayer must sign his tax form when he files his income tax return.
2. Hamilton Exports increased their revenues last year.
3. Three new procedures were used to improve the internal control system. This was the responsibility of Nancy Copeland.
4. Although financial analysts often use averaging techniques to reduce the possibilities of error, it is not essential.
5. I find the new tax forms confusing because you have so much trouble understanding them.
6. Dell's Delights has greatly increased it's advertising expense.
7. A switch to stocks usually results in a higher return over a long period of time; this would be important to our company.
8. The board of directors will hold its next meeting in July.
9. Every corporation coming under SEC regulations must follow certain procedures in preparing their financial statements.
10. Everyone registering for the convention will receive a package of information when they arrive.

Exercise 5–5

Revise the following sentences for parallel structure.

1. Three people attended the July meeting:

   - the financial analyst
   - the manager of the marketing department
   - the president also attended

2. This committee will study the problem, a recommendation for correcting it, and oversee the correction procedures.
3. The hiring decisions will be based on three criteria: experience, training, and whether the applicants have good communication skills.

Exercise 5–6

a. Complete the following chart.

SINGULAR	SINGULAR POSSESSIVE	PLURAL	PLURAL POSSESSIVE
prospectus			
company			
user			
cost			
risk			
CFA			
year			
industry			

b. Use the words from the chart to fill in these sentences. The singular form of the correct word is given in the parentheses.

1. (CFA) _____ from all over the country will be at the convention.
2. (company) Investors examine a _____ statements to determine its financial condition.
3. (cost) This company's recurring _____ are too high.
4. (analysis) Which of the _____ is in error?
5. (value) What is the present _____ of this machine?
6. (risk) Investors in these bonds must accept certain _____ .
7. (industry) Research and development are crucial in many _____ .
8. (user) Financial statements provide information for different types of _____.
9. (company) The board of directors considered the _____ pension plan.
10. (column) We are making changes in the two _____ totals.

Exercise 5–7

Punctuate the following sentences correctly.

1. Most companies base asset values on their historical cost, however, there are exceptions to this rule.
2. To provide this important information to our investors we should include projections.
3. The report was filed February 12 1998 in Washington D.C.
4. Before we can issue an opinion on these bonds we must be sure that this issue was evaluated correctly.
5. The report was signed by the analyst, the director of financial planning, and the vice president.
6. The analysis revealed several problems in Hudson Hat Company's financial situation such as its cash collection its handling of bad debts and its inventory accounting.
7. The presidents letter contained the following warning "If our revenues don't increase soon the plant may be forced to close"
8. "We're planning a new sales strategy" the manager wrote in reply.
9. We have decided not to invest in new trucks at this time instead we are considering subcontracting our deliveries.
10. Although our revenues increased during June expenses rose at an alarming rate.

Exercise 5–8

Identify and correct any misspelled words in the following list. Look up any words you are unsure of; not all of these words were included in the chapter.

1. believe
2. receive
3. occured
4. separate
5. accural
6. benefitted
7. existence
8. principle (the rule)
9. cost (plural)
10. mislead (past tense)
11. advise (the noun)
12. effect (the noun)
13. thier

NOTES

1. Timothy J. Gallagher and Joseph D. Andrew, Jr., *Financial Management: Principles and Practice* (Upper Saddle River, N.J.: Prentice Hall, 1996): 25.
2. Ibid.

6

Format for Clarity: Document Design

How a document looks at first glance can make a big difference in how the reader reacts to it. An attractive document generally gets a positive response, but a paper that is not pleasing to the eye may never be read. Good design will also help you create a document that looks polished and professional, which is the sixth tip for effective writing, as shown in Figure 1–1.

This chapter looks at techniques of document design that make letters, memos, and reports more attractive. A good design does more for the readers than appeal to them visually. A well-planned format also contributes to the clarity of documents by making them easier to read.

Later chapters cover the conventions and formats specific to particular kinds of documents, such as the standard parts of letters, memos, and reports. The techniques covered in this chapter are ones you can use for any kind of document. We consider ways to make documents look professional and attractive, such as the choice of paper and print and the use of white space. We also show how techniques of formatting, such as headings, lists, and graphic illustrations, can make your documents clearer and more readable.

GOOD DESIGN: AN ILLUSTRATION

To illustrate the difference good design can make in the readability of a document, study the example in Figures 6–1 through 6–3, which are three versions of the same memo. Figure 6–1 shows straight text, with no divisions for paragraphs, headings, or other features of good document design. Figure 6–2 divides the text into readable paragraphs with a little more white space, and Figure 6–3 uses additional white space, headings, and a set-off list. Which version of the memo do you think is most effective? Does the version in Figure 6–3 suggest formatting techniques you can use in your own writing?

A PROFESSIONAL APPEARANCE

If you already have a job, you may find models of well-designed documents by looking at papers written by people with whom you work. In fact, your employer may expect all documents to be written a certain way—in a standard format, for example, and on the company's letterhead and standard stock paper. You will seem more professional if you learn your employer's expectations for document design and then adhere to them.

Often, however, whether you're on the job or still in school, you will have a fair amount of leeway in how you design your documents. The remainder of this chapter looks at techniques you can use to give your documents a professional appearance. For example, a professional-looking document uses high-quality material—the best paper and the best print. It incorporates an attractive use of margins and white space, and it is perfectly neat.

Paper and Print

If you're already employed, you may not have any choice about the paper; you probably use your company's letterhead stationery and standard stock for all your documents. If you are still a student, however, you need to select a paper that makes a good impression. For the final copy of a paper you submit for a grade, your instructor may prefer you to use 8½ × 11-inch paper of a high-quality bond, about 24-pound weight, in white or off-white. Never submit a paper printed on the large green-and-white striped computer paper (unless you have your instructor's permission), and never use erasable bond paper.

The print of your document is another consideration. After you prepare your final manuscript on a word processor, print it on a good printer (laser or ink jet) that gives a professional appearance.

FIGURE 6–1   *Memo for Comparison (see Figures 6–2 and 6–3)*

TO: John S. Lang
FROM: Lee A. McGrady
DATE: February 19, 1998
SUBJECT: Personal Investment Portfolio Objective and Strategy

The investment objective is to accumulate, in 30 years, enough money in the portfolio to generate $3,000 income each month in 1998 dollars. Assuming inflation averages 3% a year during the next 30 years, the nominal amount the portfolio must provide at maturity is $7,282 a month. Assuming a retirement portfolio is able to earn 7% annually in 30 years, $1,248,306 in assets will be required to produce the $7,282 a month. Therefore, the portfolio objective, or target, is $1,248,306 in 30 years. The current amount of cash available, $5,000, is not enough to grow to the target in 30 years without additional contributions. If it is assumed that the portfolio will return 13% on average during the next 30 years, then it will be necessary to invest an additional $231 every month in order to reach the target. To reach the target, follow this strategy: Invest 80% of the portfolio in stock mutual funds, 10% in bond mutual funds, and 10% in money market funds. These percentages are based on the assumption that during the next 30 years stock funds will return, on average, 15% a year, bond funds will return 11%, and "cash" (that is, short-term liquid debt securities) will return 5%. If these assumptions prove to be true, and if the portfolio target distribution is maintained, then the portfolio's average annual rate of return will be 13.6%. To implement the strategy, set up the portfolio as a self-directed IRA. Rebalance the portfolio annually, in April, after the results of the previous year have been calculated. Hold all assets purchased for at least three years (barring some obvious reason to sell early). Once each year, evaluate the performance of all assets held more than three years. Note the worst-performing asset in each group (as measured by average annual return during the entire holding period). If an asset is the worst in its group two years in a row, sell it and replace it with the fund in same category having the best five-year performance according to the financial press. Exception: if the reported performance of the best-performing fund is worse than the record of the candidate for replacement in the portfolio, disregard this requirement.

FIGURE 6–2   *Memo for Comparison (see Figures 6–1 and 6–3)*

TO: John S. Lang
FROM: Lee A. McGrady
DATE: February 19, 1998
SUBJECT: Personal Investment Portfolio Objective and Strategy

The investment objective is to accumulate, in 30 years, enough money in the portfolio to generate $3,000 income each month in 1998 dollars. Assuming inflation averages 3% a year during the next 30 years, the nominal amount the portfolio must provide at maturity is $7,282 a month. Assuming a retirement portfolio is able to earn 7% annually in 30 years, $1,248,306 in assets will be required to produce the $7,282 a month. Therefore, the portfolio objective, or target, is $1,248,306 in 30 years.

The current amount of cash available, $5,000, is not enough to grow to the target in 30 years without additional contributions. If it is assumed that the portfolio will return 13% on average during the next 30 years, then it will be necessary to invest an additional $231 every month in order to reach the target.

To reach the target, follow this strategy: Invest 80% of the portfolio in stock mutual funds, 10% in bond mutual funds, and 10% in money market funds. These percentages are based on the assumption that during the next 30 years stock funds will return, on average, 15% a year, bond funds will return 11%, and "cash" (that is, short-term liquid debt securities) will return 5%. If these assumptions prove to be true, and if the portfolio target distribution is maintained, then the portfolio's average annual rate of return will be 13.6%.

To implement the strategy, set up the portfolio as a self-directed IRA. Rebalance the portfolio annually, in April, after the results of the previous year have been calculated. Hold all assets purchased for at least three years (barring some obvious reason to sell early).

Once each year, evaluate the performance of all assets held more than three years. Note the worst-performing asset in each group (as measured by average annual return during the entire holding period). If an asset is the worst in its group two years in a row, sell it and replace it with the fund in same category having the best five-year performance according to the financial press. Exception: if the reported performance of the bestperforming fund is worse than the record of the candidate for replacement in the portfolio, disregard this requirement.

FIGURE 6–3   *Memo for Comparison (see Figures 6–1 and 6–2)*

TO: John S. Lang
FROM: Lee A. McGrady
DATE: February 19, 1998
SUBJECT: Personal Investment Portfolio Objective and Strategy

Investment Objective

The investment objective is to accumulate, in 30 years, enough money in the portfolio to generate $3,000 income each month in 1998 dollars. Assuming inflation averages 3% a year during the next 30 years, the nominal amount the portfolio must provide at maturity is $7,282 a month. Assuming a retirement portfolio is able to earn 7% annually in 30 years, $1,248,306 in assets will be required to produce the $7,282 a month. Therefore, the portfolio objective, or target, is $1,248,306 in 30 years.

The current amount of cash available, $5,000, is not enough to grow to the target in 30 years without additional contributions. If it is assumed that the portfolio will return 13% on average during the next 30 years, then it will be necessary to invest an additional $231 every month in order to reach the target.

Strategy

Allocate funds in the portfolio as follows:

Stock Mutual Funds........... 80%
Bond Mutual Funds........... 10%
Money Market Fund.......... 10%

These percentages are based on the assumption that during the next 30 years stock funds will return, on average, 15% a year, bond funds will return 11%, and "cash" (that is, short-term liquid debt securities) will return 5%. If these assumptions prove to be true, and if the portfolio target distribution is maintained, then the portfolio's average annual rate of return will be 13.6%.

Implementation

To implement the strategy, set up the portfolio as a self-directed IRA. Rebalance the portfolio annually, in April, after the results of the previous year have been calculated. Hold all assets purchased for at least three years (barring some obvious reason to sell early).

FIGURE 6–3   *Memo for Comparison (see Figures 6–1 and 6–3) (cont'd)*

> Once each year, evaluate the performance of all assets held more than three years. Note the worst-performing asset in each group (as measured by average annual return during the entire holding period). If an asset is the worst in its group two years in a row, sell it and replace it with the fund in same category having the best five-year performance according to the financial press. Exception: if the reported performance of the best-performing fund is worse than the record of the candidate for replacement in the portfolio, disregard this requirement.

Whatever word processor program and printer you use, you will probably have a choice of type sizes and font styles. Choose a 10- or 12-point type size and a standard font, such as New Times Roman, throughout your document. Your type sizes and fonts should be easy to read, but they should not draw attention to themselves, so be conservative in your choices. Never use unusual fonts for business documents.

White Space and Margins

White space is the part of a page that does not have any print. White space includes margins, the space between sections, and the space around graphic illustrations.

A document with visual appeal will have a good balance between print and white space. White space also makes a document easier to read. The space between sections, for example, helps the reader to see the paper's structure.

There are no hard-and-fast rules for margin widths or the number of lines between sections. As a general guideline, plan about a one-inch margin for the sides and bottoms of your papers. The top of the first page should have about a two-inch margin; subsequent pages should have a one-inch margin at the top.

Leave an extra line space between the sections of your document. A double-spaced page, for example, would have three lines between sections.

For any document that is single-spaced, be sure to double-space between paragraphs.

Neatness Counts!

Whatever you write, the final copy should be error-free and extremely neat. A word processor, especially one with a spell-checker, enables you to find errors and make corrections with ease. Sloppiness in a document is unprofessional and careless.

FORMATTING

Some writers think of the format of their document only in terms of straight text: page after page of print unbroken by headings or other divisions. If you look at almost any professional publication, including this handbook, you will see how various formatting devices, such as headings, lists, and set-off material, make pages more attractive and easier to read.

Headings

For any document longer than about half a page, headings can be used to divide the paper into sections. Headings make a paper less intimidating to readers because the divisions break up the text into smaller chunks. In a sense, headings give readers a chance to pause and catch their breath.

Headings also help the readers by showing them the structure of the paper and what topics it covers. In fact, many readers preview the contents of a document by skimming through it to read the headings. For this reason, headings should be worded so that they indicate the contents of the section to follow. Sometimes headings suggest the main idea of the section, but they should clearly identify the topic discussed. If you look through this book, you will see how headings suggest the content of the chapters. Chapter 1 even uses questions for headings, which is a good technique if not overused.

Headings can be broken down into several levels of division. Some headings indicate major sections of a paper and others indicate minor divisions. In other words, a paper may have both headings and subheadings. In this chapter, for example, "A Professional Appearance" indicates a major section of the chapter; "Paper and Print" marks the beginning of a subtopic, because it is just one aspect of a document's appearance. Generally, a short document needs only one heading level, but this rule can vary depending on what you are writing.

The style of the heading (how the heading is placed and printed on the page) varies with the levels of division. Some styles indicate major headings; other styles indicate subheadings. For this chapter, the major headings are printed in all capital boldfaced letters at the left margin, and subheadings are boldfaced, with only the initial letter of each main word capitalized and at the left margin, as follows:

FIRST LEVEL: LEFT MARGIN, ALL CAPS, BOLD FONT

Second Level: Bold Font, Initial Letters Capitalized

Here is another example of heading styles and the corresponding levels of division.

FIRST LEVEL: CENTERED, ALL CAPS

Second Level: Centered, Underlined

Third Level: Centered, Not Underlined

Fourth Level: Left Margin, Underlined

If you use fewer than four levels, your headings may follow this last system using any of the four styles, as long as they are in descending order. For example, you might use second-level headings for main topics and fourth-level headings for subtopics. If you are using only one level of headings, any style is acceptable.

It's possible to overuse headings. You would not, for example, put a heading for every paragraph.

Lists and Set-Off Material

Another formatting technique that can make a document easier to read is set-off material, especially lists. Mark each item on the list with a number, a bullet, or some other marker. Double-space before and after the list and between each item. The items may be single- or double-spaced.

Here is an example using bullets:

Your firm should update its systems in these areas:

- Budgets
- Payrolls
- Fixed assets
- Accounts payable
- Accounts receivable

Set-off lists not only improve the appearance of the paper by providing more white space, but they may also be more readable. The following example[1] presents the same information as straight text and in a list format. Which arrangement do you prefer?

Firms often base their credit decisions on the *Five C's of Credit*, which are *Character,* indicating the borrower's willingness to pay; *Capacity,* indicating the borrower's ability to pay; *Capital*, indicating how much wealth the borrower has to fall back on; *Collateral*, indicating what the lender will get if the borrower defaults; and *Conditions*, indicating the state of the borrower's business situation.

Firms often base their credit decisions on the *Five C's of Credit*

Character: the borrower's willingness to pay
Capacity: the borrower's ability to pay
Capital: how much wealth the borrower has to fall back on
Collateral: what the lender will get if the borrower defaults
Conditions: the state of the borrower's business situation

The letter in Figure 8–4 shows other examples of set-off lists.

Occasionally you will use set-off material for other purposes besides lists. Long direct quotations are set off, and rarely you may set off a sentence or two for emphasis. Chapters 2–6 use this technique to emphasize the guidelines for effective writing.

Pagination

The next formatting technique is a simple one, but it's overlooked surprisingly often. For every document longer than one page, be sure to include page numbers. They may be placed at either the top or the bottom of the page, be centered, or be placed in a corner. Begin numbering on page 2.

GRAPHIC ILLUSTRATIONS

Graphic illustrations such as tables, graphs, and flowcharts can make a document more interesting and informative. They may enable you to summarize a great deal of information quickly and help readers identify and remember important ideas.

Tables are an efficient way to summarize numerical data in rows and columns. The yield information shown in Table 6–1 is an example of a table.

When you use a table, be sure you label the rows and columns, indicate the units of measure you are reporting, and align the figures.

TABLE 6–1   Yields on Selected Securities

	YESTERDAY	PREVIOUS DAY	YEAR AGO
3-month T-bill	5.18	5.17	no change
1-year T-bill	5.67	5.67	5.38
30-year T-bond	6.88	6.85	6.66

Source: *The Washington Post*, March 13, 1997, p. E6

A pie chart shows how a whole is divided into parts, just as a pie is divided into slices. The pie chart in Figure 6–4 shows how the expenses of Gabe's Technologies, Inc., for the fourth quarter of 1997 might be displayed. The circle represents total expenses and the slices show the portions of each individual expense.

When you use a pie chart, label the wedges and show what percentages of the whole they represent.

Graphs, which may take several forms, are useful for comparisons. Two of the most common types of graphs are bar graphs and line graphs. Bar graphs compare quantities or amounts. The bar graph in Figure 6–5 shows the net sales for the Lands' End company as presented in Lands' End's 1996 annual report.[2] This graph shows that sales grew at an average compound annual growth rate of 10.9% between 1992 and 1996.

A line graph, which also compares quantities, is helpful for showing trends. A line graph may have a single or multiple lines. The line graph in Figure 6–6 compares the sales performance of Winston's Sports, Inc., as compared with the sales of its two top competitors. This graph shows how sales for the three companies have changed individually over the past five years, and it also makes clear that Winston's sales trend has outstripped those of its competitors.

Another type of graphic illustration is a flowchart, which shows the steps in a process or procedure. Figure 6–7 shows a typical example.

FIGURE 6–4   *Gabe's Technologies, Inc. Expense Distribution*

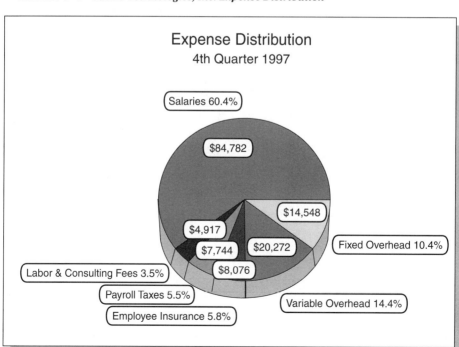

FIGURE 6–5 *Lands' End's Net Sales[2]*

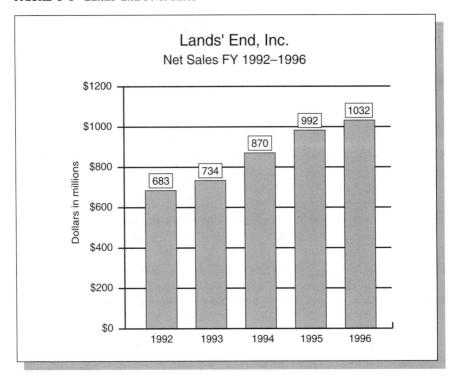

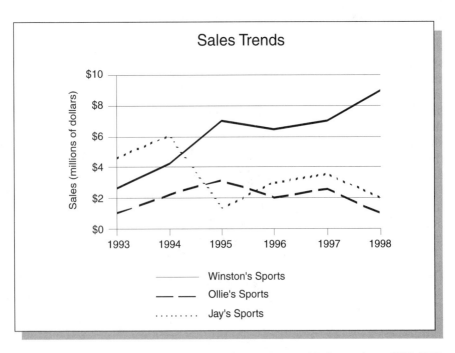

FIGURE 6–6 *Winston's Sports, Inc., Sales Comparisons with Competitors, 1993–1998*

FIGURE 6–7   *The Cash Flow Estimation Process in Capital Budgeting*

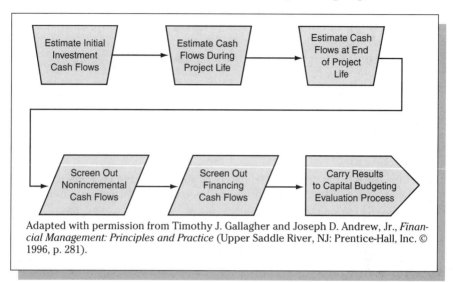

Adapted with permission from Timothy J. Gallagher and Joseph D. Andrew, Jr., *Financial Management: Principles and Practice* (Upper Saddle River, NJ: Prentice-Hall, Inc. © 1996, p. 281).

If you use a flowchart in your documents, use boxes or other shapes to show activities or outcomes; label each box or shape and arrange them so that the process flows from left to right, from the top to the bottom of the page; and use arrows to show the direction of the flow.

If you include graphic illustrations in the documents you write, whether flowcharts, graphs, or tables, there are certain guidelines to follow. Be sure to number them and give them descriptive titles. Tables should be called Tables (such as *Table 6–1*), and graphs and flowcharts should be called Figures (such as *Figure 6–7*). Graphic illustrations should be labeled sufficiently so that they are self-explanatory, but they should also be discussed in the text of the document. This discussion should refer to the illustration by name or description and number. The discussion should precede the illustration. The illustrations may be placed either in the body of the document, close to the place in the text where they are discussed, or in an appendix.

Finally, if you use a graphic illustration from another source, be sure to identify the source fully at the bottom of the illustration, or with a footnote or endnote.

DOCUMENT DESIGN
AT THE COMPUTER

Many of the formatting techniques we've talked about in this chapter are easily done with a word processor. Word processors make it easy to change margins, arrange set-off materials, add white space, and design headings. In addition, software programs can help you produce graphic illustrations of an excellent quality. Because the computer will make corrections to the text before you print your final draft, you will be able to submit a document that is flawless and professional.

This chapter has completed the guidelines for effective writing.

1. **Analyze the purpose of the writing and the needs and expectations of the readers.**

2. **Organize your ideas so that readers will find them easy to follow.**

3. **Write the draft and then revise it to make the writing polished and correct.**

4. **Make the writing unified. All sentences should relate to the main idea, either directly or indirectly. Eliminate digressions and irrelevant detail.**

5. **Use summary sentences and transitions to make your writing coherent.**

6. **Write in short paragraphs that begin with clear topic sentences.**

7. **Develop paragraphs by illustrations, definition, detail, and appeals to authority.**

8. **Be concise—make every word count.**

9. **Keep it simple—use simple vocabulary and short sentences.**

10. **Write with active verbs and descriptive nouns.**

11. **Use jargon only when your readers understand it. Define technical terms when necessary.**

12. **Be precise—avoid ambiguous and unclear writing.**

13. **Be concrete and specific. Use facts, details, and examples.**

14. **Use active voice for most sentences.**

15. **Vary vocabulary, sentence lengths, and sentence structures. Read the writing aloud to hear how it sounds.**

16. **Write from the reader's point of view. Use tone to show courtesy and respect.**

17. **Proofread for grammar, punctuation, spelling, and typographical errors.**

18. **Use formatting techniques to give your writing clarity and visual appeal.**

EXERCISES

Exercise 6–1

Collect examples of effective and ineffective formatting (personal correspondence as well as professional publications). How could the ineffective documents be improved?

Assume you are the supervisor of your company's finance department. Write a memo to the staff suggesting ways they might improve the design of the documents they write. Use some of the examples you've found to illustrate your memo.

Exercise 6–2

Choose a paper you've already written for a class assignment or on the job. Revise the paper, using at least two of these techniques:

- Headings
- Set-off lists
- Graphic illustrations
- Improved use of white space

NOTES

1. Adapted from Timothy J. Gallagher and Joseph D. Andrew, Jr., *Financial Management: Principles and Practice* (Upper Saddle River, N.J.: Prentice Hall, 1996): 467.
2. Adapted from data contained in Lands' End, *1996 Annual Report,* p. 1.

7

Financial Research

Sometimes finance people need to conduct research as part of the preparation of a report or other written document. This research which may be done at least in part via electronic media, may also involve books or other printed sources, such as the *Value-Line Investment Survey, Standard & Poor's' Stock Reports,* or government publications, such as the *Economic Report of the President.* Financial people also read professional literature such as journal articles, public documents, and monographs on topics of current interest.

This chapter discusses how to write a research paper. Much of the material will be review for students or professionals who have written term papers or documented reports. However, the suggestions should be helpful to anyone who must research professional literature and then summarize the results of that research in a written form.

HOW TO START

If you are writing a paper that requires research of the literature, chances are you already know something about the topic. If you don't, or if your memory is vague, do some initial reading so that you have a basic familiarity with your subject. A finance textbook may be a good place to start.

Once you have a general idea of what your topic involves, you need to look for additional information.

Surfing the Web

Often the next step will be to search the Internet for material related to your topic. In recent years there has been an explosion of information available on the Internet's World Wide Web. You have probably already used a Web browser program such as *Netscape*™ or Microsoft's *Internet Explorer*™ to visit hundreds of popular home pages. Search engines such as Excite™, Infoseek™, Lycos™, Web Crawler™, and Yahoo™ are accessible with your Web browser and enable you to locate documents ("pages") on the Web. Once you have selected a search engine, follow the directions given to tailor the search to your needs using key words or phrases associated with your research topic.*

The Internet may lead you to publications available at your library or to documents that you can download to your computer. Read the material you find on the Internet carefully and take accurate notes of your findings, including references to the sources you are using. A later section of this chapter discusses note taking and how to properly indicate references in more detail. It is good practice to print out useful material you may find unless the volume of a particular source makes this impractical.

Appendix A to this chapter shows some of the better Web sites available on the Internet that offer finance-related information and links to other useful sites.

Library Research

Although electronic sources can provide excellent sources for your research, it's probably not a good idea to limit your research to electronic sources because not everything is available in electronic form as yet. Some research papers require an in-depth search for additional source materials in the library. It's a good idea to consult a librarian to see what help is available. Most libraries now have computer search facilities and staff who will work with you to help find the materials you need.

One reference you may find in the library is the *Infotrac* computer database, which lists articles published in many periodicals. Be imaginative in looking for articles on your topic; consider the different headings they could be listed under.

The library will probably have other references and databases you may find helpful. For example, many newspapers, including *The Wall Street Journal*, publish an index. Many of these indices are available as both reference books and computerized reference services. A librarian

---

*If you omit this step, your search will probably produce more than you want. A recent search for *futures*, for example, recently produced 3,746 references, most of which had nothing to do with finance. Searching for "stock index futures," on the other hand, produced 39 references with more promise.

can help you find references that will help you to prepare your paper. Appendix B to this chapter contains a list of popular computerized reference services and databases. Appendix C contains a list of some of the popular printed sources of financial information.

NOTE TAKING

Once you have located a useful source, take notes on what you read. For this step in your research you will need two sets of cards—3 × 5-inch cards for the bibliography and 4 × 6-inch (or 5 × 8-inch) cards for the notes. Using these cards will save time and trouble in the long run, even though they may seem like a bother while you are reading. They will help you keep track of your sources and notes, and they will be easy to use when you write your draft.

Let's look first at a bibliography card, which is illustrated in Figure 7–1.

Be sure to include on the card all the information you will need for your bibliography (see "Documentation" later in this chapter). It's frustrating to make an extra trip to the library just to check on a date or page number.

Note cards contain the information you will actually use in your paper. Notice the parts of the note card in Figure 7–2.[1] The numbers in the upper right-hand corner give the source (from the bibliography card) and the pages or paragraph numbers where this information was found. The heading gives you an idea of what this note card is about. The note itself is taken from the source. It is the material you will use in your paper. The outline code corresponds with the section in your outline where the note fits in.

FIGURE 7–1   *Bibliography Card*

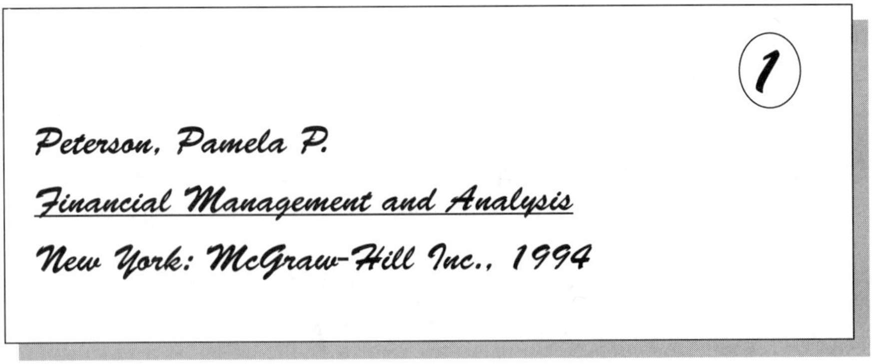

Peterson, Pamela P.
Financial Management and Analysis
New York: McGraw-Hill Inc., 1994

(1)

FIGURE 7–2 *Note Card*

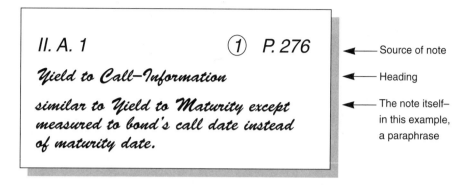

DIRECT QUOTATION AND PARAPHRASE

You can take notes in two ways: as a direct quotation (the exact words from the source) or as a paraphrase (your words and sentence structures). It may be best to take the notes in your own words if you do not plan to use any direct quotations. If you take the time to paraphrase as you research, you will save time when you write your draft.

Here is a good way to paraphrase. Read a section from your source, perhaps several short paragraphs. Then look away from the page and try to remember the important ideas. Write them down. Then look back at your source to check your notes for accuracy.

Occasionally you may want to use a direct quotation. When you copy a quotation on a note card, use quotation marks so you'll know later that these are someone else's words. Copy the quotation exactly, including capitalization and punctuation. It's important that direct quotations be accurate in every way and that paraphrases be your own words and sentence structures, not just a slight variation of your source.

It's also important to give credit for material you borrow from another writer. If you don't, you'll be guilty of plagiarism. *The Harbrace College Handbook* contains the following discussion of plagiarism:

> If you fail to acknowledge borrowed material, then you are plagiarizing. Plagiarism is literary theft. When you copy the words of another, be sure to put those words inside quotation marks and to acknowledge the source with a footnote. When you paraphrase the words of another, use your own words and your own sentence structure, and be sure to . . . [cite] the source of the idea. A plagiarist often merely changes a few words or rearranges the words of the source. As you take notes and as you write your paper, be especially careful to avoid plagiarism.[2]

The *MLA Handbook* defines plagiarism as "the act of using another person's writing without acknowledging the source."[3] The most obvious form of plagiarism is to use another person's words, but sometimes plagiarism is more subtle:

> Other forms of plagiarism include repeating someone else's particularly apt phrase without appropriate acknowledgment, paraphrasing another person's argument as your own, and presenting another's line of thinking in the development of an idea as though it were your own.[4]

Plagiarism, therefore, can involve the unacknowledged (undocumented) use of someone else's idea—not just the use of their exact words.

The key to avoiding plagiarism is to document your sources adequately with either internal documentation or notes (see the section on documentation). In actual practice, however, there may be situations when you will not know whether you should identify the source of information you wish to use in your paper. The difficulty arises because information that is considered common knowledge in a given field need not be documented.

Obviously the problem is to decide what is common knowledge. One guideline says that if you can find the same information in three different sources, that information is considered common knowledge and therefore need not be documented.

There are many gray areas when it comes to issues of plagiarism. Perhaps the safest rule is to document your sources whenever there is any question of possible plagiarism.

THE OUTLINE: ORGANIZING YOUR NOTES AND IDEAS

As you are taking notes, you will probably form some idea of the major divisions of the paper. That is, you should be getting a rough idea of its outline.

Go ahead and write down your ideas for an outline. The more reading you do, the more complete the outline will become. Stop and evaluate the outline from time to time. Are you covering all the important areas of your topic? Is the outline getting too long? Should you narrow the topic? Are some sections of the outline irrelevant to the topic? Answering these questions will guide you as you continue your research.

Once your research is complete, or nearly so, you should refine your outline. Be sure that the topic is covered completely and that the ideas are arranged in the most effective order. Think about the introduction and conclusion to your paper, and any other relevant parts. For example, do you want to include charts, tables, or graphs?

Next, arrange the note cards in the order of the outline and write the outline code in the upper left-hand corner of the card.

With a completed outline and an orderly stack of note cards, you are ready to write the draft.

THE DRAFT: INTEGRATING NOTES INTO YOUR WRITING

The draft of a research paper is written just like that of any other kind of writing, except that you are incorporating notes taken from your sources into your own ideas. If you have already paraphrased the notes, your task is much easier.

Include in your draft an indication of where your notes came from. In other words, you must give credit for words or ideas that are not your own. In the final version of your paper, these references will be footnotes, endnotes, or parenthetical citations. In the draft, you can indicate your sources with a parenthetical notation like this: *([1] p. 403)*. The numbers come from the note card and refer to the source and page or paragraph number of the note.

REVISING

After you have completed the draft, you will need to revise it to perfect the organization, development, style, grammar, and spelling. It may also be a good idea to have a colleague review your paper and suggest ways it can be improved.

DOCUMENTATION

Any information you get from a source other than your own knowledge must be documented; that is, you must say where you got the information. Styles for documentation vary, but we will look at two of the most common: internal documentation and notes.[5] The format we illustrate for both styles is consistent with *The Chicago Manual of Style*[6] and Kate L. Turabian's *A Manual for Writers of Term Papers, Theses, and Dissertations.*[7] You may want to consult one of these works as you write your paper.

Internal Documentation

Many writers prefer to use internal documentation, which places abbreviated information about sources within the text, using parentheses ( ), followed by a list of references at the end of the paper. What goes between the parentheses depends on the kind of source you are using. Appendix D at the end of this chapter gives sample citations and reference list entries for sources typically used by finance people.

It's a good idea to introduce quotation or paraphrases within the text itself:

> According to Block and Hirt, current assets are "items that may be converted to cash within one year (or within the normal operating cycle of the firm)" (1996, 27).

Information you include in the introduction to the quotation or paraphrase does not need to be repeated within the parentheses. Thus in this example, Block and Hirt was left out of the parenthesis because the authors were mentioned in the introductory phrase. If readers check the reference list at the end of the paper, they will find . . .

> Block, S., and G. Hirt. 1996. *Foundations of financial management,* 8th ed. Chicago: Irwin Publishing.

Note also that the end punctuation for the quotation, in this case the period, comes after the parentheses.

Here's one reminder about the use of technical sources. Consider whether the readers of your paper will be familiar with the literature cited. If they aren't, it's helpful to identify the source more fully and possibly give a brief explanation of its significance.

Endnotes and Footnotes

The other style of documentation in wide use is endnotes or footnotes. The difference between these two note forms is that footnotes come at the bottom of the page where the references occur, whereas endnotes come at the end of the paper. Most authorities consider endnotes quite acceptable. If you prefer footnotes, however, your word processor probably has the ability to place footnotes on the right pages, in acceptable format. With either endnotes or footnotes, you may also use an optional bibliography at the end of your paper listing your sources in alphabetical order.

Appendix E at the end of this chapter gives examples of notes and bibliographical entries for typical finance sources.

As with internal documentation, you should introduce your paraphrased or quoted material:

> According to a recent article in *The Wall Street Journal*, many accounting firms find the poor writing skills of their new employees a serious problem.[8]

The introduction to this paraphrase tells generally where the information came from; the note and bibliographical entry give complete information about the source.

Citing Electronic Sources

Electronic sources have recently become so important to the research process that the chances are high you will need to cite material that you have found on-line, on CD-ROM, or on magnetic disk.

An acceptable form of citation for documents available from electronic sources usually resembles the general pattern of citations for hard-copy sources, but you will need to provide additional information so that your readers can find the file or document on-line.

It's important to provide the date you accessed the document because the document may be modified or even removed from on-line availability after you have accessed it. For the same reason, it's also a good idea to print out and keep a hard copy of the document you are citing unless the size of the document makes this impractical.

Electronic sources of information may come from the World Wide Web (www), File Transfer Protocol (FTP) sites, telnet sites, gopher sites, listservs, newsgroups, and e-mail. Examples of citations for sources on the World Wide Web are illustrated in Appendices C and D to this chapter.

TECHNICAL RESEARCH IN FINANCE

Finance people involved with investments, financial services, and corporate finance often engage in technical research. Stock analysts, for example, need company historical data, industry information, and economic statistics in order to evaluate a company's earnings potential. Loan officers need information about companies' credit history, debt position, and income outlook before they can approve financing. Corporate financial officers need comparative information on other companies in order to assess the performance of their firms.

The following discussion will give you an idea of the complexity of this kind of research, as well as a strategy you can use when faced with a difficult financial problem.

Steps in the Financial Research Process

Financial research involves a number of steps:

1. Determine the relevant facts.
2. Identify the issues involved.
3. Research the financial literature.
4. Identify alternative solutions and arguments for and against each.

5. Evaluate alternative solutions and choose the one that can be best defended.
6. Communicate the results of your research to the interested parties.

Let's discuss these steps one at a time.

DETERMINE THE RELEVANT FACTS. Determining the relevant facts is often fairly straightforward. If you realize that research is necessary, you're probably already aware of most of the facts of the situation. Be sure you have all the facts before you begin your research. Do you fully understand the situation? What are the goals and objectives of the parties involved? What environmental factors are relevant? If there is a contract or other documents involved, be sure you have examined them thoroughly.

To illustrate, suppose your company is considering the acquisition of another company. What are the relevant facts? To begin with, you would want to obtain financial statements of the other company for several recent years. Information about the other company's debts and pending litigation would be extremely important. You would need to know what terms the members of the other company were seeking and whether the acquisition is to be handled as a cash purchase or a stock swap. Does your company have the capacity to complete the acquisition? Before taking any irrevocable steps, you would want to establish that your company will be able to arrange the necessary financing for the acquisition.

Due Diligence. A special part of determining the facts in financial research is called a "due diligence" evaluation (or simply "due diligence"). Due diligence involves visiting a company that may be acquired and investigating whether the financial information available fairly represents actual conditions. Due diligence evaluations are often conducted by teams of analysts who spend up to a week on the premises of a company, testing the validity of its financial records.

IDENTIFY THE ISSUES INVOLVED. It often comes as a surprise to many people to find that identification of the issues can be one of the more difficult steps in the financial research process. It's not uncommon for facts (or a lack of facts), terminology, and bias of the researcher to obscure some issues rather than to clarify them.

For example, consider the case of a client who has recently sold a home for a large amount of money. The client wishes to "do something with the money," and has come to you for advice. What are the issues?

A quick reading of the facts presented may suggest that the issue is to decide where to invest the client's money to achieve the highest return. Certainly the question of return is important, but it is by no means the central issue. First, the client's situation must be reviewed. How old is the client? What liquidity needs does the client have? What income requirements does the client have? What is the client's tolerance for risk?

These are fundamental issues that must be addressed before choosing specific investments.

To illustrate, imagine that your 70-year-old grandmother realized $300,000 from the sale of her home and she has asked you, a famous Wall Street stock analyst, what she should do with the money. To earn the highest return, you might steer her into stock options or perhaps pork-belly futures, but are these investments really the ones you would recommend for your grandmother? Of course not. To begin with, you would want to find out how much income your grandmother would need to withdraw from the portfolio each month for living expenses. If she would need $2,000 a month, for example, you certainly wouldn't suggest that she invest all her money in zero-dividend-paying growth stocks. Instead, you would limit your recommendations to investments expected to produce $2,000 a month in cash.

Another important issue is the client's investment objective. This is vital since the client's objective shapes the entire investment process. For example, if your grandmother's objective is to use the proceeds from the sale of her house to provide a college education for her only great-grandchild (your son, now age three), you might recommend that she invest the money in zero-coupon bonds that are expected to grow in value to the amount needed in 15 years' time. On the other hand, if your grandmother's objective is to use the money to provide income for living expenses, you might recommend that she invest in AAA rated bonds, which are relatively safe and which provide interest income. The point is, your investment recommendation is determined by your client's investment objective. Therefore, you must identify the objective before making the recommendation.

RESEARCH THE LITERATURE.   Once you have identified the issues, you must research the appropriate literature to gather all relevant material. A good starting point for most issues is the search engines on the World Wide Web that we discussed earlier (Excite™, Infoseek™, Lycos™, Web Crawler™, and Yahoo™).* Once you have selected a search program, follow the directions given to tailor the search to your needs, using key words or phrases associated with your research topic.

If the issues involve theoretical questions, as is quite possible, you might consult a number of professional journals. If the issues involve investments and portfolio management, a wide array of investment literature is available. (At the very least, in the case of investments, you would research pricing information in the financial press.) In corporate finance, trade publications and business magazines such as *Forbes* and *Fortune* often contain articles bearing directly or indirectly on the issues. On-line

---

*You may also purchase special search programs that automatically search all the popular search engines listed here. One such program is *WebFerret* by FerretSoft LLC. You can get more information about this program at http://www.ferretsoft.com.

and CD-ROM databases such as those listed in Appendix B will often point the way to most of the material bearing on the issues.

Sometimes you may find useful information in an unrelated area. For example, if you are researching an issue in the software industry, an article covering the music industry or some industry even further removed from the software industry may contain logic or guidance that could serve as a basis for a solution.

It's possible that your research may take you beyond the materials just discussed. The *Federal Reserve Bulletin,* the *Statistical Abstract of the United States*, the *Economic Report of the President*, and even the *World Almanac* may all prove useful. Appendix C to this chapter contains a list of some of the more popular printed sources of financial information available at most libraries.

Finally, don't overlook the finance textbooks that served you so well during your college courses. These books can frequently act as handy sources of reference on a wide variety of issues.

IDENTIFY ALTERNATIVE SOLUTIONS AND ARGUMENTS FOR AND AGAINST EACH. It's important to realize that if you're engaged in technical financial research, you're probably dealing with issues for which there are no established solutions. It is up to you to identify all alternative solutions, determine the best solution, and defend that solution against all others.

EVALUATE ALTERNATIVE SOLUTIONS AND CHOOSE THE ONE THAT CAN BE BEST DEFENDED. In the end, you must be able to present a well-reasoned defense of your solution. Although finance is not law (except as governed by the SEC), just as a lawyer may prepare a well-reasoned defense of an issue using legal precedent and logic, a finance professional doing technical financial research must use many of the same skills in preparing a defense of a proposed solution to a finance issue. Indeed, although we all hope it will never happen, it's possible that the solution you choose may have to be defended in a court during some legal proceeding.

COMMUNICATE THE RESULTS OF YOUR RESEARCH TO THE INTERESTED PARTIES. You will usually communicate the results of your research in a report, letter, or a memo, although occasionally you may report orally as well. However you report your research, incorporate all the elements of effective communication discussed in this book. Audience analysis, precision, clarity, and logical development are particularly important.

EXERCISES

Exercise 7–1

Choose one of the following topics and narrow it if necessary. (For example, you might select "Careers in banking" rather than "Careers in finance.") Write a documented research paper on your topic, using the steps discussed in this chapter.

- History of the finance profession
- Government regulation in finance
- Finance in international businesses
- Careers in finance
- Mutual funds
- Capital budgeting techniques
- Use of computers in finance
- Finance in nonprofit organizations.
- Relating risk and return

Exercise 7–2

Assume you are a financial analyst for a software development company. The company's leading product is a tax-preparation program designed for use by individuals and small businesses. Until now, all the company's sales have been on a cash basis. Recently, the VP for marketing suggested that the company could improve sales if it offered credit terms to its customers. The idea has gained support among company managers, but some are reluctant to go along, claiming that the delay in cash collections, coupled with inevitable bad-debt losses, would more than offset any gains in sales.

Research this technical finance problem using the steps discussed in this chapter and write a memo to your boss, Susan Chase, recommending what should be done and why.

NOTES

1. Information on note card quoted from Pamela P. Peterson, *Financial Management and Analysis* (New York: McGraw-Hill, Inc., 1994), 276. Reprinted by permission.

2. John C. Hodges and Mary E. Whitten, *Harbrace College Handbook*, 8th ed. (New York: Harcourt Brace Jovanovich, Inc., 1977), 372.

3. Joseph Gibaldi and Walter S. Achtert, *MLA Handbook for Writers of Research Papers*, 2d ed. (New York: The Modern Language Association of America, 1984), 20.

4. Ibid., p. 21.

5. There are many documentation styles in current use. The sample entries in this chapter illustrate acceptable usage, but you may use another acceptable style as long as you're consistent within each paper.

6. *The Chicago Manual of Style*, 14th ed. (Chicago: University of Chicago Press, 1993).

7. Kate L. Turabian, *A Manual for Writers of Term Papers, Theses, and Dissertations*, 6th ed. (Chicago: The University of Chicago Press, 1996).

8. Lee Burton, "Take Heart, CPAs: Finally a Story That Doesn't Attack You as Boring," *The Wall Street Journal*, (13 May 1987): 33.

Appendix 7–A

Sources of Financial Information on the Internet

Business news network services:
  CNNfn   http://www.cnnfn.com

Business newspapers:
  Financial Times of London   http://www.ft.com
  The Wall Street Journal Interactive Edition   http://www.wsj.com

Business magazines:
  Fortune Magazine (available at)   http://www.pathfinder.com
  Money Magazine (available at)   http://www.pathfinder.com
  Worth Magazine   http://www.worth.com

Data on the economy, industries, market
indexes, and financial statistics—domestic
and foreign:
  Bloomberg Personal Magazine   http://www.bloomberg.com
  Briefing.Com   http://www.briefing.com
  Data Broadcasting Company   http://www.dbc.com
  Dow Jones   http://www.djmarkets.com
  New York Federal Reserve Bank   http://www.frb.org/pihome/
    —exchange rates   mktrates/forex10.shtml

Information about stocks—company
performance; corporate financial data,
charts, company home pages, etc.:

Appendix 7–A: Sources of Financial Information on the Internet (cont.)

Wall Street Research Net	http://www.wsrn.com
Quicken Financial Network	http://www.quicken.com
Yahoo Financial Research	http://www.yahoo.com
EDGAR (available at)	http:www.sec.gov
INVESTools	http://www.investools.com
Morningstar International Stocks on Demand	http://www.investools.com/ cgi-bin/Library/msis.pl
Stockguide	http://www.stockguide.com
StockMaster	http://www.stockmaster.com

Information about bonds:
Bonds Online	http://www.bonds-online.com
Quote.com	http://www.quote.com

Information about mutual funds:
Morningstar Mutual Funds on Demand	http://www.investools.com/ cgi-bin/Library/msmf.pl
Mutual Fund Cafe	http://www.mfcafe.com
Mutual Funds Interactive	http://www.brill.com
Standard and Poor's Rating Service	http://www.ratings.standard poor.com/funds
StockMaster	http://www.stockmaster.com

Academic research:
Financial Economists Network	http://www.SSRN.Com

Securities Exchanges and SEC:
American Stock Exchange (AMEX)	http://www.amex.com
NASDAQ	http://www.nasdaq.com
New York Stock Exchange (NYSE)	http://www.nyse.com
U.S. Securities and Exchange Commission	http://www.sec.gov.

Links to Finance journals, academic research, research centers, and a wealth of other excellent finance-related sites:
Research Resource in Finance—Ohio State University	http://www.cob.ohio-state. edu/~fin/journal/ jofsites.htm

Appendix 7–B

Computerized Reference and Database Services

CD-ROM DATABASES

Business Index, by Information Access Co. Contains indexing of more than 800 business and trade journals and selective indexing of 3,000 other magazines and newspapers.

Business Indicators, by Slater Hall Information Products. Includes national income and product accounts from 1929 to present; state income and employment data from 1958 to present; and business statistics from 1961 to present corresponding to the Survey of Current Business.

Business Source, by EBSCO Information Services. Provides citations and abstracts to articles in about 600 business periodicals and newspapers. Full text is provided from 49 selected periodicals covering accounting, communications, economics, finance, management, marketing, and other business subjects.

WILSONDISC: Wilson Business Abstracts, by H. W. Wilson Co. Provides CD-ROM "cover-to-cover" abstracting and indexing of over 400 prominent business periodicals. Indexing is from 1982 to present and abstracting is from 1990 to present.

Appendix 7–B: Computerized Reference and Database Services (cont.)

ON-LINE DATABASES

ABI/INFORM, by UMI/Data Courier. Provides on-line indexing to business-related material occurring in over 900 periodicals from 1971 to the present.

Banking Information Source, by UMI. Provides indexing and abstracting of periodical and other literature from 1982 to date, with weekly updates. Covers the financial services industry, including banks, savings institutions, investment houses, credit unions, insurance companies, and real estate organizations. Emphasis is on marketing and management.

CITIBASE (Citicorp Economic Database), by FAME Software Corp. Presents over 6,000 statistical series relating to business, industry, finance, and economics. Time period is 1947 to date, with daily updates.

Compustat, by Standard and Poor's. Financial data for the most recent 20 years on publicly held U.S. and some foreign corporations.

Disclosure SEC Database, by Disclosure, Inc. Provides information from records filed with the Securities and Exchange Commission by publicly owned corporations, 1977 to present. Updated weekly.

DRI Financial and Credit Statistics, by DRI/McGraw-Hill, Data Products Division. Contains U.S. and international statistical data relating to money markets, interest rates, foreign exchange, banking, and stock and bond indexes.

Economic Literature Index, by the American Economic Association. Covers the worldwide literature of economics as contained in selected monographs and about 400 journals. Subjects include microeconomics, macroeconomics, economic history, inflation, money, credit, finance, accounting theory, trade, natural resource economics, and regional economics.

NAARS, by the American Institute of Certified Public Accountants. National Automated Accounting Research System. Financial statements, authoritative accounting literature, most current five years on-line, 1972 to present off-line.

InvesText, by Thomson Financial Services. Contains full text of investment research reports from more than 300 sources, including leading brokers and investment bankers. Reports from 1982 to date are available on approximately 25,000 U.S. and international corporations. Separate industry reports cover 53 industries.

Source: James Way, ed., *Encyclopedia of Business Information Sources,* 1997-98, 11th ed. (Detroit: Gale Research, 1996), 295–301.

Appendix 7–C

Other Printed Sources of Financial Information

Business news, articles, market data, stock, bond, mutual fund price quotes:

Barron's
USA Today

The Wall Street Journal

Business news, articles:

Business Week
Forbes

Fortune
Money

Data on the economy and industries; financial and economic statistics:

Business Conditions Digest
Economic Report of the President
Federal Reserve Bulletin
Standard & Poor's Industry Surveys

Standard & Poor's Statistical Surveys
Statistical Abstract of the United States
US Industrial Outlook
World Almanac

Summary data about industries, companies; advice on industries, stocks; analysis and forecasts:

Appendix 7–C: Other Printed Sources of Financial Information (cont.)

Standard & Poor's Outlook   *Value-Line Investment Survey*

Stock information, company
performance, corporate financial
data:

Annual reports of companies   *Moody's OTC Manual*
Moody's Bank & Finance Manual   *Moody's Public Utility Manual*
Moody's Bond Record   *Moody's Transportation Manual*
Moody's Bond Survey   *Standard & Poor's Corporation*
Moody's Handbook of Common   *Records*
  Stocks
Moody's Industrial Manual   *Standard & Poor's Stock Reports*
Moody's International Manual

Bond information:

Moody's Bond Record   *Moody's Bond Survey*

Mutual fund information:

Morningstar Mutual Funds   *Weisenberger's Current Performance &*
Weisenberger's Management Results   *Dividend Record*

Appendix 7–D

Internal Documentation Style

C = Citation within the text
R = Entry in reference list

Book—Single Author
C   (Pacter 1994, 12)
R   Pacter, P. 1994. *Reporting financial information by segment.* London: International Accounting Standards Committee.

Book—Single Editor
C   (Frankel 1994, 64)
R   Frankel, J. A., ed. 1994. *The internationalization of equity markets.* Chicago: University of Chicago Press.

Book—Two Authors
C   (Gallagher and Andrew 1996, 403)
R   Gallagher, Timothy J., and Joseph D. Andrew. 1996. *Financial management: principles and practice.* Upper Saddle River, N.J.: Prentice Hall.

Book—Three or More Authors
C   (Kiger, Loeb, and May 1987, 602)
R   Kiger, Jack E., Stephen E. Loeb, and Gordon S. May. 1987. *Principles of accounting,* 2d ed. New York: Random House.

Appendix 7–D: Internal Documentation Style (cont.)

Book—Author Is an Association, Institution, or Organization
C   (AICPA 1993, 2)
R   American Institute of Certified Public Accountants (AICPA). 1993.
     *The information needs of investors and creditors: A report on the
     AICPA special committee's study of the information needs of
     today's users of financial reporting, November, 1993.* New York:
     AICPA.

Article in a Journal—Single Author
C   (Grossman 1988, 20)
R   Grossman, Sanford J. 1988. Program trading and market volatility:
     A report on interday relationships. *Financial Analysts Journal* 44,
     no. 4 (July/August): 18–28.

Article in a Journal—Two Authors
C   (Diamond and Verrecchia, 1330)
R   Diamond, D., and R. Verrecchia. 1991. Disclosure, liquidity, and the
     cost of capital. *Journal of Finance* 46, no. 4 (September):
     1325–1359.

Article in a Journal—Three or More Authors
C   (Schneider, May, and Shaffer 1994, 80)
R   Schneider, Douglas K., Gordon S. May, and David R. Schaffer. 1994.
     On the credibility of GAAP: Do preparers, auditors, and users see
     eye to eye? *The Journal of Applied Business Research* 10, no. 4
     (Fall): 77–87.

Article in a Magazine
C   (Blinder 1988, 25)
R   Blinder, Alan S. 1988. Dithering on hill is crippling a key agency.
     Business Week, 26 September, 25.

Article in a Newspaper—Author Not Identified
C   (*Wall Street Journal,* 16 July 1986)
R   *Wall Street Journal,* 16 July 1986, Words count.

Article in a Newspaper—Author Identified
C   (May 1987)
R   May, Gordon S. 1987. No accounting for poor writers. *The Wall
     Street Journal,* 29 May, letters to the editor.

Annual Report for a Corporation
C   (Lands' End, Inc. 1996 Annual Report, 12)
R   Lands' End, Inc., *1996 Annual Report Lands' End Direct Merchants.*
     Dodgeville, Wis.

Appendix 7–D: Internal Documentation Style (cont.)

Primary Source Reprinted in a Secondary Source
C   (FASB, *SFAC 1*, par. 3)
R   Financial Accounting Standards Board (FASB). 1978. *Objectives of financial reporting by business enterprises, statement of financial accounting concepts no. 1.* Stamford, Conn.: FASB. Reprinted in *Accounting Standards: Original Pronouncements as of June 1, 1996.* Vol. II. New York: John Wiley & Sons, 1996.

Legal Citation
C   (*Aaron v. SEC*, 446 U.S. 680, 1980)
R   Aaron v. SEC, 446 U.S. 680 (1980).

Internal Revenue Code Section
C   (*Internal Revenue Code* Sec. 6111(a))
R   *Internal Revenue Code.* Sec. 6111(a).

Government Document
C   (SEC 1995, 3)
R   United States Securities and Exchange Commission (SEC). 1995. *Self-regulatory organizations; notice of filing and order granting accelerated approval of proposed rule change by the National Association of Securities Dealers, Inc., relating to an interim extension of the OTC Bulletin Board (R) service through September 28, 1995.* Securities Exchange Act Release No. 35918, 60 FR 35443. Washington, D.C. (July 7).

Federal Register
C   (61 Fed. Reg. 1996, 208:55264)
R   "Revision to NASA FAR supplement coverage on contractor financial management reporting." *Federal Register* 61, no. 208 (25 Oct. 1996): 55264.

World Wide Web
C   (Creswell 1997)
R   Creswell, Julie. 1997. Stock flow for week declines to just $1 billion. *Wall Street Journal Interactive Edition,* 8 March [on-line]. Available from <http://www.wsj.com>; accessed 8 March 1997.

Listserv Message
C   (MONEYDAILY, 25 March 1997)
R   MONEYDAILY, 25 March 1997, <moneyadm@PATHFINDER.COM>. Fed raises rates/Save on home office equipment. Available from <dailymail@listserv.pathfinder.com>; accessed 25 March 1997.

Appendix 7–D: Internal Documentation Style (cont.)

E-Mail
C   (May, 28 April 1997)
R   May, Claire B., 28 April 1997, <cmay@jaguar1.usouthal.edu>. Citation style, E-mail; accessed 29 April, 1997.

More than One Work in Reference List by Same Author or Authors—Different Years
R   Lang, M., and R. Lundholm. 1993. Cross sectional determinants of analyst ratings of corporate disclosures. *Journal of Accounting Research* 31, no. 2 (Autumn): 246–271.
———. 1996. Corporate disclosure policy and analyst behavior. *The Accounting Review* 71, no. 4 (October): 467–192.

More than One Work in Reference List by Same Author or Authors—Same Year
C   (Frost and Pownall, 1994b, 61)
R   Frost, C. A., and G. Pownall. 1994a. Accounting disclosure practices in the United States and United Kingdom. *Journal of Accounting Research* 32, no. 1 (Spring): 75–102.
———. 1994b. A comparison of the stock price response to earnings measures in the United States and the United Kingdom. *Contemporary Accounting Research* 11, no. 1 (Summer): 59–83.

Appendix 7–E

Endnotes or Footnotes and Bibliography Style

N = Endnote or footnote; B = Bibliographical entry*

Book—Single Author

N   [1]P. Pacter, *Reporting Financial Information by Segment* (London: International Accounting Standards Committee, 1994), 12.

B   Pacter, P. 1994. *Reporting Financial Information by Segment.* London: International Accounting Standards Committee, 1994.

Book—Single Editor

N   [1]J. A. Frankel, ed., *The Internationalization of Equity Markets* (Chicago: University of Chicago Press, 1994), 64.

B   Frankel, J.A., ed. *The Internationalization of Equity Markets.* Chicago: University of Chicago Press, 1994.

Book—Two Authors

N   [1]Timothy J. Gallagher and Joseph D. Andrew, *Financial Management: Principles and Practice* (Upper Saddle River, N.J.: Prentice Hall, 1996), 403.

B   Gallagher, Timothy J. and Joseph D. Andrew. *Financial Management: Principles and Practice.* Upper Saddle River, N.J.: Prentice Hall, 1996.

*A Footnotes preceded by a superscript numeral; endnotes preceded by full-size arabic numerals.

Appendix 7–E: Endnotes or Footnotes and Bibliography Style (cont.)

Book—Three or More Authors
N [1]Jack E. Kiger, Stephen E. Loeb, and Gordon S. May, *Principles of Accounting,* 2d ed. (New York: Random House, 1987), 602.
B Kiger, Jack E., Stephen E. Loeb, and Gordon S. May. *Principles of Accounting,* 2d ed. New York: Random House, 1987.

Book—Author is an Association, Institution, or Organization
N [1]American Institute of Certified Public Accountants (AICPA), *The Information Needs of Investors and Creditors: A Report on the AICPA Special Committee's Study of the Information Needs of Today's Users of Financial Reporting, November, 1993.* (New York: AICPA, 1993), 2.
B American Institute of Certified Public Accountants (AICPA). *The Information Needs of Investors and Creditors: A Report on the AICPA Special Committee's Study of the Information Needs of Today's Users of Financial Reporting, November, 1993.* New York: AICPA, 1993.

Article in a Journal—Single Author
N [1]Sanford J. Grossman, "Program Trading and Market Volatility: A Report on Interday Relationships," *Financial Analysts Journal* 44, no. 4 (July/August 1988): 20.
B Grossman, Sanford J. "Program Trading and Market Volatility: A Report on Interday Relationships." *Financial Analysts Journal* 44, no. 4 (July/August 1988): 18–28.

Article in a Journal—Two Authors
N [1]D. Diamond and R. Verrecchia, "Disclosure, Liquidity, and the Cost of Capital," *The Journal of Finance* 46 (Sept. 1991): 1330.
B Diamond, D., and R. Verrecchia. "Disclosure, Liquidity, and the Cost of Capital." *The Journal of Finance* 46 (Sept. 1991): 1330–1359.

Article in a Journal—Three or More Authors
N [1]Douglas K. Schneider, Gordon S. May, and David R. Shaffer, "On the Credibility of GAAP: Do Preparers, Auditors, and Users See Eye to Eye?," *The Journal of Applied Business Research* 10, no. 4 (Fall 1994): 79.
B Schneider, Douglas K., Gordon S. May, and David R. Schaffer. "On the Credibility of GAAP: Do Preparers, Auditors, and Users See Eye to Eye?" *The Journal of Applied Business Research* 10, no. 4 (Fall 1994): 77–87.

Appendix 7—E: Endnotes or Footnotes and Bibliography Style (cont.)

Article in a Magazine

N   [1]Alan S. Blinder, "Dithering on Hill Is Crippling a Key Agency," *Business Week*, 26 September 1988, 25.

B   Blinder, Alan S. "Dithering on Hill Is Crippling a Key Agency." *Business Week,* 26 September 1988, 25.

Article in a Newspaper—Author Not Identified

N   [1]*The Wall Street Journal,* 16 July 1986, "Words Count."

B   *The Wall Street Journal,* 16 July 1986. "Words Count."

Article in a Newspaper—Author Identified

N   [1]Gordon S. May, "No Accounting for Poor Writers," *The Wall Street Journal,* 29 May 1986, letters to the editor.

B   May, Gordon S. "No Accounting for Poor Writers." *The Wall Street Journal,* 29 May 1986, letters to the editor.

Annual Report for a Corporation

N   [1]Lands' End, Inc., 1996 Annual Report, 12.

B   Lands' End, Inc. "1996 Annual Report Lands' End Direct Merchants." Dodgeville, Wis.

Primary Source Reprinted in a Secondary Source

N   [1]Financial Accounting Standards Board (FASB). *Objectives of Financial Reporting by Business Enterprises, Statement of Financial Accounting Concepts No. 1.* (Stamford, Conn.: FASB, 1978), par. 3; reprinted in *Accounting Standards: Original Pronouncements as of June 1, 1996,* Vol. II. (New York: John Wiley & Sons, 1996), 1005–1020.

B   Financial Accounting Standards Board (FASB). *Objectives of Financial Reporting by Business Enterprises, Statement of Financial Accounting Concepts No. 1.* Stamford, Conn.: FASB. Reprinted in *Accounting Standards: Original Pronouncements as of June 1, 1996,* Vol. II, 1005–1020. New York: John Wiley & Sons, 1996.

Legal Citation

N   [1]Aaron v. SEC. 446 U.S. 680 (1980).

B   Aaron v. SEC. 446 U.S. 680 (1980).

Internal Revenue Code Section

N   [1]*Internal Revenue Code* Sec. 6111(a).

B   *Internal Revenue Code.* Sec. 6111(a).

Appendix 7–E: Endnotes or Footnotes and Bibliography Style (cont.)

Government Document

N   [1]United States Securities and Exchange Commission (SEC), *Self-Regulatory Organizations; Notice of Filing and Order Granting Accelerated Approval of Proposed Rule Change by the National Association of Securities Dealers, Inc., Relating to an Interim Extension of the OTC Bulletin Board (R) Service Through September 28, 1995.* Securities Exchange Act Release No. 35918, 60 FR 35443 (7 July 1995): 3.

B   United States Securities and Exchange Commission (SEC). *Self-Regulatory Organizations; Notice of Filing and Order Granting Accelerated Approval of Proposed Rule Change by the National Association of Securities Dealers, Inc., Relating to an Interim Extension of the OTC Bulletin Board (R) Service Through September 28, 1995.* Securities Exchange Act Release No. 35918, 60 FR 35443 (7 July 1995).

Federal Register

N   [1]"Revision to NASA FAR Supplement Coverage on Contractor Financial Management Reporting," *Federal Register* 61, no. 208 (25 Oct. 1996): 55264.

B   "Revision to NASA FAR Supplement Coverage on Contractor Financial Management Reporting." *Federal Register* 48, no. 208 (25 Oct. 1996): 55264.

World Wide Web

N   [1]Julie Creswell, "Stock Flow for Week Declines to Just $1 Billion," *Wall Street Journal Interactive Edition* (8 March 1997) [on-line]. Available from <http://www.wsj.com>; accessed 8 March 1997.

B   Creswell, Julie. "Stock Flow for Week Declines to Just $1 Billion," *Wall Street Journal Interactive Edition* (8 March 1997) [on-line]. Available from <http://www.wsj.com>; accessed 8 March 1997.

Listserv Message

N   [1]MONEYDAILY, <moneyadm@PATHFINDER.COM>, "Fed raises rates/Save on home office equipment," 25 March 1997. Available from <dailymail@listserv.pathfinder.com>; accessed 25 March 1997.

B   MONEYDAILY, <moneyadm@PATHFINDER.COM>, "Fed raises rates/Save on home office equipment," 25 March 1997. Available from <dailymail@listserv.pathfinder.com>; accessed 25 March 1997.

E-Mail

N   [1]May, Claire B., <cmay@bigcat.usouthal.edu>, "Citation style," 28 April 1997. Accessed 29 April, 1997.

B   May, Claire B., <cmay@jaguar1.usouthal.edu>, "Citation style." 28 April 1997. E-mail; accessed 29 April, 1997.

Appendix 7–E: Endnotes or Footnotes and Bibliography Style (cont.)

More than One Work in Bibliography by Same Author or Authors

B   Lang, M., and R. Lundholm, "Cross Sectional Determinants of Analyst Ratings of Corporate Disclosures," *Journal of Accounting Research* 31, no. 2 (Autumn 1993): 246–271.

————. "Corporate Disclosure Policy and Analyst Behavior." *The Accounting Review* 71, no. 4 (October 1996): 467–492.

8

Letters

Finance people write many letters to companies, clients, government agencies, fellow professionals, and so on. They may write letters to seek information about suppliers' credit policies, for example, or to report to investors on their portfolios' performance. They may also write letters to communicate the results of research into a technical finance problem. Any merger or acquisition activity would, of course, result in a flurry of letters between finance people in the acquiring company and in the company being acquired.

For any letter to get the best results, of course, it must be well written.

This chapter begins with some principles of good letter writing: organization, style, tone, and format. Then we look at some letters typical of those that finance people write.

PRINCIPLES
OF LETTER WRITING

Effective letters have many of the characteristics of other good writing: They contain correct, complete information, and they are usually written with specific readers in mind. They are also written in an active, direct style. In other words, they are coherent, clear, and concise. They are also neat and attractive, with a professional appearance.

Planning a Letter

Letters can vary in length from one paragraph to several pages, although many business letters are no longer than a page. Whatever the length, you should be certain about what you want to include before you begin so you won't forget something important.

As in other writing tasks, you must analyze the purpose of the letter before you write it. If you are answering another person's letter, keep that letter on hand and note any comments for which a reply is needed. Finally, jot down a brief outline to organize the material logically.

It's also important to think about the reader of your letter, especially when you write about a technical topic. The knowledge and experience of your readers determine how detailed the explanations of technical material should be.

Sometimes you must explain complex financial concepts in words a non–finance person can understand. A typical example is the net present value (NPV) concept. Although finance people refer to NPV among themselves routinely, letters to people without a background in finance should explain NPV in nontechnical terms.

> The style of a letter may range from a highly sophisticated format, with numerous technical explanations and citations, to a simple composition that uses only laypersons' terms. In many situations, of course, the best solution lies somewhere between the two extremes.[1]

Organization

Like other kinds of writing, letters are organized into an introduction, a body, and a conclusion. Each section uses summary sentences to emphasize main ideas and help the reader follow the train of thought.

The *introduction* of a letter establishes rapport with the reader and identifies the subject of the letter or the reason it was written. You can mention previous communication on the subject, such as an earlier letter or phone call, or remind the reader of a recent meeting or shared interest. The introduction should also summarize briefly the main ideas or recommendations discussed in the letter. If the letter is very long, it's also a good idea to identify in the introduction the main issues or topics the letter covers.

The *body* of the letter is divided logically into discussions of each topic. Arrange the topics in descending order of importance *from the reader's point of view*: Start with the most important issue and work your way down to the least important. Begin the discussion of each issue with a summary sentence stating the main idea or recommendation.

Paragraphs should be short, usually a maximum of four or five sentences, and each should begin with a topic sentence.

The letter's *conclusion* may be a conventional courteous closing:

Thank you very much for your help.

The conclusion is also a good place to tell your correspondent exactly what you want him or her to do, or what you will do to follow up on the subjects discussed in the letter:

May I have an appointment to discuss this matter with you? I'll be in Chicago next week, October 7–11. I'll call your secretary to set up a time that is convenient for you.

If your letter is very long, the conclusion may also summarize your main ideas and recommendations.

Conciseness and Clarity

Conciseness and clarity, qualities of all good writing, are particularly important in letters. You don't want to waste your readers' time, nor do you want them to miss important ideas. Come to the point quickly and say it in a way they will understand.

A number of the techniques already presented in this handbook are useful for writing short, clear letters. For example, your writing should be unified; that is, each paragraph in the letter with a central idea is easy to spot. The letter should also be as brief and simple as possible, while still conveying an unambiguous, precise meaning.

Tone

One of the most important characteristics of a well-written business letter is its tone, or the way it makes the reader feel. Chapter 4 discussed writing from the point of view of your readers, emphasizing their interests and needs. Courtesy and respect are also important qualities of business letters, as they are in all forms of communication.

In general, effective letters reflect a personal, conversational tone. However, the best tone to use for a given letter depends to some extent on the purpose and reader of that letter. Review the discussion of tone in Chapter 4 to see how the content of the letter and your relationship with the reader can affect the tone you choose for your correspondence.

Form and Appearance

One of the primary characteristics of an effective letter is a neat appearance. Good stationery is important: 8 1/2 × 11-inch unlined paper of a high-quality bond, about 24-pound weight. Envelopes, 4 × 10 inches, should match the stationery. White or cream is usually the best color choice.

Business letters should be printed on a letter-quality printer, either a laser or ink jet. Envelopes may be printed or typed.* Both the letter and the envelope should be free of errors. Neatness is essential!

A letter is usually single-spaced, with double-spacing between paragraphs, although letters can be double-spaced throughout (see the sample formats in Figures 8–1 and 8–2). Margins should be at least 1 inch on all sides and as even as possible, although the length of the letter will affect the margin width.

One-page letters should be placed so that the body of the letter, excluding the heading, is centered on the page or slightly above center. A word processor makes it easy to experiment with margins and spacing until you get the best arrangement.

Study the diagrams in Figures 8–1 and 8–2, which illustrate the parts of a letter and their proper placement for two formats, the block and the modified block styles. Remember also that formatting techniques, such as headings and set-off lists, can make your letters attractive and easy to read.

Parts of the Letter

HEADING   The heading contains your address (not your name) and the date of the letter. If you use stationery without a letterhead, place the heading on the left margin (for block style) or next to the right margin (for modified block style). If you use letterhead stationery, center the date below the letterhead.

INSIDE ADDRESS   The inside address is a reproduction of the address on the envelope. Place the title of the person to whom you are writing either on the same line as his or her name, or on the following line:

Anna M. Soper, President
Muffet Products
516 N. 25th Street
Edinburg, TX 78539

- or -

Anna M. Soper
President
Muffet Products
516 N. 25th Street
Edinburg, TX 78539

It's usually better to address a letter to a specific person rather than to an office or title. You can find the name for the person to whom you are

---

*Most word processing programs contain an envelope printing feature that automatically selects and prints a business address on an envelope.

FIGURE 8–1 *Diagram of a Letter Format—Block Style*

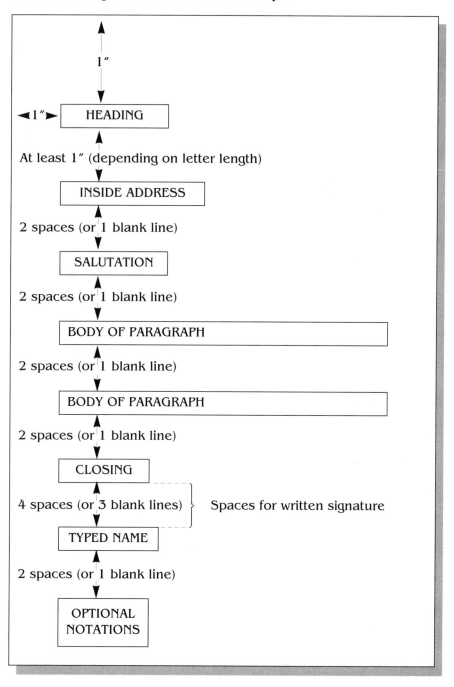

FIGURE 8–2   *Diagram of a Letter Format—Modified Block Style*

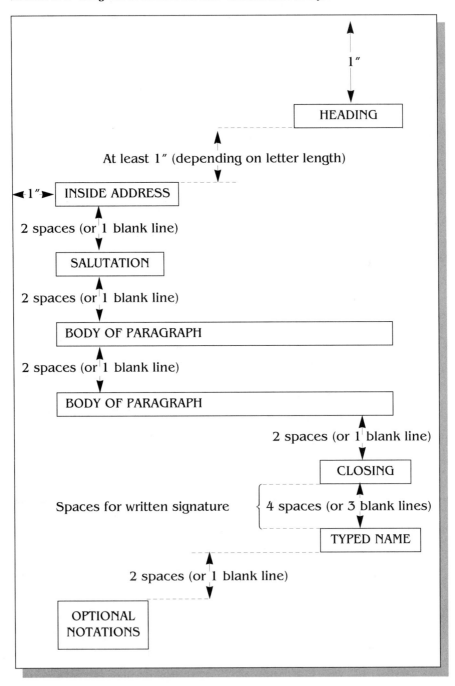

writing by phoning the company or organization. It's also a good idea to verify the spelling of the name.

SALUTATION   If possible, address your correspondent by name:

Dear Ms. Soper:

- or -

Dear Mr. Smith:

For a female correspondent, use *Ms.* unless she prefers another title.

If you know your correspondent well, you may want to use his or her first name in the salutation:

Dear Anna:

Be careful with the use of first names, however, especially when writing to an older person or one in a position of greater authority than yours. In many situations, a respectful, courteous tone requires the use of a title and last name.

If you don't know the name of the correspondent, use a salutation such as the following:

Dear Director of Personnel:

Dear Registrar:

Note that a colon (:) always follows the salutation in a business letter.

CLOSING   The formal closing of a letter is placed at the left margin for a block-style letter and next to the right margin for the modified block style. Capitalize the first word of the closing and put a comma at the end. Either of the following closings is correct:

Sincerely yours,

Sincerely,

SIGNATURE   Your name should be printed four lines below the closing; your position can be placed beneath your name. The space between the closing and printed name is for your handwritten signature:

Sincerely,

Anna M. Soper

Anna M. Soper
President

OPTIONAL PARTS OF A LETTER   Sometimes you will need additional notations below the signature, on the left margin. First, if someone else types your letter, a notation is made of your initials (all capital letters) and the typist's (all lowercase):

AMS:lc

or

AMS/lc

Second, if the letter includes an enclosure, make a notation:

Enclosure(s)

Finally, if you will distribute copies of the letter to other people, note the people who will receive a copy:

cc: John Jones

SECOND PAGE   Many business letters are only one page long. If you need to write additional pages, each should have a heading identifying the addressee, the date, and the page number. This information is usually printed at the left margin:

Mr. Richard Smith
November 18, 1997
Page 3

A second page (and any subsequent pages) should have at least three lines of text in addition to the heading and closing.

RESPONDING TO CORRESPONDENCE

When you reply to a letter written by someone else, it's important to respond in a way that will build a good working relationship between you and your correspondent. Many of the techniques for effective letters already discussed apply to responses. Here is a summary of those techniques, as well as a few pointers that apply particularly when you are answering someone else's letter:

1. Respond promptly, by return mail if possible.
2. Reread carefully the letter you received, noting questions that need answers or ideas that need your comment.
3. For the opening paragraph:
    * Refer to earlier correspondence, such as the date of the letter you received.

- If your letter is good news, or at least neutral, state clearly and positively the letter's main idea.
- If your letter contains bad news, such as the denial of a request, identify the subject of the letter in the opening paragraph. State the explicit refusal later in the body of the letter, after you have prepared the reader with some buffer material.

4. Answer all your correspondent's questions fully and cover all relevant topics in sufficient detail. However, the letter should be as concise as possible.
5. End with a courteous closing.

TYPICAL FINANCE LETTERS

Before we begin this section, we should note that many companies have standardized letters for some situations. The management of a company may have decided on the organization and even the specific wording it requires its staff to use for requests for proposal letters, payment reminder letters, and the like. If your company uses standardized letters, simply adapt the basic letter to the specific case you are concerned with, adding dates, names, figures, and other relevant facts.

Presented below are sample letters for various situations, along with some general comments on the content and organization of these letters.

Price Quotes

In the world of business-to-business sales, products and services are frequently tailored to each individual customer. Prices may thus vary from customer to customer, and may not be advertised beforehand. Finance people often write letters to obtain the prices of products and services. Figure 8–3 contains an example of a letter written to a software development company to inquire about the price of the company's project accounting software.

Letters of Agreement

Letters of agreement put into writing the arrangements made between two parties. You could call a letter of agreement a simple form of contract. These letters can confirm the arrangements for a variety of services: payroll processing, accounting services, consulting services, product distribution services, employment (as in the case of an offer letter), and so on. They may be written by either party to the agreement, depending on the situation. For example, an offer letter to a prospective employee would be written by the firm making the offer. A letter containing the terms of a consulting arrangement would probably be written by the consultant. In either case, the purpose of a letter of agreement is to clarify the mutual responsibilities of all parties and thus prevent possible misunderstandings.

FIGURE 8–3 *Sample Price Quote Letter*

Electronic Business Solutions, Inc.
2010 New Silicon Valley Drive
Reston, VA 22122

April 1, 1997

Sandy Brown, Sales Consultant
Tekstar Systems
8800 Greensboro Drive
McLean, VA 22102

Dear Mr. Brown:

I read your brochure on the Tekstar Project Accounting Software system with great interest.

For some time our company has been looking into the possibility of converting our stand-alone accounting system over to an integrated materials and financial management program. The Tekstar program, with its accounting, project, timesheet, material management, and inventory modules, looks like a promising solution.

As a first step toward a possible conversion, please send me a price quote for the Tekstar program, listing individual prices for the various modules and configurations. After we have reviewed the prices and made some preliminary selections, I will contact you to arrange for further discussions.

Please call me at (703) 555-1212 if you have any questions.

Sincerely,

Daniel Warbucks

Daniel Warbucks
Chief Financial Officer

Letters of agreement can vary a great deal in content, depending on who is writing the letter, the type of services to be provided, and the complexity of the situation.* However, most letters have similar elements:

- A description of the nature and limitations of the services to be provided
- Assistance that the client will provide, such as certain records and schedules
- A description of the outcomes expected to occur as a result of the agreement
- Important deadlines for the work
- Information about fees and payment schedules
- A space for both parties to indicate acceptance of the arrangements outlined in the agreement letter.

Figure 8–4 shows a sample letter of agreement for financial consulting.

Letters to Customers
and Suppliers

Finance people often write letters to customers and suppliers. These letters fall into two main categories: letters about payment terms and letters about why payments weren't made when expected. For example, corporate finance officers write letters to suppliers requesting credit. Suppliers write back either approving or denying the requests, and describing the terms of payment if the credit requests are approved. Circumstances may later force finance officers to write suppliers explaining why payments aren't being made on schedule.

On the customers' side, the situation is reversed. Corporate finance officers write letters to customers granting them credit and explaining payment terms. Circumstances may later force the corporate finance officers to write to customers reminding them that payment is due, or insisting that payment be made as soon as possible.

When payments are not made when expected, the tone of the letters between the parties will vary depending on the type of relationship that exists between the recipient of the letter and the writer. For example, if a small supplier is trying to collect from a large customer, and that customer is one of the supplier's major customers, the supplier will probably behave with a good deal of restraint and patience toward the customer. The tone of reminder letters from the supplier to the customer will probably be quite mild and conciliatory. On the other hand, if a very large supplier is having trouble collecting from one of a very large number of small customers, the tone of reminder letters from the supplier to the customer may be quite insistent and demanding. Figure 8–5 contains a sample letter

---

*If the terms of an agreement go beyond what can be expressed on a page or two, a formal contract would probably be prepared rather than a letter of agreement.

FIGURE 8-4 *Sample Letter of Agreement*

Dollars and Sense
Financial Consultants
1601 Pennsylvania Avenue
Washington, DC 22002

March 24, 1997

Mr. Robert Fulton
International Recreations Group
1000 White Granite Drive
Fairfax, VA 22124

Dear Mr. Fulton:

This letter confirms the arrangement we discussed for Dollars and Sense to perform a financial analysis of your company's proposed International Recreational Center project.

The analysis will contain a quarter-by-quarter cash flow projection for an eight-year period beginning July 1, 1997. It will also include an estimate of the investment return potential investors might expect from the project. Target date for completion of the analysis is May 1, 1997.

Records needed for the analysis include pricing assumptions, attendance projections, construction cost data, and historical profit and loss statements for your company. It is possible that the need for additional information may arise. If so, our analysts will request it directly from you or from the person you designate to be contacted.

Upon approval of these arrangements, two of our analysts will visit your company for approximately two days, with follow-up visits as needed. Upon completion of the work we will prepare a formal report suitable for presentation to investors.

As we discussed, our fee for this type of analysis is $25 an hour per analyst. We will invoice you upon completion of the analysis. Payment will be expected within 30 days.

Please indicate your acceptance of these terms by signing on the "accepted" line below.

FIGURE 8–4   *Sample Letter of Agreement* (cont'd)

Mr. Robert Fulton
March 24, 1997
Page 2

We are pleased that you have asked us to perform these services
for you, and we look forward to working with you and your
staff.

Sincerely,

Jack Sprat

Jack Sprat,
President Accepted by: _____ Date: _____

---

from a supplier to a customer, reminding the customer that payment is
overdue. Figure 8–6 contains a sample response from the customer.

Letters to Investors

Finance people often correspond with investors on a variety of matters. In response to an investor's request for a copy of a company's annual report, for example, a corporate finance officer may send a cover letter providing additional details not contained in the report in hopes of
encouraging the investment. Merger or acquisition activity may generate
dozens of letters between the companies merging. These will range from
letters of intent to letters containing terms of a final agreement. A sample
of one such letter, a confidentiality agreement letter,[2] is shown in Figure 8–7.

Advisory Letters

Financial consultants often write advisory letters to clients suggesting ways clients can improve their businesses. This type of letter may
contain suggestions on a variety of topics:

- Internal control
- Accounting and information systems
- Inventory control
- Credit policies

FIGURE 8–5   *Sample letter from a supplier to a customer, reminding the customer that payment is overdue on an account*

Superior Software, Inc.
516 Willow
Dallas, TX 59901

REMINDER NOTICE

September 16, 1998

Mr. Ralph Crabtree
Foremost Distributing
1221 Curvy Lane
Fort Worth, TX 59801

Re: Invoice #488, Order-Pro Program, $395

Dear Mr. Crabtree:

This is a reminder that we have not yet received payment for the Order-Pro software you purchased on August 12, 1998 (see enclosed invoice—terms net 30). We would appreciate it if you would remit the amount due, $395, as soon as possible. If you have recently mailed payment, please accept our thanks and disregard this notice.

Sincerely,

N. O. Patience

N. O. Patience
Director of Finance

FIGURE 8–6 *Sample letter from a customer to a supplier, explaining why payment has not yet been made on an account*

Foremost Distributing
1221 Curvy Lane
Fort Worth, TX 59801

September 20, 1998

N.O. Patience, Director of Finance
Superior Software, Inc.
516 Willow
Dallas, TX 59901

Re: Invoice #488, Order-Pro Program, $395

Dear Mr. Patience:

Please accept our apologies for missing the due date for payment on the Order Pro software we purchased from you in August. During the process of installing the software and integrating it with our accounting program, the invoice was misplaced.

A check for $395, representing payment in full, is enclosed.

Your *Order Pro* program has proved to be a major improvement to our internal control systems. Its use should prevent invoice misplacement in the future.

Sincerely,

Ralph Crabtree

Ralph Crabtree,
Accounts Payable Manager

FIGURE 8–7   *A Sample Confidentiality Agreement Letter*

White Airlines, Inc.
867 Hanger Bay Rd.
Atlanta, GA 30688

PERSONAL AND CONFIDENTIAL

June 1, 1998

Mr. Bill Smith, President
BLUE AIRLINES, INC.
100 Park Avenue
New York, NY 10022

Dear Mr. Smith:

We are interested in examining the business of Blue Airlines, which is a candidate for possible acquisition by our company. In connection with this examination, we will provide your company with certain financial statements and other information and documents relating to White Airlines and its business. In consideration of the conduct of this examination, we will not, directly or indirectly, divulge the fact that an examination is being conducted or any of the financial and other information you may divulge to us.

Any documents we may furnish to you contain confidential information which will at all times remain our exclusive property. You will be responsible for the safekeeping of these documents and will not reproduce, disseminate, or otherwise disclose the information contained in them to any third parties.

White Airlines would sustain irreparable injury in the event of a breach of this agreement by your company. Accordingly, in the event of any such breach, White Airlines will be entitled to seek and obtain immediate injunctive relief against your company. This agreement is binding on your company, its employees, directors, and representatives.

FIGURE 8–7   *A Sample Confidentiality Agreement Letter (cont'd)*

Mr. Bill Smith
June 1, 1998
Page 2

Please indicate acceptance of this agreement by signing this letter and returning a copy to me.

Respectfully,   Confirmed and Agreed to:
WHITE AIRLINES, INC.   BLUE AIRLINES, INC.

_____   _____
Alan Jones   Bill Smith
President   President

- Budgeting
- Tax matters
- Management of resources
- Operating procedures

Two versions of an advisory letter are presented in Figures 8–8 and
8–9. Sometimes, if the consultant includes many recommendations in the
letter, the letter may be quite long. If you write an advisory letter that is
over three pages long, consider organizing it into a report with a transmittal letter. Address the transmittal letter to the president or board of directors of the client company and summarize in the letter the major recommendations made in the report.

In any case, whether the advisory letter is a single document or a report with a transmittal letter, remember that long letters are more attractive and easier to read if they contain headings. These headings divide
the letter into logical sections.

Whatever the format of the advisory letter, write it so that it will be
helpful to the client and build a good professional relationship between
the client and your firm. The techniques for effective writing discussed so
far in this book certainly apply to advisory letters: clear and logical organization, readable style, and specific and concrete explanation.

Figure 8–8 is an example of a letter that might be sent to a relatively
sophisticated client who is familiar with financial concepts and terminol-

FIGURE 8–8   *Management Advisory Letter— Sophisticated Client*

BEASLEY AND POOLE
Financial Consultants
1553 W. Ellis Street
Atlanta, GA 30316

March 15, 1999

Mr. Robert F. Freeman, President
Southeast Manufacturing Company
24 N. Broad Street
Atlanta, GA 30327

Dear Mr. Freeman:

Our analysis of the Southeast Manufacturing Company revealed two areas where we believe you could improve your business:

- Stronger sales forecasting techniques
- More accurate determination of the company's cost of capital

The following paragraphs explain these recommendations in greater detail.

Sales Forecasting Techniques

Currently Southeast's finance department is producing sales forecasts by drawing a bar chart of sales for the previous five years, connecting the tops of the bars with a hand-drawn line, and then extending the line one more year into the future. While a rudimentary forecast can be constructed in this fashion, a more mathematically accurate method is available. Using the least squares linear regression technique, the regression equation for the line of best fit can be constructed for past sales. Future sales can then be estimated by solving the regression equation for sales in the year of the forecast. A sample sales forecast based on the least squares linear regression technique is shown in attachment 1 to this letter.

FIGURE 8–8 *Management Advisory Letter— Sophisticated Client (cont'd)*

Mr. Robert F. Freeman
March 15, 1999
Page 2

Cost of Capital

Southeast's cost of capital is currently being determined by
adding a 5 percent premium to the current prime rate of interest.
While this procedure is simple and direct, it usually does not
produce the best results. First, it does not take into account the
relative proportions of debt and equity used to supply capital,
and second, it does not adequately represent the rate of return
required by the firm's common stockholders.

We suggest using the Weighted Average Cost of Capital approach. In this method, the percent costs of Southeast's debt and
equity are combined according to their relative proportions in the
company's capital structure:

$$WACC = Wd(Kd) + We(Ke)$$

where WACC = the weighted average cost of capital
Wd = the proportion of debt in the capital struc-
ture
Kd = the after-tax cost of debt
We = the proportion of equity in the capital struc-
ture
Ke = the cost of common equity

The cost of debt component in the WACC calculation is normally the interest rate the company anticipates on future loans.

The cost of common equity component of Southeast's weighted
average cost of capital model can be developed from the Gordon Dividend Growth Model as follows:

$$Ke = \frac{D1}{P0} + g$$

where Ke = the cost of equity
D1 = the expected dividend next year
P0 = the current price of Southeast's common stock
g = the long-run constant growth rate of Southeast's
dividends

FIGURE 8–8 *Management Advisory Letter— Sophisticated Client*

Mr. Robert F. Freeman
March 15, 1999
Page 3

The disadvantage of this model is that it assumes that the company's dividend growth rate remains constant for an infinite period of time. This, as you know, is not always the case with Southeast. Furthermore, estimating any company's long-term dividend growth rate is a chancy procedure at best.

We prefer to use the Capital Asset Pricing Model (CAPM) to estimate the cost of equity:

$$Ke = Krf + B(Km - Krf)$$

where Krf = the risk-free rate of return
B = Southeast's beta
Km = the expected rate of return on the stock market

This model has the intuitive appeal of producing a cost of equity based on risk premiums. Furthermore, the terms in the CAPM are not difficult to obtain. The risk-free rate is usually established by the rate of return on short-term U.S. Treasury bills, which can be found in daily newspapers. The market expected rate of return can be established by averaging the forecasts of a selection of investment bankers, and Southeast's beta can be calculated by regressing Southeast's stock returns against those of the stock market for some representative number of periods in the past.

We will be glad to discuss these suggestions with you and help you implement them. We also look forward to seeing you at our firm's holiday reception!

Sincerely,

Roger Poole

Roger Poole

FIGURE 8–9 *Management Advisory Letter—Less Sophisticated Client*

BEASLEY AND POOLE
Financial Consultants
1553 W. Ellis Street
Atlanta, GA 30316

March 15, 1999

Mr. Robert F. Freeman, President
Southeast Manufacturing Company
24 N. Broad Street
Atlanta, GA 30327

Dear Mr. Freeman:

Our analysis of the Southeast Manufacturing Company revealed two areas where we believe you could improve your business:

- Stronger sales forecasting technique
- More accurate determination of the company's required rate of return on investment projects

The following paragraphs explain these recommendations in greater detail.

Sales Forecasting Technique

Currently Southeast's finance department is producing sales forecasts by drawing a bar chart of sales for the previous five years, connecting the tops of the bars with a hand-drawn line, and then extending the line one more year into the future. While a rudimentary forecast can be constructed in this fashion, statistical tools are available that will do a better job. One of these tools, called linear regression, is available on the computers in Southeast's finance department. We can demonstrate its use to the analysts in the finance department at your convenience

Required Rate of Return on Investment Projects

Southeast's required rate of return on investment projects is currently being determined by adding a 5 percent premium to the current prime rate of interest. While this procedure is simple

Mr. Robert F. Freeman
March 15, 1999
Page 2

and direct, it does not produce the best results because it does
not take into account the different rates of return required by
Southwest's lenders and by Southwest's stockholders. It also
does not take into account the amounts of capital supplied by
lenders and stockholders.

Mr. Robert F. Freeman
March 15, 1999
Page 2

We suggest using a technique called the *Weighted Average Cost
of Capital,* or WACC approach. In this method, the percent
costs of Southeast's loans and the percent return required by the
stockholders are combined in a weighted average formula.

To use the WACC approach, the company first estimates the interest rate anticipated on future loans. Next, the company estimates the rate of return required by the company's stockholders.
This is done by totaling up the rates of return that stockholders
require for taking on various types of risk. Starting with the
risk-free rate, which is the rate of return on short-term U.S.
Treasury Bills, we add a premium for equity investments in
general, and adjust it for the degree of risk present in Southeast
Manufacturing. The result is referred to as the cost of equity.

Once the loan rate and the cost of equity have been determined,
the two are averaged together according to the proportions of
debt and equity financing the company desires to maintain. This
final result is the WACC.

We will be glad to discuss these suggestions with you and help
you implement them. We also look forward to seeing you at our
firm's holiday reception!

Sincerely,

Roger Poole

Roger Poole

ogy. Figure 8–9 is an example of a letter on the same subject sent to a less sophisticated client who has not had any formal training in finance.

STANDARDIZED LETTERS: A CAUTION

As already mentioned, many organizations have standardized letters that they use for situations that occur often, such as payment reminder letters. These form letters save time, and they also convey the message precisely and reliably. If your employer expects you to use these standardized letters, then of course you should do so.

With the widespread use of word processors that store documents, however, there is a danger that writers will use form letters when personalized letters would be more appropriate. If you use standardized letters, be sure that they are responsive to the reader's needs and concerns.

If you know your correspondent personally, a friendly reference to a topic of mutual interest can add warmth to your letter. The last sentence of the letter in Figure 8–9 provides a friendly, personalized closing to a letter:

> We also look forward to seeing you at our firm's holiday reception!

EXERCISES

Exercise 8–1 (All Levels)

Suppose you received the letter shown in Figure 8–10. How would you react? What, specifically, is wrong with this letter? What about it is effective?

After you have analyzed the strengths and weaknesses of the letter as it is shown in Figure 8–10, revise it so that it would make a better impression on a reader.

Exercise 8–2 (All Levels)

You have always been close to your sister, an attorney, even though she is ten years older than you and now lives many miles away. She is quite interested in your education and career plans, so you have decided to write her a letter to explain why you are majoring in finance. You know she will be interested in your personal reasons for choosing this career path as well as the employment opportunities that are likely to be open to you after graduation. She would also like to hear about any plans you may have for continuing your professional education and training after you receive your undergraduate degree.

Write your sister a letter that will persuade her that a major and career in finance are good choices for you. Use the proper format, effective

FIGURE 8–10 *Letter for Exercise 8–1*

Smith, Barnum, and Bailey
Investment Counselors
301 MacDonald Place
Atlanta, GA 36095
Telephone: (306) 782-5107

May 21, 1998
Mr. John W. Simmons
254 Myers Hall, UGA
Athens, GA 30609

Dear John:

After considerable debate about our needs, we have decided to offer the internship to someone else. Our offer was excepted, so the position is now filled.

I enjoyed talking with you and felt you would of been a positive impact to our firm and would work well with our present staff.

Upon graduation we would be most interested in talking with you regarding full-time employment. If I can be of assistance in the near future, please feel free to call.

Sincerely,

Jason A. Smith

Jason A. Smith

JASjr/mlk
Enclosures

organization, and appropriate style. Invent any information you feel is necessary to make your letter complete.

Exercise 8–3 (All Levels)

Tammy Johnson, a representative from one of your company's suppliers, Megamart Office Supplies, has called to inquire why a recent invoice hasn't been paid yet. The payment was due in 30 days, and 45 days have gone by without payment. You are aware of the situation, but your company is suffering a "cash crunch" and cannot afford to pay the invoice until after the receipt of a large cash inflow, which is expected to occur in about 10 days.

Write a letter to Ms. Johnson at Megamart reassuring her that the invoice will be paid soon. Remember, your credit with this supplier is very important to your company and you don't want Ms. Johnson to have any doubts about your company's ability to pay. Use the proper format, effective organization, and appropriate style. Invent any information you feel is necessary to make your letter complete.

Exercise 8–4 (All Levels)

One of your company's customers, Buz's Sports, has not paid for a shipment of office supplies. You invoiced the company when the supplies were shipped (payment was due in 30 days) and mailed a reminder in May. At the end of June, Buz's Sports still hasn't paid the bill, and you need to write a letter to the company president, Mr. Buster Alan, requesting payment. Of course, you do not want to antagonize Mr. Alan, because the company has been a client for several years and you value the business relationship.

Write the letter to Mr. Alan asking him to pay the bill. Use the proper format, effective organization, and appropriate style. Invent any information you feel is necessary to make your letter complete.

Exercise 8–5 (All Levels)

You are preparing investment recommendations for Carol and John Land and find you need some additional information: their ages, the ages of their two children, and the age at which they plan to retire. You need this information in order to compute the average annual return the Lands' portfolio needs to achieve to reach their investment goals.

Write a letter to Mr. and Mrs. Land requesting this information. Use the proper format, effective organization, and appropriate style. Invent any information you feel is necessary to make your letter complete.

Exercise 8–6 (All Levels)

Assume you are a financial analyst working for the state government, and your office is setting up a state lottery with a $10 million jackpot. The lottery rules as you have formulated them specify that a person winning the lottery will be paid the $10 million in 10 annual payments of $1 million each. After becoming aware of this provision, Mr. Schaeffer, a prominent local attorney, has written a letter to your office expressing concern about how the $10 million necessary to support the payouts to the winner will be raised.

Write a letter to Mr. Schaeffer that addresses his concerns. Explain why the state doesn't need to raise $10 million to support the 10 annual payments of $1 million each. Use the proper format, effective organization, and appropriate style. Invent any information you feel is necessary to make your letter complete.

Exercise 8–7 (Intermediate)

John D. Stoneygal, your corporation's largest stockholder, has called your corporation's chief executive officer (CEO) because he read in *USA Today* that your company is considering cutting its annual dividend this year. The facts contained in the article are true, but in your opinion as chief financial officer (CFO) the news is favorable because your corporation has plans to use the cash that would otherwise be paid out as dividends to make a major acquisition in a new emerging market. This investment is expected to provide a much higher return to the stockholders in the long run than if the money were simply distributed as dividends.

Draft a letter for the CEO to send to Mr. Stoneygal. The letter should discuss the pros and cons of paying dividends versus retaining earnings for growth, and it should contain an explanation of how the company's new dividend policy will benefit Mr. Stoneygal. Use the proper format, effective organization, and appropriate style. Invent any information you feel is necessary to make your letter complete.

Exercise 8–8 (Intermediate)

The chief executive officer (CEO) of Visionary Enterprises, Ms. Seem Dim, has offered to purchase your company, Future-Bright, for $300,000 cash, which is the net worth of the firm as shown on its most recent balance sheet. However, you are not willing to sell so cheaply because your company's accountants have told you that the fair market value of the company's net separately identifiable assets is about $700,000 more than is shown in the balance sheet. In addition, there is at least $300,000 in goodwill that would-be purchasers should be willing to pay for.

Write a letter to Ms. Dim explaining why the figures in the balance sheet do not reflect the market value of Future-Bright. Include an explanation of what goodwill is and why it is not currently listed on the balance sheet. You may assume your client is an astute businessperson but with no background in accounting. Use the proper format, effective organization, and appropriate style. Invent any information you feel is necessary to make your letter complete.

Exercise 8–9 (All levels)

Carla Bryant wants to invest in an annuity for her son, Charles, who is 10 years old. She wants the annuity to pay exactly $10,000 a year for five years, beginning when Charles turns 21. She wants to know how much money she will have to invest now, assuming the money will earn interest, compounded annually, of 8 percent.

Write a letter to Ms. Bryant explaining annuities and the amount she would need to invest now to set up the plan she has in mind. Use the proper format, effective organization, and appropriate style. Invent any information you feel is necessary to make your letter complete.

Exercise 8–10 (All levels)

An ad in today's paper introduces a new payroll servicing company, Fast-Pay, Inc. According to the ad, when companies like yours sign up with Fast-Pay, all they have to do is ensure that sufficient funds are available in a payroll checking account at the bank, and Fast-Pay does the rest—issues checks and handles all withholding and tax payments.

Write a letter to George Brown of Fast-Pay, Inc., asking for details about Fast-Pay's services and asking that one of its agents call you. Include specific questions about how the arrangement would operate. Use the proper format, effective organization, and appropriate style. Invent any information you feel is necessary to make your letter complete.

Exercise 8–11 (All Levels)

Write a letter to the president of Steller Software indicating your firm's desire to acquire the rights to Steller's computer game program *Thermonuclear Revenge*. During a recent telephone conversation, Steller's president, Sally Salvo, indicated that her firm would be willing to sell the rights to the popular program for $2,000,000. Marketing analysts in your company indicate the rights are probably worth about $1,500,000. Include this information in your letter. Use the proper format, effective organization, and appropriate style. Invent any information you feel is necessary to make your letter complete.

Exercise 8–12 (Intermediate)

Suppose you were a financial analyst at a consulting firm and received the letter in Figure 8–11 from a client.[3] Write a letter in reply. Use the proper format, effective organization, and appropriate style. Invent any information you feel is necessary to make your letter complete.

Exercise 8–13 (Intermediate)

Write an engagement letter to the city of Fargo, North Dakota, in which you agree to perform a financial analysis of a proposal to construct a ski area upon the mountain of trash that is piling up at the city dump.* You may mention other services that your consulting firm agrees to provide. Use the proper format, effective organization, and appropriate style. Invent any information you feel is necessary to make your letter complete.

Exercise 8–14 (Intermediate)

One of your company's major stockholders, Mr. Buffy Low, has written you, the Chief Financial Officer, to express his dismay about the decline in value of the corporation's stock. He cannot understand how such a thing could occur in view of the constant increases in profits the com-

*Don't laugh! This has been done in Michigan.

FIGURE 8–11   *A Letter from a Client (Exercise 8–12)*

KEN-L-PRODUCTS, INC.
749 E. Peartree St.
Manhattan, KS 66502

May 1, 1999

Ms. Ellen Acker
Common Cents Consultants
331 J. M. Tull Street
Manhattan, KS 66502

Dear Ms. Acker:

As you well know, it is becoming impossible to conduct business without the constant threat of litigation. This year our company is faced with several lawsuits. We are unsure how these suits should be treated in our financial statements and would like your advice about how to record them.

Here are the details:

1. Several show dog owners have filed a class-action suit concerning the product "Shampoodle." The plaintiffs claim that severe hair loss has occurred as a result of product use. The suit is for a total of $2 million. However, our attorneys claim that it is probable that we will have to pay only between $500,000 and $1 million.

2. For quite sometime we have been producing a dog food called "Ken-L-Burgers." Recently we changed the formula and advertised the product as "better tasting." A consumer group known as "Spokesman for Dogs" has filed suit claiming that humans must actually eat the product in order to make the claim of better taste. Our lawyers say that the chance of losing this suit is remote. The suit is for $6 million.

3. One of our workers lost a finger in the "Ken-L-Burger" machine. Our attorneys believe that we will probably lose this suit but are unsure about the amount.

FIGURE 8–11   *A Letter from a Client (Exercise 8–12) (cont'd)*

Ms. Ellen Acker
May 1, 1999
Page 2

4. My brother's company, House of Cats, is being sued for
$4 million. His lawyers say that it is not likely that he will lose.
However, Ken-L-Products, Inc., has guaranteed a debt he owes
to a bank. It he loses, he will not be able to pay the bank.

5. A grain company sold us several tons of spoiled grain
used as filler in our products. Because the company will not re-
imburse us for the spoilage, we have sued for $2 million. Our
attorneys say we will probably win the case.

6. We aired several commercials that claimed Wayne Newton's dog uses our products. Mr. Newton told us that his dog
hates our products and that if we show the commercials again
he will probably sue us.

If each of these items is material, should we show them on
the financial statements?

Thank you for your help on these matters.

Sincerely,

Ken L. Price

Ken L. Price

pany has reported for the last five years. Mr. Low is an intelligent, well-
educated person, but he knows very little about business or accounting.

Write a letter to Mr. Low explaining how stock prices can be down
despite rising profits. Use the proper format, effective organization, and
appropriate style. Invent any information you feel is necessary to make
your letter complete.

Exercise 8–15

Imagine you are a loan officer for a bank, Nation's Trust. One of the local businesses, Glovco, has applied for a loan of $200,000 for six months. The company has offered to put up the building in which its manufacturing operations are located as collateral for the loan. Local real estate agents estimate the building is worth at least $200,000.

Write a letter to Sam Thomas, President of Glovco, explaining why Nation's Trust does not wish to accept the building as collateral for this loan. Propose two alternative assets that your bank would accept as collateral.[4] Use the proper format, effective organization, and appropriate style. Invent any information you feel is necessary to make your letter complete.

Exercise 8–16

Imagine you are Sam Thomas, President of Glovco and the recipient of the bank loan officer's letter referred to in Exercise 8–15. Respond to the letter with a reply that proposes to use the Glovco's accounts receivable as collateral for the loan. Include an accounts receivable aging schedule in your letter. Use the proper format, effective organization, and appropriate style. Invent any information you feel is necessary to make your letter complete.

Exercise 8–17 (Management Information Systems)

Parker's Shoe Store has been owned and managed by a very conservative individual who is intimidated by computers. The money from cash sales is kept in an old-fashioned cash register, and clerks keep track of the shoes sold by recording pertinent information (brand, style number, price, and size) on a yellow legal pad.

The owner of the store is planning to retire soon and his daughter, Sue Parker, will then be the full-time manager. She believes a computer system could help her run the store more efficiently, and she hires you to evaluate the store's needs and explain how a computer system could help her manage the business.

Write a letter to Ms. Parker explaining the benefits to the store of a computer system, as well as its limitations. Remember that although she is open-minded about the usefulness of computers, she knows very little about them. Use the proper format, effective organization, and appropriate style. Invent any information you feel is necessary to make your letter complete.

Exercise 8–18 (Management Information Systems)

Your company, a small service business with ten office employees, plans to purchase a database package for use with the office's personal computers. Select two database packages and evaluate them for your company's needs. Consider the advantages and disadvantages of both packages, including the ease with which the staff will be able to learn the new system. You should consider basic features of the database package as well as advanced functions.

Write your evaluation in the form of a letter to the company's president, Heather Owen. Use the proper format, effective organization, and appropriate style. Invent any information you feel is necessary to make your letter complete.

NOTES

1. Ray M. Sommerfeld, G. Fred Streuling, Robert L. Gardner, and Dave N. Stewart, *Tax Research Techniques*, 3rd. ed., Revised (New York: American Institute of Certified Public Accountants, 1989), pp. 163–164. This source provides information on letters that tax accountants may write, such as tax protest letters and requests for rulings.

2. Adapted from an example in Paul S. Sperry and Beatrice H. Mitchell, *The Complete Guide to Selling Your Business* (Chicago, Ill.: Upstart Publishing Company, 1992).

3. Adapted from William R. Pasewark, "Writing Assignment for Intermediate Accounting" unpublished class assignment, University of Georgia, 1987.

4. Adapted from an exercise in Timothy J. Gallagher and Joseph D. Andrew, Jr., *Financial Management: Principles and Practice* (Upper Saddle River, N.J.: Prentice Hall, 1996).

9

Memos

Memos, also called memoranda or memorandums, are often used for communication within an organization—between departments, for example, or between a supervisor and other members of the staff. Memos may be of any length, from one sentence to several pages. They may be less formal than letters written to people outside the organization, but well-written memos have the same qualities as good letters: clarity, conciseness, coherence, and courtesy.

This chapter first discusses some of the general characteristics of effective memos. Then we look at special kinds of memos that finance people often write, including memos to clients' files, memos to customers and suppliers, and memos that become a part of working papers.

MEMOS: SOME BASIC PRINCIPLES

Often memos are quite short—from one sentence, perhaps, to several paragraphs. Figure 9–1 is an example. Notice the heading of the memo: the person or persons addressed, the writer, the subject, and the date. Often the writer's initials replace a formal signature.

Sometimes memos are much longer than the one in Figure 9–1; in fact, they may be used for short reports. For longer memos, organization

FIGURE 9–1 *Sample Memo*

> To: Fourth-floor employees
> From: Skip Waller
> Subject: Scheduled painting
> Date: September 12, 1997
>
> Our painting contractors are scheduled to repaint the offices and public areas on our floor next week, September 18–22. The contractors understand that we will continue to work in the offices during this time and will try to disturb us as little as possible. But the work is bound to be somewhat disruptive, so let's all stay flexible and keep a sense of humor during this time that is bound to be somewhat inconvenient.
>
> Thanks for your cooperation as we complete this much-needed maintenance.

and structure are more complicated, so you need to think of writing the memo in terms of the writing process discussed in Chapter 2. You need to spend some time planning your memo: analyzing its purpose, considering the needs and interests of your readers, perhaps doing some research, and finally organizing the material to be covered into a good outline. Once you have planned the memo, you can then draft and revise it using the techniques covered in Chapters 2–7.

The Parts of a Memo:
Organizing for Coherence

Like most kinds of writing, a memo is organized into an introduction, a body, and a conclusion. Summary sentences are used throughout the memo to make it more coherent.

Even very short memos have this structure. The memo in Figure 9–1, which contains only two paragraphs, begins by summarizing the main idea of the memo. The remainder of the first paragraph provides additional information, and the final paragraph, which is only one sentence, concludes by thanking the readers for their cooperation.

INTRODUCTION Most introductions are from one sentence to one paragraph long, although for a longer memo the introduction may be two or three short paragraphs. The introduction should identify what the memo is about and why it was written. If the memo will discuss more than one topic or be divided into several subtopics, the introduction should identify all the most important issues to be covered. The introduction might contain a sentence such as the following to indicate the memo's contents:

> This memo explains how to establish values for patents, copyrights, and trademarks.

An introduction should also identify the main ideas or recommendations of your memo. Sometimes the main idea can be summarized in one or two sentences, but for longer memos, you may need an entire paragraph. If the summary of your main ideas is longer than a paragraph, it's often better to put it in a separate section immediately following the introduction. This section would have a heading such as "Summary" or "Recommendations."

BODY   The body of the memo can be divided into sections, each with a heading that describes the contents of that section. Remember to begin by summarizing the main idea of the section.

A section may have one or many paragraphs. Paragraphs should usually be no more than four or five sentences long, and each should begin with a topic sentence.

CONCLUSION   Memos often end with a conclusion, which may be very brief.

> Let me know if you have any further questions about these procedures.

A conclusion such as this one brings the memo to a close and ends in a courteous, helpful tone. Here's a word of caution, though, about conclusions like the one just given: Be careful not to end all your memos with the same sentence (or some slightly altered variation). The conclusion should be a *meaningful* addition to the memo, not just an empty string of words added out of habit. Also, be sure your conclusion (like the rest of the memo) is appropriate to your reader. Why would the conclusion above be unsuitable for a memo you're sending to your boss?

The sample memos in this chapter show several different kinds of conclusions; all are appropriate to the content of the memo and the reader.

One misconception some people have about conclusions is that they should always repeat the memo's main ideas. For short memos, this repetition is usually not necessary, although for memos longer than about three or four pages, such an ending summary may be helpful.

Whatever the length of the memo, the conclusion is a good place to tell your readers what you want them to do, or what you will do, to follow up on the ideas discussed in the memo. The memo in Figure 9–1 has such a conclusion.

Concise, Clear, Readable
Memos: Style and Tone

Memos should be as concise as possible: no unnecessary repetitions or digressions and no wordiness. They should be written in clear, direct style, so that readers find them interesting and informative. Finally, memos should have flawless grammar and mechanics.

Memos can vary considerably in tone, depending on what they are about and how they will be circulated. Some memos, such as the one in Figure 9–1, are quite informal. For these memos, a conversational, personal tone is appropriate.

Other memos are more formal and may serve as short reports. Some memos, such as the one in Figure 9–5, may report the results of research or work performed, and may thus become part of the permanent records in a file. These memos are usually written with a more impersonal, formal tone, but whether formal or informal, all memos should be written in a vigorous, readable style.

Formats

Memos can be written in a variety of formats, as the examples in this chapter show. The memo in Figure 9–2 is typical of the format used in many organizations. Notice especially how the headings and set-off list make this memo attractive and easy to read.

Some organizations prefer another format that has become customary within the organization. You should prepare your memos according to your employer's expectations. The examples in Figures 9–3 and 9–5 illustrate formats sometimes preferred when the memos are part of a client's file.

SAMPLE MEMOS

The memo shown in Figure 9–2 was written in response to the hypothetical situation described below.[1]

Situation:

Floyd Jones is the proprietor of the company for which you work. Mr. Jones wants to acquire a competitor's business, Sheraton Manufacturing. Sheraton's owner insists that Jones pay not only for the identifiable net assets of the business, but also for something called "goodwill." Mr. Jones says to you: "What is this goodwill stuff? Should I pay for it or not? If I should pay for it, how much should I pay?"

Study the memo in Figure 9–2 to see how it illustrates the principles of memo writing already discussed. Do you think Mr. Jones will be pleased with the memo?

FIGURE 9–2 *A Memo*

MEMORANDUM   August 16, 1998

TO: FLOYD JONES
FROM: DENNIS SMITH
SUBJECT: PURCHASING SHERATON MANUFACTUR-
ING

This memo is in response to your questions concerning the purchase of Sheraton Manufacturing. The memo will first explain goodwill and then discuss how to determine its value. By determining the value of Sheraton's goodwill you will have a dollar amount to help you determine how much you want to offer for the company as a whole.

What Is Goodwill?

Goodwill is an intangible asset made up of items that may contribute to the value and earning power of a company but that are not listed on the company's balance sheet. Some possible items that may make up goodwill for Sheraton Manufacturing are:

1) Highly capable engineering staff
2) Strong reputation for quality work
3) Good management
4) A large number of loyal customers

These items are not listed on Sheraton's balance sheet. However, they obviously have value and, therefore, should be included in the purchase price of the business.

Determining the Value of Goodwill

The value of goodwill is established by comparing the present value of future cash earnings with the fair market value of a firm's other assets less liabilities. The difference between the two is the value of goodwill.

The key to determining the value of goodwill is, of course, estimating the present value of future cash earnings. In the case of Sheraton Manufacturing, we can do this by accomplishing a cash flow analysis similar to the ones we perform in our capital budgeting process.

Let me know if you have any further questions about goodwill or the Sheraton Manufacturing acquisition.

Memos to Clients' Files

Financial analysts who serve clients often record information about a client's situation in a memo that is placed in the client's file for later reference. Other members of the staff may refer to the information recorded in these memos months or even years later, so the information must be recorded clearly, accurately, and correctly.

For example, a firm employing financial analysts may have been asked by a client to appraise another business it might purchase. Several individuals may be assigned to an appraisal team, each working on separate issues involving the appraisal. As information is gathered and opinions are generated by members of the appraisal team, they may record both in memos which are then included in the client's file for the other members of the appraisal team to review.

Figure 9–3 is an example of a memo that might be placed in a client's file.

Memos to Customers' and Creditors' Files

Corporate financial analysts may record information about their company's customers and suppliers in memos that are kept in customers' and creditors' files. For example, a creditor may write or call a corporation about a financing question. The person receiving the letter or handling the call will write a memo to record the pertinent facts of the call. Later, if a reply is called for, the details of the original call will be readily available.

A sample memo written for a creditor's file appears in Figure 9–4.

Memos as Part of Working Papers

When finance people prepare working papers as part of their work on large projects, they usually include memos summarizing the work they've performed, what they've observed, and the conclusions they've reached. In a business appraisal, for example, the appraisal team members prepare memos describing each major area of the appraisal. Then a supervisor, perhaps the senior appraiser or senior financial analyst, will often prepare a summary or review memo that includes comments on the entire appraisal process.

These memos must be clear, accurate, and complete. Other members of the firm, or lawyers on either side of a court case who review the working papers later,* may need to know exactly what procedures the appraisers performed. Thus, the memos should be written in a direct, active style: "I [the person writing the memo] performed a physical inventory of

---

*Business appraisals are frequently done to support legal actions.

FIGURE 9–3 *Memo in a client's file*

April 27, 1999

TO: Appraisal team
FROM: Joe Prior
SUBJECT: Smith-Cochran Tower Systems Valuation

After an examination of Smith-Cochran's business situation, I recommend we rely on the income approach to valuation for these reasons:

1. Since the assets of Smith-Cochran are not being liquidated, the liquidation value approach is inappropriate. Given the low liquidation value of communications towers due to disassembly and removal costs, this method would not measure the true market value of the Smith-Cochran company in any case.

2. The market approach cannot be used due to a lack of data. Because the communications tower industry is dominated by small entrepreneurs ("Mom and Pop" operations), no publicly traded companies similar to Smith-Cochran could be located. There is no trade association for communications tower operators, and no compiled data for sales of private companies. The market approach is simply unworkable given the situation.

3. The income approach, in which the company's future income is analyzed, projected over a specified time frame, and discounted to the present using an appropriate capitalization rate, is clearly the best approach.

assets on May 31, 1999. A copy of the inventory was delivered to Mr. Sanchez, CEO, on June 6."

The memo in Figure 9–5 was written to record an analysis of inventory procedures.[2] This memo has a different organization and format from the sample memos given earlier in the chapter, yet it illustrates qualities essential for effective writing: coherence, conciseness, and clarity. What specific techniques make this memo effective?

FIGURE 9–4 *Sample Memo in a Creditor's File*

MEMORANDUM

March 3, 1998

TO: Bob Martin
FROM: Joe Boswick
SUBJECT: Interest rate on Andy Randall's note

Andy Randall called today about the terms of his note. As you know, he is willing to make $125,000 available to our company under the following terms:

- He will establish a "revolving credit" limit of $125,000 against which our company may take "advances."
- Our company is to pay interest (calculated on a daily basis) on the unpaid principal amount of the advances taken until the due date, August 31, 2000.
- The interest rate will be 12%, compounded daily, payable on the due date.
- A "facility fee" of 30% of the maximum cumulative advances taken by our company is to be paid on the due date, August 31, 2000.

If we took the maximum amount of advances over a 12-month period and then paid it all back at the due date, the effective interest rate we would pay would be 70% a year! The problem is the "facility fee," which could add up to $49,500 to the cost of the funds.

I believe we need to get back to Andy and renegotiate the terms.

E-MAIL

With the explosion of information technology, many memos are now written in the form of e-mail messages. E-mail is extremely convenient: with the click of a mouse, a memo can be sent to a colleague in the next office or a business partner in Hong Kong.

FIGURE 9–5 *A Memo as a Part of Working Papers*

Prepared by: C.J.G. Date: 1/05/99
Reviewed by: A.C.E. Date: 1/11/99

Highlight Company
Inventory Procedures Memorandum—Wayne Plant A
12/31/98

1. Observing client's inventory taking. Four members of our staff arrived at the Wayne plant at 7:40 A.M. on 12/31/98 for an analysis of the company's inventory procedures. All manufacturing and shipping operations had been shut down for the day. All materials had been neatly arranged, labeled, and separated by type.

Two teams of staff members were assigned to different parts of the plant. Each team observed the care with which the client's personnel made the inventory counts and the control being exercised over the inventory count sheets. In every case, it appeared that the client's inventory instructions were being followed in a systematic and conscientious manner.

2. Making test counts. Each team made numerous test counts, which were recorded in our work papers. The test counts covered approximately 22 percent of the inventory value and confirmed the accuracy of the client's counts.

3. Identifying obsolete and damaged goods. Each team made inquiries concerning obsolete, damaged, or slow-moving items. Based on our observations and inquiries, we have no reason to believe that any obsolete or damaged materials remained in inventory. We identified certain slow-moving items, portions of which on further investigation were excluded from the inventory.

4. Observing cutoff controls. We observed that receiving reports were prepared on all goods received on the inventory date and recorded the number of the last receiving report prepared. No goods were shipped on 12/31. We recorded the number of the last shipping document used on 12/30. These numbers were subsequently used in our purchases and sales cutoff tests.

5. Conclusions. Based on our observation of the procedures followed by the client, it is my opinion that an accurate count was made of all goods on hand at 12/31/98 and that all obsolete, damaged, or slow-moving items were appropriately identified.

Carl Good

A number of special considerations should be observed when you use e-mail:

- Address messages carefully. Stories of messages being sent to unintended recipients abound. This often occurs when a memo is addressed to "staff" or some other general address, when the intended recipient is one individual. The results are sometimes humorous, as when an employee sends a love note to the entire corporation; or they can be disastrous, as might occur when the plans for a new product are sent by mistake to the firm's competitors. The lesson is to "think twice and click once" when addressing and sending e-mail messages.

- Remember that even though an e-mail message is addressed and sent to one individual, it may still be read by unintended recipients. E-mail messages are not private. They are sent over computer communications networks where they can be easily intercepted. That nasty message you sent to your friend criticizing your boss might end up on your boss's desk without your knowledge! In general, you should assume that every e-mail message you write may be read by anyone and everyone else. Compose your e-mail accordingly.

- Remember that all e-mail messages can be saved and used as proof that the communication took place. There are no "off-the record" e-mails. Generally this is not a problem, because presumably the reason you are sending a memo by e-mail is to record some information for the record; but occasionally, people fall into the trap of treating e-mail like phone calls. For example, they may say in an e-mail something like "Steve thinks he's going to exercise his options for $4,000, but it'll never happen as long as I'm the CFO." Imagine how this CFO will feel if Steve turns up with a copy of the e-mail message. Again, the best advice is assume that every e-mail message you write will be read by everyone else. Compose your messages accordingly.

- Avoid junk e-mail. People, even financial professionals, constantly send e-mail to people other than their intended addressees simply because they click on group addresses out of habit. "Tom, I'll be out of town Monday. Handle the meeting, will you? Thanks, Bill." is an example of a memo that has meaning only for Tom. What may happen, however, is that Bill will send the message to "Corporate Staff," or something similar, because that is the button he is used to clicking on when he sends e-mail. Consequently, perhaps 40 people will receive Tom's message and must take time to access it and then delete it (worse—sometimes they will reply to it, perpetuating the problem).

When your job requires you to write a memo, remember the techniques of effective writing stressed throughout this book. *Coherent* memos are logically organized and easy to follow; *concise* memos cover essential information in as few words as possible; and *clear* memos are precise, readable, and grammatically correct. *Courteous* memos help ensure that you maintain good relationships with your colleagues.

EXERCISES

Exercise 9–1 (All Levels)

You work in the finance department of Midsouth Corporation. The company's Chief Executive Officer, Mary Sanders, has asked you to be in charge of your department's fundraising for the United Way campaign.

Write a memo to your coworkers asking them to contribute to this year's campaign. The memo will accompany a pledge card that they may fill in and sign. Make the memo persuasive, and add any details you think would make the memo effective.

Exercise 9–2 (Intermediate)

You are newly hired as a financial analyst for the O-Y-Me Corporation, a small service business which has no formal capital budgeting system. The president of your company, Mr. Now U. Donit, has requested that you write a memo to him explaining what the discounted cash flow of investment evaluation is, how it differs from simply projecting the rate of return, and why O-Y-Me should use the discounted cash flow method for capital budgeting purposes instead of projected rates of return.

Exercise 9–3 (All Levels)

You are a loan officer at Gotham City National Bank. The proprietors of two businesses, Butler Department Store and Susan Nielsen Home Decorators, have sought business loans from you. To decide whether to make the loans, you have requested their balance sheets, which are shown in Figure 9–6. Based solely on these balance sheets, which entity would you be more comfortable loaning money to? Explain fully, citing specific items and amounts from the balance sheets. Write your answer in the form of a memo to the bank's vice president, Edward Barth.[3]

Exercise 9–4

You are a financial analyst at Conner Company. Today you discovered that the Deelay Company, which purchased $1,000 worth of software from Conner under terms of net 30, has not yet paid for the software, even though 50 days have passed since the software was shipped. Write a memo for Deelay's customer file noting this fact, and reporting that you have reached only voice mail during the three times you have called Deelay.

Exercise 9–5

You are a financial analyst for the Deelay Corporation. Fifty days ago, Deelay purchased software from the Conner Corporation under terms of net 30. Due to an unfortunate cash crunch, the $1,000 due has not yet been paid. Recently, people from Conner have been calling to inquire about payment, but in each case you have been "out of the office." Write a memo for Conner's creditor file, noting the company's calls and describing why payment has been delayed.

Exercise 9–6

Delores Deelay, your boss at the Deelay Corporation, has informed you that the company expects to receive $100,000 in capital within a week from outside sources. This is good news because a continuing cash

FIGURE 9–6 *For Exercise 9–3*

Butler Department Store
Balance Sheet
August 31, 1998

Assets		Liabilities	
Cash	$ 1,000	Accounts payable	$12,000
Accounts receivable	14,000	Note payable	18,000
Merchandise inventory	85,000	Total liabilities	30,000
Store supplies	500		
Furniture and fixtures	9,000	Owner's Equity	
Building	90,000		
Land	14,000	Roy Butler, capital	183,500
		Total liabilities	
Total assets	$ 213,500	and owner's equity	$213,500

Susan Nielsen Home Decorators
Balance Sheet
August 31, 1998

Assets		Liabilities	
Cash	$11,000	Accounts payable	$ 3,000
Accounts receivable	4,000	Note payable	18,000
Office supplies	1,000	Total liabilities	21,000
Office furniture	6,000		
Land	19,000	Owner's Equity	
		Susan Nielsen, capital	20,000
		Total liabilities	
Total assets	$41,500	and owner's equity	$41,500

crunch has forced the company to delay payment of many bills. Because the $100,000 will not cover all requirements, Ms. Deelay requests that you, as senior financial analyst, provide her with a prioritized list of items for which the money should be used. Write a memo to Ms. Deelay listing and justifying your prioritized recommendations. You are aware of the following pressing requirements:

Taxes owed on Jan 1 payroll	$11,500
Jan 15 payroll	40,000
Rent for Dec and Jan	20,000
Legal expenses	22,000
Employees' expenses	12,000
Note payable payment due	12,000

Software Purchases
   (including one very overdue bill
   from Conner Corporation)
	21,000

Telephone bill	6,000

Exercise 9–7

You are the controller of the Red Mesa Ranch and are preparing the ranch's financial statements for the year. You requested information from the cattle manager, Tuf Cowan, about the value of the ranch's livestock assets. Mr. Cowan sent you the memo in Figure 9–7, which asks you some questions about how to classify the livestock. Write a memo to answer Mr. Cowan's questions.[4]

Exercise 9–8

You are the head of finance for Ms. Ima Astute, who owns a small business. Ms. Astute is considering the purchase of a competing business. The sum of the fair market values of the separately identifiable assets of the business she may purchase is $350,000. Ms. Astute determined this amount by having an appraisal made before making an offer. The offer she made was equal to this amount—that is, $350,000. The owner of the business she wants to purchase has declined the offer and indicated he thinks his business is worth at least $400,000 considering the goodwill that exists. Ms. Astute cannot understand how the business can be worth more than $350,000, considering this was the amount of the appraisal.

Write a memo to Ms. Astute explaining what goodwill is, why it may exist for the business she wants to purchase, how to determine what to pay for it, and the effects on future financial statements she may expect.

Exercise 9–9

Daniel Gordon, the president of the Skinner company, is considering a bond issue to raise $1,000,000 for the company. Mr. Gordon notes that long-term T-Bonds are yielding 8% right now, and he thinks that is a pretty good loan rate. Before proceeding with the bond issue, however, Mr. Gordon wants to know more about it. Specifically, he wonders what the annual interest payments would be on the bonds.

You are a financial analyst at Skinner Company. Write a memo to Mr. Gordon explaining what the interest payments on a $1,000,000, 20-year bond issue would be, if the bonds were issued at an 8% yield. Also explain

FIGURE 9–7   *Memo for Exercise 9–7*

RED MESA RANCH
OFFICE MEMO

To: Ian Greenberg, Controller
From: Tuf Cowan, Cattle Manager
Date: June 28, 1998
Subject: Classification of livestock on the balance sheet

I have received your request to value our livestock assets for
the balance sheet for the year ending June 30, 1998. Based on
available commodity prices, I can easily determine the dollar
value of the livestock. However, I am unable to determine
whether the following livestock categories should be shown as
inventory or as long-term assets:

1. Bulls—kept for breeding purposes; average useful life of
   ten years.
2. Steers—held for approximately 15 months from birth,
   then sold for slaughter.
3. Heifers—most kept for breeding purposes; average useful
   life of five years, then sold for slaughter.
4. Calves—less than one year old, certain percentage sold as
   veal, others used for breeding or grazed and sold later for
   slaughter.

Would you please assist me by specifying how I should classify each of these categories?

---

in your memo why the Skinner company would probably not be able to
issue the bonds at 8%.

Exercise 9–10

Imagine you work for a consulting firm that specializes in business
appraisals. These appraisals are intended to determine the market value
of private companies (companies whose stock is not publicly traded).
The basic procedure that your firm uses to determine a company's market value is to project the operating cash flows the company can reason-

ably be expected to receive for the foreseeable future, then to discount those cash flows back to the present at an appropriate capitalization rate. The result is the company's present value.

One of your firm's clients has called to ask how this procedure works. Someone has told him the procedure is based on the "time value of money" concept, and he would like to know what that is.

Write a memo to the client explaining why the value of his business is the sum of the present values of all the future cash flows the business will receive. Remember, the client has no formal training in finance.

Write another memo for the client's file recording the client's call and outlining your response.

Exercise 9–11

During a telephone conversation this morning, the sole stockholder for your company told you that he had borrowed $150,000 from a private individual in the corporation's name. He instructed you, the chief financial officer, to make sure the loan got recorded in the corporate books. You are mystified, as the stockholder apparently used the funds for his own purposes—none of the cash found its way into the corporate checking account. Obviously the company president needs to know about this situation, and a written record of the event needs to be created. Write a memo to the president notifying her of the phone conversation and what it was about. Include your recommendation for handling the matter.

Exercise 9–12

Your company gives tax advice from time to time to clients who are regular customers. Mark Rood has asked you to help him with his income tax return for the tax year ending December 31, 1998. His records indicate that he received wages and commissions of $30,000 from his job as a salesperson. The records also indicate that Rood did the following during the year:

1. Transferred one-half of his 100 shares of IMP stock, bought in 1989 for $12 a share and worth (on the date of the transfer) $26 a share, to his divorced wife as part of their property settlement.
2. Sold 50 shares of the IMP stock in March of 1998 for $29 per share.
3. In March of 1998, bought a rare Mongolian coin for $1,000 to add to his collection. In August, he sold the coin for $1,800.
4. Bought a Ghanian coin for $2,500 in September and sold it in November for $1,000.

Assuming these are Rood's only capital assets transactions during the year, what is his adjusted gross income?

Write a memo to Rood's file in which you answer this question. Be sure to show the step-by-step computation of his gains and losses.[5]

Exercise 9–13 (E-mail)

Recently you have noticed that your "in-basket" on the local area network in your company accumulates 8–10 messages a day that are jokes and humorous stories downloaded from the Internet. Most of these messages are not very funny, but they all take time to delete, and sometimes you delete important messages by accident. Clearly, the situation has gotten out of hand. Write a memo to the staff about the problem and ask that the practice of distributing humorous e-mail messages be discontinued. Be sure to explain your reasoning so you won't come across as dictatorial. You expect to send your memo as an e-mail message.

NOTES

1. This memo is based on a student paper written by Pete Wardlow at the University of Georgia in 1987.
2. Adapted by permission, from pp. 490–491 in *Modern Auditing* by Walter G. Kell and Richard E. Ziegler. Copyright © 1980 by John Wiley & Sons, Inc.
3. Adapted with permission from Charles T. Horngren and Walter T. Harrison, *Accounting* (Englewood Cliffs, N.J.: Prentice Hall, Inc., 1989): 36–37.
4. From William R. Pasewark, "Writing Assignment for Intermediate Accounting" (unpublished class assignment, University of Georgia, 1987).
5. Adapted with permission from Prentice-Hall, *1988 Federal Tax Course* (Englewood Cliffs, N.J.: Prentice-Hall, Inc., © 1987): 279.

10

Reports

Sometimes finance people prepare formal reports, such as a financial consultant's report for a client or an investment analysis report for publication. Corporate financial managers might prepare reports for other departments in their firm or perhaps for a group of managers with a particular need.

A report usually analyzes a finance problem and applies finance principles to a particular situation. It may also require some research of professional literature or other material, so the research techniques discussed in chapter 7 are often part of report preparation.

Reports vary in length, but all reports should meet certain basic criteria. The finance content should be accurate, the organization should be coherent, the report should be presented attractively, and the writing style should be clear and concise. Like all forms of writing, a report should be designed and written with the readers' needs and expectations in mind.

PLANNING A REPORT

If you are preparing a report on the job, the organization for which you work may have an established format for you to follow for all reports. Be sure to find out the expectations and policies of your organization before you begin work on your report. Even if the organization doesn't require employees adhere to a certain format, you may find your job easier if you use several well-written reports as models.

If you are free to design your own report format, or if you are preparing the report for a class assignment, the format presented in this chapter can serve as a model. It is a generic model, typical of those used in business and industry.

In planning the report, you must also consider the purpose of the report and who its readers will be. The analysis of purpose and audience for a report may be more difficult than it is for letters and memos. A report may have many groups of readers, and each group will have different interests and needs.

For example, a report from the finance department recommending that a firm invest in a new computer system might be circulated to the information management systems (IMS) department, the accounting department, the departments that would actually use the system, and senior management. Of course, the finance department itself would be interested in the finance aspects of the acquisition as well as how the system could be used for various financial tasks. The IMS department would be interested in the technical features of the system and how it would affect IMS personnel. Other departments would want to know how the system would make their work easier or more difficult, whether it would affect their budgets, and whether their personnel would have the training to use the system. Senior management, on the other hand, would be interested in a bigger picture, such as how the system would affect the firm's efficiency, competitiveness, and cash flow.

To write this report, you would need to identify who the readers are and what information they want the report to include. You would obviously be writing to readers with different degrees of knowledge about technical features of the new system and with different interests and concerns as well. The way to handle this complicated situation is to write different parts of the report for different groups of readers.

Fortunately, many reports are not as difficult to plan and write as this one would be, but this example shows how important it is to analyze carefully the needs and expectations of different groups of readers.

Most reports require a great deal of research. They may report the results of empirical studies or pilot projects, or report research involving technical literature. Organizing this research into a coherent outline is essential. Review the principles of organization discussed in chapter 3, and then apply the following questions to your report as you are planning the outline and structuring your draft.

1. Is the subject covered adequately?
   - Background information when necessary
   - Adequate explanations, supporting data, and examples
   - Citations from authorities, as needed
   - Application to the specific needs and interests of the readers

2. Is the report too long?
   - Digressions—off the subject
   - Too much explanation or detail
   - Repetitions or wordiness
3. Is the report organized logically?
   - In order from most to least important, from the readers' point of view
   - Summary sentences where helpful
   - Transitions to link ideas
   - Short, well-organized paragraphs with topic sentences

The format of a report—how its various parts are put together—also determines how coherent the report is.

THE PARTS
OF A REPORT

Reports can be presented in a variety of formats, any of which should make the report easy to read. The format presented in this handbook is typical of the ways in which reports are structured.

A report may include these sections:

Transmittal document
Title page
Table of contents
List of illustrations
Summary section
Introduction
Body of the report
Conclusion
Appendices
Notes
Bibliography
Graphic illustrations

Transmittal Document

The transmittal document can be either a letter or memo, depending on whether you are sending your report to someone outside your organization or to someone within it. This document is a cover letter or memo: It presents the report to the people for whom it was written and adds any other information that will be helpful.

The transmittal document will not be long, but it should include essential information: the report's title, its topic, and its purpose. It's usually a good idea to summarize the main idea or recommendation of the report if you can do so in about one or two sentences. You may want to add other comments about the report that will be helpful to the readers, but always end with a courteous closing.

Whereas the style of the actual report is usually formal and impersonal, the transmittal document can usually be more conversational, including the use of personal pronouns.

Title Page

In a professional report, the title page may look something like this:

Title of Report
Prepared for . . .
Prepared by . . .
Date

For a student report, the instructor may prefer information such as this:

Title of Report
Student's Name
Course and Period
Instructor
Date

Table of Contents

The table of contents should be on a separate page and should have a heading. The contents listed are the major parts of the report, excluding the transmittal document, with the appropriate page numbers.

List of Illustrations

The list of illustrations, if applicable, includes titles and page numbers of graphs, charts, and other illustrations.

Summary Section

All formal reports should have a section at the beginning of the report that summarizes the main ideas and recommendations. This section can vary in length from one paragraph to several pages, and it can come either immediately before or immediately after the introduction. The summary section may be called an executive summary, abstract, synopsis, summary, or some other term.

An executive summary is especially helpful for long reports. This section gives the readers an overview of the report's contents without the technical detail. Busy managers may read the executive summary to decide whether they should read the entire report.

The executive summary identifies the purpose and scope of the report and possibly the methods used for research. It includes the major findings of the research, the conclusions of the researcher, and the recommendations, if any.

The length of an executive summary varies with the length of the report, but it is generally about one to three pages long. It should begin on a separate page following the table of contents or list of illustrations, and should be titled *Executive Summary*. The sample report at the end of this chapter uses this kind of summary.

For shorter reports, a section right after the introduction can provide a summary of the report's main ideas and recommendations. This section is usually one or two paragraphs long and should be labeled *Summary*.

Introduction

The introduction of a formal report is longer than that of a letter or memo. It is usually at least two or three short paragraphs, and for long reports may even be longer than a page.

The introduction should identify the subject of the report and may state why it was written—who requested or authorized it, or for whom it was prepared. The introduction should state the purpose of the report in specific terms:

> The purpose of this report is to discuss the feasibility of offering a stock bonus plan to employees of Gulf Coast Industries.
>
> NOT: The purpose of this report is to discuss stock bonus plans.

Sometimes an introduction includes additional information to help the reader. For example, it may give a brief background of the report's topic. However, if it's necessary to include very much background information, this material should be presented in a separate section in the body of the report.

Finally, the introduction of a report should end with a plan of development that gives the reader an overview or forecast of the topics the report covers and the order in which they are presented. A simple plan of development may be in sentence form:

> This report describes the proposed pension plan and then discusses its costs and benefits.

Sometimes a set-off list makes the plan of development easier to read:

> This report discusses the following topics related to the proposed pension plan:
>
> - Major provisions
> - Benefits to employees
> - Benefits to the corporation
> - Cost
> - Accounting for the plan

Body of the Report

The body of the report should be divided into sections and possibly subsections, each with an appropriate heading. Remember to begin each section with a statement that summarizes the main idea to be covered in that section.

The body of the report may also contain graphic illustrations, as discussed below.

Conclusion

In addition to the summary section at the beginning, a report should have a conclusion to remind the reader of the report's main ideas and recommendations. This section may be from one paragraph to several pages long.

Appendices (optional)

Depending on the report's audience and purpose, you may want to place technical information and statistics in appendices at the end of the report. If you use an appendix, give it a title and refer to it in the body of the report.

Notes and Bibliography

What to put at the end of the report depends in part on the style of documentation you use. If you use endnotes, they should be labeled *Notes*.

Almost all reports have some sort of bibliography or reference list. This list identifies the sources you cited in your paper, and it may also include additional references the reader might wish to consult. This section should follow the notes (if any), and should have a title such as *Bibliography* or *References*.

Chapter 7 demonstrates the proper form for endnotes and bibliographical entries.

Graphic Illustrations

Sometimes graphic illustrations, such as graphs or tables, make a report easier to read and more interesting, especially if you are presenting statistical or numerical data or if the subject of the report concerns a process. You can place graphic illustrations either in an appendix or in the body of your report, just after the place in the text where they are discussed.

Graphic illustrations are discussed more fully in chapter 6.

APPEARANCE

It's important to present your report as attractively as possible. Use good quality paper, such as 24-lb. bond, and be sure that the report is printed with a letter-quality printer.

Reports may be single-spaced or double-spaced, depending on the situation. Students' reports are usually double-spaced to provide space for annotations when they are graded. In all reports, the transmittal document and any set-off material are single-spaced. Pages should be numbered, using lowercase Roman numerals for front matter (table of contents, list of illustrations, executive summary) and Arabic numerals for the remainder of the report, from the introduction through the end matter.

STYLE AND TONE

The tone of a formal report should usually be just what its name implies: formal, and therefore impersonal. For example, you probably would not use personal pronouns or contractions in a formal report. However, a formal style should still be readable and interesting, so you should use the techniques of effective style discussed in chapter 4. Even a formal document can be written simply, clearly, and concretely.

Unlike the actual report, the transmittal document may be written in a personal, more informal style.

The report in Figure 10–1 that begins on page 193, illustrates many of these techniques of effective report writing.

FIGURE 10–1 *A Report*

B&H Financial Consultants
125 Easy Street
Athens, Georgia
August 8, 1998

Mr. Sam Hamilton
Hamilton Manufacturing
1890 Meerly Avenue
Atlanta, Georgia 30306

Dear Mr. Hamilton:

Enclosed is the report about convertible bonds that you requested in your letter of July 21. The report, titled *Convertible Bonds: Financial and Accounting Considerations*, examines the nature of convertible debt, the pros and cons of such an issue, and the accounting treatment of the securities.

The report shows that convertible bonds may represent a relatively less expensive method of raising capital than nonconvertible bonds. Another advantage is that if the convertible bonds are converted, the existing shares of common stock will not be diluted as severely as they would be if common stock had been issued. However, as the report makes clear, these effects are by no means certain.

I believe the report will provide you with the information you need. If you have any further questions, however, don't hesitate to give me a call.

Sincerely yours,

Joyce Byron

Joyce Byron

jhw

FIGURE 10–1   *A Report (cont.)*

CONVERTIBLE BONDS:
FINANCIAL AND ACCOUNTING CONSIDERATIONS

Prepared for Hamilton Manufacturing

by

JOYCE BYRON

AUGUST 8, 1998

FIGURE 10–1   *A Report (cont)*

CONTENTS

i

FIGURE 10–1   *A Report (cont.)*

EXECUTIVE SUMMARY

This report provides information about convertible bonds for the managers of Hamilton Manufacturing. Included is information about the nature of convertible bonds, financial advantages and disadvantages of issuing such bonds, and their accounting treatment.

A convertible bond is a debt security that carries the option of exchange for an equity security, usually common stock. The bond indenture specifies when the bonds may be converted and a conversion price or ratio. The conversion price is usually 10 to 20 percent above the market price of the common stock at the time of issue. Both the issuer and the investor expect the market price of the stock to rise above the conversion price; therefore, bondholders are likely to convert the bond into equity.

Convertible bonds would offer Hamilton three advantages:

- The company could issue the bonds at a premium or at a low stated interest rate, which investors would accept because of the conversion privilege.
- The company could avoid another stock issue now, when the price of Hamilton's stock is low.
- Management would avoid possible conflict with its major stockholder.

There are also potential disadvantages management should consider before issuing the convertible bonds:

- The uncertain conditions of the economy make a future increase in the market price of the company's stock uncertain. If conversion does not occur, Hamilton may have difficulty meeting the debt requirements.
- Bond conversion will reduce earnings per share and operating leverage. Conversion will also increase Hamilton's income tax liability because of the loss of interest expense.
- The required accounting treatment of convertible bonds may have an unfavorable effect on the company's financial statements: a high level of debt may be presented alongside a lowered diluted earnings per share (DEPS).

ii

FIGURE 10–1   *A Report (cont.)*

CONVERTIBLE BONDS:
FINANCIAL AND ACCOUNTING CONSIDERATIONS

Introduction

The purpose of this report is to provide information for the management of Hamilton Manufacturing about an increasingly popular form of
financing: convertible debt. Convertible debt is an issue of debt securities (bonds) that carry the option of exchange for equity securities (usually common stock).

Three major topics make up the report: (1) The nature of convertible
bonds, (2) financial advantages and disadvantages Hamilton could expect if it issues the bonds, and (3) accounting treatment for the bonds.

Nature of Convertible Bonds

When convertible bonds are issued, the bond indenture specifies a period of time after issuance during which the bonds may be converted.
The indenture also specifies a conversion price, "the amount of par value
of principal amount of the bonds exchangeable for one share of stock"
(Bogen 1968, 31). If a conversion ratio, rather than a conversion price, is
specified, the effective price of stock to the bondholder may be determined by dividing the par value of the bond by the number of shares exchangeable for one bond.

The conversion price, which is determined when the bonds are sold, is
usually from 10 to 20 percent above the prevailing market price of the
common stock at the time of issue. Both the issuing firm and the investor
expect that the market price of the stock will rise above the conversion
price and that the conversion privilege will then be exercised by most or
all bondholders.

The indenture typically includes a call provision so that the issuing
firm can force bondholders to convert. Therefore, it is evident that firms
issuing convertible debt often truly want to raise equity capital. The reasons that they choose convertible debt are discussed below.

1

FIGURE 10–1   *A Report (cont.)*

Financial Advantages and Disadvantages

Advantages
Use of convertible debt would offer Hamilton advantages over straight debt or stock issues.

Bonds that are convertible into stock are in demand. Therefore, bond buyers are willing to accept a low stated interest rate on such bonds, to pay a premium and accept a lower yield, or to accept less restrictive covenants. Hamilton could thus obtain funds at a lower cost than would be possible if it issued bonds without the conversion privilege.

The advantages of a convertible bond issue over a common stock issue relate to timing. Although Hamilton might be willing to take on more equity in the future, current economic conditions make this an unfavorable time to sell stock. One authority has explained this advantage as follows:

To sell stock now would require giving up more shares to raise a given amount of money than management thinks is necessary. However, setting the conversion price 10 to 20 percent above the present market price of the stock will require giving up 10 to 20 percent fewer shares when the bonds are converted than would be required if stock were sold directly (Brigham 1978, 532).

Another possible advantage to Hamilton of issuing convertible bonds is that the company could avoid creating a possible conflict with the major stockholder, who would probably want to maintain his controlling interest. The stockholder might vote against a large issue of stock. However, the bond issue could be convertible into a number of shares small enough not to injure significantly the stockholder's interest.

Disadvantages
Most of the disadvantages of convertible bonds are related to the uncertainty of the conversion and its timing. If Hamilton's stock price does not rise, conversion will not occur and the company will not obtain the equity financing it desired. Hamilton might then have difficulty meeting the unplanned-for obligations of debt.

Other disadvantages arise, however, if the conversion does occur. When the debt becomes equity, basic earnings per share (BEPS) is reduced, operating leverage is reduced, and income taxes increase because interest expense is reduced.

2

FIGURE 10–1   *A Report (cont.)*

Accounting Treatment

The Accounting Principles Board (APB) has ruled that convertible bonds "which are sold at a price or have a value at issuance not significantly in excess of the face amount" must be treated in the same manner as other bonds (1969, par. 1). That is, "no portion of the proceeds from the issuance . . . should be accounted for as attributable to the conversion feature" (par. 10). The expectation that some or all of the bonds will be converted into stock is not recognized in the accounts.

Because convertible bonds are normally sold at a premium, the amount of the cash proceeds from the issue is greater than the face value of the bonds. The premium is amortized over the life of the bonds. The effect of the amortization is that the interest expense recorded by Hamilton each period would not equal the amount of the interest <u>payment</u>, but would reflect the effective yield to the bondholders.

When the bonds are converted, Hamilton will remove from the accounts the balance associated with those bonds. Two methods can be used to record the common stock issued in exchange for the bonds. Under one method, the stock is assigned a value equal to the market value of the stock or the bonds. If this value differs from the book value of the bonds (the balance associated with the bonds, mentioned above), then a gain or a loss is recorded. Under the other method, which is more widely used, the value assigned to the stock equals the book value of the bonds and no gain or loss is recognized or recorded (Chasteen, Flaherty, and O'Connor 1995, 693).

If Hamilton decides to retire its convertible bonds for cash before their maturity date, the transaction will be recorded in the same way as the early bonds and the cash paid to retire them will be a gain or a loss on the income statement.

Although convertibles are accounted for solely as debt, Hamilton must also consider the equity characteristics of such issues in computing diluted earnings per share (DEPS). The Financial Accounting Standards Board (FASB) requires that corporations having issued securities that are potentially dilutive of EPS, such as convertible bonds, must present both basic earnings per share (BEPS) and diluted earnings per share (DEPS) in their financial statements (1997, par. 36).

The DEPS figure represents EPS <u>as if</u> the bonds had been converted into stock. If they had been converted, the removal of the bonds would have caused a reduction of interest expense, which would have increased earnings. However, the positive effect of the earnings adjustment may not offset the negative effect of the shares adjustment. Thus, convertibles reduce reported DEPS.

3

FIGURE 10–1   *A Report (cont.)*

Conclusion

In the decision whether to finance with convertible debt, Hamilton must consider whether it would benefit from using convertibles rather than straight debt or stock issues and whether it can meet the debt requirements, should conversion not occur as expected. In addition, management should analyze carefully the effect of the issue on readers of the financial statements, because until the bonds are converted, a possibly high level of debt will exist alongside a lowered presentation of DEPS.

WORKS CITED

Accounting Principles Board 1969. *Accounting for convertible debt and debt issued with stock purchase warrants.* Opinion no. 14. New York: AICPA.

Bogen, J. I., ed. 1968. *Financial handbook,* 4th ed. New York: Ronald Press.

Booker, J. A., and B. D. Jarnagin. 1979. *Financial accounting standards: Explanation and analysis.* Chicago: Commerce Clearing House.

Brigham, E. F. 1978. *Fundamentals of financial management.* Hinsdale, Ill.: Dryden Press.

Chasteen, L. G., R. E. Flaherty, and M. C. O'Connor. 1995. *Intermediate Accounting,* 5th ed. New York: McGraw-Hill.

Financial Accounting Standards Board. 1997. *Earnings per share.* Statement of financial accounting standards no. 128. Stamford, Conn.: FASB.

4

EXERCISES

Exercise 10–1

One of your clients, Albert P. Moneybags, III, has recently inherited a portfolio of stocks in various Fortune 500 companies. He has received the annual reports of these companies, which of course include the income statement, balance sheet, statement of cash flows, and statement of retained earnings.

Mr. Moneybags knows very little about these statements. He has asked you to write a report that explains the statements so that he can use them to manage his investments.

Prepare the report for your client. Supplement your discussion with sample financial statements that you construct yourself or find in the annual report of an actual company.

Exercise 10–2

A client, Robert Gutierrez, has just inherited some money and has decided to begin investing in a stock portfolio. He is not interested in mutual funds because he prefers to have personal control over his stock investments. He also realizes that over time he will need to have a diversified portfolio, but for now he wants to begin his investment strategy by purchasing stock in one company. Your client wants to invest about $10,000, and he wishes to keep his risk as low as possible.

Mr. Gutierrez has asked you to evaluate the annual reports of several corporations as possible investment options. Choose three corporations whose stock is traded on the New York Stock Exchange and whose annual reports you can study. Compare the information found in these reports and then write a report for Mr. Gutierrez that explains which of the companies is likely to be his best investment. Explain your conclusions thoroughly, quoting from the annual reports as necessary.

Exercise 10–3
(valuation, assuming an
unsophisticated client)

You have received an inquiry from a prospective client, Armchair Shopping, Inc., concerning the valuation of the business. Betsy Johnson, owner of Armchair, wants to sell the business, but before she offers it for sale she wants to get an idea of what the business is actually worth. Write a report for Ms. Johnson, explaining briefly the various methods of establishing a market value for a private company. Remember that your client has no formal training in finance.

Exercise 10–4
(valuation, assuming
a sophisticated client)

Carol Loudermilk and Russell Williams own a mall music store that will carry CDs, tapes, posters, and T-shirts. As part of a major expansion effort, they have applied for $600,000 in bank financing for which they propose to use the music store as collateral. Since the music store is to be used for collateral, the lender, Stargate National Bank, a small bank with limited staff, is very interested in the market value of the music store's assets. Accordingly, Ms. Mary Moneypenny of Stargate has contacted your firm and asked if a determination of the store's market value is feasible, and, if so, how the market value would be established. Write a report for Ms. Moneypenny, explaining briefly the various methods of establishing a market value for a private company. Remember that your client is a finance professional.

Exercise 10–5

Twice a year, as a part of your financial consulting company's "empower employees" program, someone is asked to write a report on a subject of interest to the other members of the company. This time, it's your turn. Your boss has asked you to write a report about risk (a subject of great interest to finance people). Write a report describing the types of risks businesses face. Include in your report a discussion of how risk is measured and what businesses do to reduce risk. Assume that you are writing the report for your colleagues, who are all familiar with financial theory.

Exercise 10–6

Assume that you work for the firm discussed in Exercise 10–5 above and that one of your colleagues wrote the report about risk in business. In the report, the role of *actuaries* in finance was mentioned briefly, and you have become curious about them. It occurs to you that your fellow employees probably don't know much about actuaries either, and that the actuarial field would be a good subject for the next report in the "empower employees" program. In fact, you decide to write the report now in order to have it all ready by the time the next report is due. Write the report, including in it what actuaries are, what they do, how they do it, how one becomes an actuary, and how companies may benefit from their services.

Exercise 10–7

Select a publicly traded company from the business references in the library. Write a report analyzing the financial aspects of the business including (1) liquidity, (2) profitability, (3) productivity, and (4) debt management. If your analysis uncovers any problems, include recommendations on how they may be overcome.

11

Writing Essay Exams: Academic Courses and Professional Certification Exams

One of the more interesting developments to affect the finance profession in recent years is the decision of professional organizations to evaluate the writing skills of candidates seeking professional certification. These organizations recognize that the ability to "crunch numbers" is not enough. Finance people must also be able to explain their findings. Therefore, writing skills are now evaluated explicitly on a number of professional certification exams.

This chapter discusses strategies you can use to answer essay exams successfully. Because you may also encounter essay or discussion questions in finance courses, the chapter suggests ways to prepare for and answer those questions.

ACADEMIC ESSAY EXAMS

Essays or discussion questions that appear on school exams may cause you some anxiety, but they give you a chance to practice for the professional examinations you may take later in your career. You can learn how to study for an essay exam as well as how to develop strategies for writing your answer and managing the pressure. You can also learn how to write an answer that ensures that you receive full credit for what you know.

Preparation

Although much of your studying for an objective examination will also help prepare you for essay questions, you need to do a different kind of studying as well. Remember that a discussion or essay question requires that you show mastery of ideas. You may be asked to explain a concept, compare or contrast two methods of doing something, evaluate alternative treatments for a given situation, or justify a recommendation. Thus, when you are reviewing your class notes and assigned reading material, you should note concepts and explanations that would lend themselves to answering these types of questions.

One good way to prepare is to outline notes given in class, especially lecture notes. It's also a good idea to highlight and then outline key ideas and explanations from assigned readings.

Once your notes and outlines are ready, review them and try to guess questions that might appear on the exam, paying particular attention to concepts the instructor has stressed in class or important discussions in the text. Then make outlines of the information you would include in an answer to those questions. With any luck, you will predict at least a few of the questions that will appear on the exam, especially after you have taken the first exam given by your instructor and have a better idea of the kinds of questions usually asked.

It is also helpful to study in a small group of students, after all of you have prepared your notes and outlines. This group can brainstorm possible questions and answers and check that everyone in the group understands the material that will be covered on the exam.

Taking the Exam

Actually writing the answer to an essay or discussion question is easier if you have a strategy for using your time and composing your answer.

BUDGET YOUR TIME. Managing your time well is a crucial part of your strategy. You may not have as much time as you would like to plan in detail, revise extensively, and then copy your answer over to create a perfect paper. Make the time you do have work to your advantage by following the three steps of the writing process: planning, writing, revising.

First, take a few minutes to read the question carefully to be sure you know what is being asked. It may be helpful to underline key phrases in the question so that your answer won't overlook something important. Then jot down the main ideas you want to include in the answer. Put numbers by these ideas or draw arrows to arrange them in the most effective order. If you have 30 minutes to answer a question, planning your answer (the first step in the writing process) should take about five minutes.

The next step, writing your answer, should take most of the remaining time. Write as legibly as possible and write on every other line of your paper to allow room for editing. Write as well as you can, but don't spend much time looking for the perfect word or phrase if it doesn't come quickly. The most important objective is to get the ideas down on paper in order to get credit for what you know.

Finally, allow at least five minutes to edit your answer. When you edit, check that all words are correctly spelled and that sentences are grammatically correct and clearly constructed. It's acceptable to cross out words and write your revisions in the line above as long as the essay remains legible.

Time is a big factor in answering essay and discussion questions, so use it wisely. Budget your time so that you can plan, write, and then revise.

ORGANIZE YOUR ANSWER.   The goals in organizing your answer are to help the instructor read it easily and to receive full credit for what you know. Thus, you should apply one of the primary recommendations emphasized throughout this book: Use summary sentences so that main ideas stand out. In an essay or discussion question, the key is to begin the answer with a thesis statement and to use topic sentences at the beginning of each paragraph.

The thesis statement should echo the question and summarize the main ideas of your answer. Suppose you find this question on an exam:

Explain the capital budgeting process in finance.

Your answer to this question might begin this way:

The capital budgeting process consists of selecting projects for capital investment and allocating capital among them.

For short discussion questions, your answer might be only one paragraph long. In this case, the thesis statement for the answer would also function as the topic sentence for the paragraph. For more extensive questions, organize your answer into several paragraphs, each discussing one aspect of your answer. Each paragraph will have a topic sentence that provides a transition from the last paragraph, where needed, and that summarizes the main idea to be discussed in the new paragraph. Suppose you're asked this question on an exam:

Discuss the goal of corporate financial management. Include in your answer an explanation of why the maximization of profits is not thought to be an acceptable goal.

Your answer might be organized like this:

Thesis (first paragraph of your answer):

The goal of corporate financial management is to maximize the wealth of the corporation's common stockholders.

Topic sentence for paragraph 2:

<u>Wealth</u> maximization involves directing management efforts toward activities that enhance the stock market's perception of the long-term prospects of the company.

Topic sentence for paragraph 3:

<u>Profit</u> maximization is not acceptable because it fosters a short-term focus on revenues and expenses alone. In so doing, it neglects long-term investment, research, risk, and the timing of cash flows.

One final reminder about organization: In deciding how many paragraphs to use for your answer, remember that readers usually find shorter paragraphs easier to read, as long as you provide adequate transitions so that they can follow your train of thought.

For further discussion of organization, review Chapter 3.

Use Document Design.   Sometimes the best way to include a number of points in your answer in a minimum amount of time is to use the principles of document design explained in Chapter 6, especially set-off lists and headings. The sample answer to a question from the CFA exam[1] given in Figure 11–1 shows how to use a list to organize the answer to a short question. For a longer essay, headings may be a good way to divide your answer into its main components.

Qualities of a Good Essay

The discussion so far has already suggested several qualities of an effective answer to an essay or discussion question. Here is a summary of those qualities, plus a few additional pointers:

- Your handwriting should be legible and your pages neat and easy to read. Corrections, additions, and deletions should be made as neatly as possible.
- Main ideas should be easy to identify; the flow of thought should be easy for the grader to follow.
- Answer the question asked directly and completely. Supply adequate details and examples to support your assertions.
- Sentences should be concise, clear, and readable. Grammatical and mechanical errors should not distract the reader.

These qualities of a good essay and the strategy you use to prepare for and write an academic essay exam also apply to professional examinations, with a few modifications.

FIGURE 11–1 *Sample Answer, CFA Exam*

QUESTION 4

Each of the following can be useful in evaluating Big River Technology's (BRT) management and business plan.

1. Venture Advisors' (VA) Current Venture Capital Investments

   VA may want to discuss its investment in BRT with the management of some of its existing portfolio companies, particularly those in closely related industries. These companies may be customers, potential customers, suppliers, or potential suppliers of BRT. Having an existing relationship with these companies may allow VA to obtain valuable information about BRT and its plausibility as an investment.

2. Other Venture Capital Investment Managers

   VA may want to talk with other venture capital management firms. In the process of reviewing various proposals and investments, other venture capitalists may have gained experience that would be useful to VA. In particular, VA may want to talk to a venture capital management firm that specializes in technology or computer software.

3. Pro Forma Analysis

   VA would analyze pro forma financial projections prepared by BRT to assess BRT's potential earnings growth. Such an analysis will provide VA with data to estimate the current value of BRT as compared with similar companies. In addition, VA can use the analysis to derive an estimate of potential value to be received when VA exits the investment. Due to the risk involved, VA may want to prepare a scenario analysis to determine how well BRT will do under various scenarios. VA may also want to determine if or when BRT may require additional funds. If BRT needs additional funds, VA should determine the amount and the best way to acquire these funds.

Finally, the pro forma analysis can be used to assess the competence of management.

PROFESSIONAL CERTIFICATION EXAMS

A number of professional certification exams in finance require candidates to write answers to essay questions as well as to questions requiring short answers. As we mentioned earlier, the professional associations sponsoring these exams recognize that it is not enough for a finance professional to be able to "crunch numbers." They must be able to communicate their findings to others as well.

The quality of the writing on any professional exam affects whether candidates receive credit for what they know. You are more likely to receive full credit for the content of your answer if the grader has an easy time reading and understanding what you've written.

Even when an answer is not evaluated explicitly for writing skills, how well it is written can influence the score. Graders of these exams have a lot of work to do in a short amount of time. Their job is to determine whether the candidates know the answers to the questions asked. Thus, graders appreciate essays that enable them to spot main ideas quickly and easily. They also appreciate sentences that are clear and readable.

Like readers of business documents, graders of professional exams want essays to be coherent (main ideas easy to identify, flow of thought easy to follow), concise (no wasted words), and clear (no guesswork about meaning, no distractions by nonstandard English). Thus, the writing skills emphasized in this book apply to professional exams as well as to more common forms of business writing.

Preparing For and Taking the Exam

Preparing for professional examinations is much more involved than studying for an exam in a course. You will study many long hours, perhaps with the help of an exam review text or course. However, the types of questions you are asked may resemble those in your course exams: possibly to explain a concept, describe a process, or analyze a situation, for example.

MANAGE YOUR TIME. The pressure of time constraints in a professional examination may be even greater than the stress you feel during a course exam because your ability to be a certified financial professional depends on how well you do. However, strategies for managing this stress remain the same regardless of what kind of exam you're taking. The keys are to budget your time so that you can plan your answer, draft the essay, and edit what you've written.

USE THE QUESTION TO ORGANIZE YOUR ESSAY. As with the essays and discussion questions you write for your finance courses, you can help

FIGURE 11–2   *Sample Question and Answer from the CFA Exam*

QUESTION 20 IS COMPOSED OF THREE PARTS, FOR A TOTAL OF 10 MINUTES

20. WAH is considering the purchase of stores from a regional competitor that is experiencing financial difficulty. The purchase and refurbishment of these stores would cost $250 million (excluding land and buildings). The required funds would be obtained by selling WAH's entire portfolio of marketable securities and by borrowing $200 million to be repaid over 10 years. WAH intends to remain a private company.

WAH is concerned about financial flexibility—the ability of a firm to take actions to meet its financial obligations during periods of stress. As direct competition with other large retailers increases, price competition will increase, putting pressure on profit margins and cash flows.

   A. **List and briefly discuss** *three* examples of how WAH's financial flexibility would be reduced by this purchase. (6 minutes)

   B. **Describe** *two* actions that WAH could take to moderate the negative impact that the purchase of the stores would have on its financial flexibility. (4 minutes)

Guideline Answer

   A. The following are examples of how WAH's financial flexibility would be reduced by purchasing stores from a regional competitor that is experiencing financial difficulty.

      1. Reduction of liquidity. WAH's portfolio of marketable securities provides a source of cash to supplement operating cash flows and increases its liquidity. For example, by having these marketable securities, WAH can cut prices to meet competitive pressures and still have funds available to cover overhead expenses. Using the entire portfolio of marketable securities to buy stores reduces WAH's liquidity because it would no longer have these assets to generate income or to convert into cash.

      2. Debt service requirements. Borrowing $200 million will require WAH to make future cash payments on schedule for the next ten years. These debt service requirements will decrease WAH's ability to compete on price, to increase its advertising budget, or to buy equipment that might increase its productivity and competitiveness.

FIGURE 11–2   *Sample Question and Answer from the CFA Exam (cont'd)*

> 3. The $200 million of additional debt uses up some of WAH's debt capacity. The additional debt increases WAH's financial leverage ratios (i.e., debt/equity and debt/assets) and decreases its interest coverage ratios. The changes decrease WAH's ability to raise additional debt in the future.
>
> B. The following are actions that WAH could take to moderate the negative impact that buying the stores would have on its financial flexibility:
>
>   1. Sell noncore assets. WAH could sell unneeded assets for generating cash to reduce debt or to increase liquidity. WAH should have a well-defined strategy for such action because sales during periods of financial distress do not generally bring the best price.
>
>   2. Sell common stock through a private placement. Although WAH wants to remain private, it can potentially sell additional shares to private investors.

graders of professional exams identify your main ideas if you write in short paragraphs with strong topic sentences. The question itself can suggest the wording of the topic sentences. Sample questions and answers from past exams show how this strategy works. Figures 11–2, 11–3, and 11–4 contain CFA exam questions and unofficial answers suggested by the AIMR.[2]

The answers to parts A and B in Figure 11–2 clearly address the specific questions posed. The command words *list, briefly discuss,* and *describe* in bold print dictate the content of your answers. In part A you *list* and *discuss* the factors that would decrease WAH's financial flexibility. In part B you *describe* how WAH might alleviate the effects of the purchase.

A portion of another question from a past CFA exam is shown in Figure 11–3. As in the previous question, the requirements specify the organization of the answer. Each paragraph of the answer focuses on the command words in bold print in the question. The discussion is divided into short paragraphs, each beginning with a strong topic sentence (in this case, a heading identifying the calculation the paragraph contains).

USE FORMATTING TECHNIQUES TO MAKE YOUR ESSAYS EASY TO READ.   Good document design makes it easier for graders to read your essays and give you full credit for them. Although you are obviously limited to what you

FIGURE 11–3 *Sample Partial Question and Answer from the CFA Exam*

QUESTION 2 IS COMPOSED OF FOUR PARTS, FOR A TOTAL OF 29 MINUTES

2. Your supervisor, Kelly Smith, CFA, is the pharmaceutical analyst for Stone Partners, a large investment management firm that is a major holder of WDC shares. Smith has read negative comments regarding the earnings per share dilution expected from the proposed combination with SPL. He also wants to determine which of the two scenarios is better for WDC shareholders.

To consider these issues, Smith asks you to use the information in Tables I and II on pages 8 and 9 and the Introduction on page 4 to answer the following questions.

A. Calculate the level of SPL's 1995 earnings per share required to avoid pro forma dilution for WDC shareholders from the combination under *each* of the following two scenarios:

    i. Cash Purchase Scenario, and
    ii. Stock Merger Scenario.

Show your calculations. (8 minutes)

Guideline Answer:

A. The following explains how to calculate the level of SPL's 1995 earnings per share (EPS) required to avoid pro forma dilution for WDC shareholders from the combination under each of the following two scenarios:

    1. Cash Purchase Scenario
    Add $0.12 to the EPS in the Cash Purchase Scenario column of Table II so that $0.12 × 170 million shares = $20.4 million of net income required. Adding $20.4 million to actual 1995 results of SPL would add $0.204 [$20.4 million/100 million shares] to SPL earnings per share. Therefore, the required SPL EPS equals $2.004 ($1.80 plus $0.204).

    2. Stock Merger Scenario
    With a share-for-share pooling, SPL must have the same $2.12 of earnings per share as WDC.

FIGURE 11-4 *AIMR Advice for Answering Essay Questions—Partial List of Tips*

Think over the question and *organize (or briefly outline) your answer*. The examination is designed so that each question's time allocation includes enough time for you to read and reflect before you answer. When you write your answer, clearly state your assumptions. Be sure to answer the question that is asked.

Show all your calculations in the answer booklet even if the question doesn't specifically instruct you to do so. You will be able to check your work this way. Also, if your answer is wrong, the grader can give partial credit where warranted if you show your calculations. If the question specifically says, "Show your work," you must present your calculations and, for full credit, they must be correct.

Answer the questions with curriculum assignments in mind. When preparing the CFA exam, the Council of Examiners is guided by the assigned reading materials and the Learning Outcome Statements.

Pay close attention to the command words and number instructions in the question. The command words are in bold type, and the number instructions are italicized.

Take nothing for granted. Assume nothing and state the obvious even if the obvious is in the question itself.

Provide a direct answer to the question asked. The questions are straightforward and never designed to trick you.

[Exam] questions are specific and should be answered specifically. Determine the significance and intent of each question, pay attention to the command words, note the various points raised, and address each point in a consistent and succinct manner.

... examination questions have been written with the expectation that you will respond with answers that are strictly relevant to the question and that are logically and internally consistent. Providing more than the required number of responses will not earn extra points. The required number of responses will be graded in the order you present them. Additional responses will be ignored. For example, if the question asks you to "discuss three reasons" and you discuss five, only the first three reasons will be graded. Furthermore, if your answers are partly inconsistent or illogical, you will not score full credit. For example, if the question asks you to recommend and justify, the second part (justification) must be consistent with the first part (recommendation) to earn the maximum number of points.

can accomplish quickly with a paper and pen, formatting techniques such as bullets and set-off lists may make it easier for graders to spot main ideas and follow your train of thought.

For example, Part A of the answer to the CFA exam question shown in Figure 11–3 uses numbered paragraphs to identify each of the sections called for in the answer.

Qualities of a Good Answer

The Association for Investment Management and Research (AIMR) gives candidates advice for answering the essay questions on the Level II and Level III exams. A partial list of tips from the AIMR is given in Figure 11–4.[3]

When you are studying for professional certification exams, you may find it helpful to review the chapters of this book that discuss qualities of effective writing. These chapters would probably be the most useful to you:

Chapter 2: Writing appropriately for the reader and responding to the requirements of the questions

Chapter 3: Organizing for coherence

Chapter 4: Writing with a style that is clear and concise

Chapter 5: Writing in standard English

Chapter 6: Formatting techniques

EXERCISES

Exercise 11–1

The information in Figure 11–5 comes from questions on a past CFA exam.[4] One of the requirements on the exam was as follows:

> **Create** and **justify** an investment policy statement for <u>Hope Ministries</u> based solely on the information provided. Be specific and complete as to the objectives and constraints. (10 minutes)

Respond to this requirement using the techniques discussed in this chapter. You should plan, write, and revise your answer in about 10 minutes.

Exercise 11–2

The information in Figure 11–5 comes from questions on a past CFA exam.[5] One of the requirements on the exam was as follows:

> **Create** and **justify** an asset allocation for the Hope Ministries portfolio, considering both the requirements of the policy statement created [in Exercise 11–1] and the returns which are required by the prevailing security market

FIGURE 11–5   *CFA Exam Question Information for Exercises 11–1 and 11–2*

INTRODUCTION
Hope Ministries

Hope Ministries is a tax exempt charitable organization which was established to provide financial assistance to homeless people. The Foundation's charter requires that all income earned from its endowment fund must be used in operations; any increase in the value of the principal of the endowment fund, whether realized or not, must be retained in the endowment fund. Hope currently requires $90,000 annual income from its $1,500,000 endowment fund.

The Omega Trust Company uses the CAPM in managing investment portfolios, combining U.S. Treasury bills (as a proxy for the risk-free rate) and co-mingled funds having differing characteristics. A summary of prevailing expectations for selected capital markets and for each of Omega's co-mingled funds are outlined in Table VIII below

Table VIII
Omega Trust Company Investment Choices

INVESTMENT	EXPECTED RETURN		BETA
U.S. Treasury Bills (risk-free rate)	4.0%		0.0
S&P 500 (the equity market portfolio)	12.0%		1.0
Fund A (aggressive equity)	16.5%	(including 1.0% from dividends)	1.7
Fund B (diversified equity)	13.0%	(including 3.0% from dividends)	1.1
Fund C (global fund)	8.0%	(including 8.0% from dividends)	0.5

line. Use only the three co-mingled funds (A, B, C) shown in [Figure 11–5]. (5 minutes)

Respond to this requirement using the techniques discussed in this chapter. You should plan, write, and revise your answer in about 5 minutes.

NOTES

1. 1997 CFA Level II Candidate Readings, CFA Level II Exams and Guideline Answers 1994, 1995, and 1996 (Charlottesville, Va.: The Association for Investment Management and Research), 1996 Level II Guideline Answers, Morning Section, p. 9. Used with permission. All rights reserved.

2. Ibid. For Figure 11–2: CFA Level II Examination Question Pamphlet, Afternoon Section, June 3, 1995, p. 14, 1995 Level II Guideline Answers, Afternoon Section, p. 32. For Figure 11–3: CFA Level II Examination Question Pamphlet, Morning Section, June 1, 1996, p. 6, 1996 Level II Guideline Answers, Morning Section, p. 4. Used with permission. All rights reserved.

3. The Institute of Chartered Financial Analysts, CFA Study Guide, Level II (Charlottesville, Va.: The Association for Investment Management and Research, 1992), p. 76. Used with permission. All rights reserved.

4. 1997 CFA Level II Candidate Readings, CFA Level II Exams and Guideline Answers 1994, 1995, and 1996 (Charlottesville, Va.: The Association for Investment Management and Research), CFA Level II Examination Question Pamphlet, Afternoon Section, June 1, 1996, pp. 12 and 14. Used with permission. All rights reserved.

5. Ibid.

12

Writing for Employment: Résumés and Letters

One of the greatest concerns for most finance students is the need to find a job after graduation. Communication skills can be your greatest asset in finding that job. This chapter focuses on several important skills you will need to get a good job: researching a targeted company, preparing a résumé and letter of application, and writing a thank-you letter to follow an interview.

STARTING THE JOB SEARCH: RESEARCHING POSSIBLE EMPLOYERS

How you begin your job search depends to some extent on where you are when you begin. If you are still a student in a large university, for example, you will probably work with the school's job placement office, faculty, and the recruiters who visit campus. If you are a student in a small school, opportunities for on-campus interviews may be more limited, and you may find it helpful to work with the finance faculty to identify potential employers. If you have already graduated, then you may be on your own in locating potential jobs and establishing initial contacts with employers, although the placement office of the school from which you graduated may still work with you.

Regardless of how you begin your job search, you will need to write certain documents to secure the job, including a letter of application, a résumé, and a thank-you letter after an interview. For all these documents, knowledge of the targeted employer is important because you should tailor what you write to the potential employer's needs. You also want to show the people who read these documents that you are familiar with the company and that you did the preparation necessary to make a good impression. (By now you probably recognize the strategy that underlies this preparation: Analyze the reader's interests and needs.)

Once you have decided to apply for a job at a particular company or organization, find as much information as possible about both the organization as a whole and the particular job for which you are applying.

If there is a specific job opening, you will probably have general information about the position in a job announcement. Read the announcement carefully in order to learn as much as possible about the requirements of the position and the credentials for which the employer is looking. This information can guide you in preparing your résumé and letter of application.

You will also need general information about the organization. Your school's job placement office may have a file of information on the company. You can also visit the library or search the Internet to look for articles and news items in the financial press, and you can talk with business faculty about the organization. Perhaps you will be fortunate enough to meet recruiters from the organization on campus at meetings of finance clubs or job fairs. If so, listen carefully to what the recruiters say about their organization and ask any questions that seem appropriate. Show in your polite, attentive listening that you are interested in what the recruiters have to say. Remember the names of the people you meet!

All this information about the organization or company, the names of individuals you have met, and the requirements for particular job openings are important when you write your letter of application and edit your résumé.

PREPARING A RÉSUMÉ

Preparing a résumé may be one of the most important steps you take in finding a good job. A tongue-in-cheek saying actually has some truth when applied to résumés: "An ounce of image is worth a pound of performance." Of course, good performance in school and in previous jobs is essential, but if the résumé doesn't project a professional, competent image, your performance won't be considered seriously. Take the time and the care necessary to do a good job.

Figure 12–1 is an illustration of an effective résumé, and you may want to use it as a model for preparing your own. You should realize, however, that this example is not the only way to prepare a good résumé.

FIGURE 12–1   *Sample Résumé*

Shane W. Brown

1324 Horsetooth Road   Phone: (970) 435-1234
Fort Collins, Colorado 80125   e-mail: sbrown@csu.edu

CAREER   A finance position that will allow me to build on
OBJECTIVE   my academic and employment background and pro-
                    vide opportunities for professional growth and de-
                    velopment. Willing to travel.

QUALIFICA-   Degree in finance; honor student; experience with
TIONS   corporate staff; experienced in customer service;
                    computer literate.

EDUCATION   Bachelor of Science in Business Administration,
                    Colorado State University, June 1998.
                    Major: Finance
                    GPA: 4.0 in major, 3.55 overall

WORK
EXPERIENCE:

June 1998–   **Hewlett-Packard; Executive Office,** Fort Collins,
September 1998   Colorado
                    Finance Internship
                    • Assisted in the preparation of quarterly report
                      to stockholders.
                    • Worked on depreciation schedules; updated
                      property, plant, and equipment accounts.
                    • Participated in the development of fourth quar-
                      ter 1998 sales forecast.
                    • Prepared product cost analyses.

March 1997–   **Colorado State University Business Computer**
June 1998   **Lab,** Fort Collins, Colorado
                    Laboratory Assistant
                    • Supervised foreign language students using the
                      laboratory.

September 1996–   **U.S. West Communications Systems,** Fort
March 1997   Collins, Colorado
                    Support Services
                    • Assisted U.S. West employees with their mail-
                      room needs.

June 1995–   **Albertson's,** Fort Collins, Colorado
September 1996   *Courtesy Clerk, Produce Department*
                    • Promoted to Produce Department in July 1995.

FIGURE 12–1   *Sample Résumé (cont'd)*

HONORS AND **ACTIVITIES**	Financial Management Association Honor Society; listed in *Who's Who Among Students in American Colleges and Universities, 1997;* Beta Gamma Sigma (Business Honor Society); Phi Kappa Phi (Academic Honor Society); Dean's List (three terms); Tau Epsilon Phi (Social Fraternity); Finance Club; College Republicans; Intramural Softball, Volleyball.
INTERESTS	Skiing, current events, travel, music.

You may find other models in business communication texts or in materials supplied by your school's job placement office. We will consider the résumé in Figure 12–1 to be a generic model you can adapt to your own situation.

Using a Word Processor

As with all business documents, you should prepare your résumé on a word processor and use a letter-quality printer. A word processor allows you to experiment with layout, headings, and fonts, as well as the wording and organization of the text. Another advantage of using a word processor is that you can tailor the résumé for a particular job. For example, you may want to emphasize the experience that fits the requirements the employer is seeking.

Some applicants have their résumés printed professionally if they don't have access to equipment that produces flawless copy. If you decide to have your résumé printed professionally, you may also receive advice on the design and content. You can find professional help with your résumé at a copy center or an agency that prepares résumés.

Even if you use professional help, keep the following guidelines in mind to make sure your résumé is properly prepared.

Format

First of all, look at the design of the résumé in Figure 12–1. Notice the placement of text on the page and the pleasing use of white space, headings, fonts, and bullets. The résumé is arranged so that it has an attractive, professional appearance. It is also easy to read because it's not crowded and important information is easy to find. You'll see how these design techniques can be used with the various parts of a résumé.

NAME AND ADDRESS.   Center your name in bold print at the top of the page. On the next line, put your address at the left margin and your phone number (including your area code) at the right margin, as shown in Figure 12–1. If you have a fax number or an e-mail address, list it with your phone number. Then place a horizontal line under this portion to separate your identifying data from your qualifications.

CAREER OBJECTIVE.   Be as specific as possible about the kind of job you're looking for so the employer will see whether your goals match available openings. For example, you might indicate a finance specialty such as banking, investments, or insurance. At the same time, you don't want to close any doors you will later wish you had left open, so consider describing your objective in a way that allows for all reasonable possibilities of employment for which you're qualified. As an alternative, edit your résumé so that your objective fits specific openings for which you're applying.

SUMMARY OF QUALIFICATIONS.   Employers who receive a large number of résumés (and that covers just about everyone) do not have time to study the detailed information the résumés contain. Therefore, it is important to provide a "snapshot" of your qualifications that will immediately catch the employer's eye. Notice Shane Brown's Summary of Qualifications section in Figure 12–1. In one quick phrase she sums up why the employer should pick her for the job.

EDUCATION.   Beginning with your most recent degree or school, provide information in reverse chronological order about your education to show your qualifications for employment. Include the following information:

- Degrees you have completed or are working on
- Complete name of the school granting these degrees
- Date of each degree, or expected graduation date
- Major and, if applicable to the job, your minor
- Grade point average, if it is above 3.0 on a 4.0 scale. (Figure your GPA several ways to try to reach at least a 3.0: cumulative GPA, GPA in your major course work, GPA in upper-level courses, etc., and then label it accordingly.)
- Approximate percentage of your college expenses you financed yourself, if this amount is significant

If you have attended several colleges or universities, include information about all of them, especially if you received a degree. If you attended schools without completing a degree, give the dates of your attendance.

You probably would not include information about your high school education on your résumé, unless that information would be relevant to a potential employer. If you're applying for summer employment but still have some time before you graduate from college, then it may be a good idea to list your high school and date of graduation.

WORK EXPERIENCE.   Again in reverse chronological order, provide information about the jobs you have held, both full- and part-time. List volunteer work if it is relevant to the job for which you're applying. For each job you list, provide the following information:

- Dates of employment. You may decide to put the dates in the left margin, as in the sample résumé. Let the overall appearance of the résumé when printed be your guide.
- Name and location of the organization for which you worked
- Your position
- A description of your responsibilities, with emphasis on the ones that show you are qualified for the job you are now seeking. Note any promotions or honors you received. Describe your responsibilities using active-voice verbs whenever possible, such as *assisted, completed, prepared*, and *supervised.*

HONORS AND ACTIVITIES.   List the organizations you belonged to, the honors you received, and any other activities that show you to be a well-rounded, active person. List these activities from most important to least important *from the point of view of your employer*. If you held an office in an organization or had significant responsibilities, add this information as well. Finally, if an organization or honor is not self-explanatory, give a brief explanation of its significance. For example, you might explain the importance of honorary societies.

INTERESTS.   Information about your hobbies and interests is optional on a résumé. The advantage of including this information is that it also can show that you are a well-rounded person with interests that are similar to those of other people in the firm.

REFERENCES.   Whether to list your references on your résumé is sometimes a difficult decision. If you provide the names, addresses, and phone numbers of your references, the employer can contact them easily. On the other hand, you run the risk that an employer will call your reference at an inconvenient time, or that the reference will not immediately recall detailed information about you. As a general rule, do not include references unless they are specifically requested. However, you will normally be asked to list references when you fill out a formal job application, so it is important to have some.

Normally, if you do not include references on your résumé it is a good idea to indicate on the résumé that references are available on request. The best solution, if you are enrolled or recently graduated from a college or university, is to have letters on file with your school's job placement office. Then your résumé can have a line such as this one:

References available on request from

Placement Office
University of Manhattan
Manhattan, Alabama 36678

One final word about references. Never list people as references without first asking their permission. You should ask people to be references who are likely to remember you well and have favorable things to say about you. Former instructors and employers are good candidates.

What *Not* to Put on a Résumé

Remember that there are laws against hiring discrimination on the basis of age, sex, race, religion, marital status, or national origin, so do not put information of this nature on a résumé. Also, when preparing resumes try to avoid phrases such as

- gets along well with coworkers
- pleasant disposition
- always eager to please

These phrases make you sound like you are applying to be a pet rather than an employee! "Fluff" in the form of phrases like these is guaranteed to send your résumé straight to the bottom of the pile.

Generally, employers who are considering hiring someone for a finance position are interested in two things: what you know and what you can do. Therefore your résumé should specifically state what you know and what you can do.

WRITING A LETTER
OF APPLICATION

Often you will mail your résumé to a potential employer with a formal letter of application or to follow up some earlier communication. Like the résumé, the letter must be professional and well researched.

Your letter should follow the general advice for letters discussed in chapter 8, including these guidelines:

- Address the reader by name. Get the appropriate name over the telephone or by other means, if possible.
- Give your letter an attractive, professional appearance. Use good stationery and a letter-quality printer. The letter and résumé should be printed on matching paper.
- Write in short, concise paragraphs and clear sentences. A courteous, conversational tone is best.
- The spelling, grammar, and mechanics of your letter should be perfect.

The content of your letter depends on your particular situation. If you have already discussed the job or possible employment with an employee of the company, you should refer to this person by name and say exactly why you're sending the résumé. You might write a sentence such as this one:

Sara Evans suggested that I write you about a possible opening in your finance department. I had the pleasure of meeting Ms. Evans at a meeting of our Finance Club here at the University of Central California.

As you will see in my enclosed résumé, . . .

For a formal letter of application, you might begin with a sentence such as this:

I would like to apply for the financial analyst position that you advertised in the June 25, 1997, issue of the *Denver Post*. My résumé is enclosed.

After the introduction to your letter, you will need to show the reader two things: that you are familiar with the organization and that you have the credentials they are looking for. Thus, you can refer briefly to what you've learned about the company from your research and highlight the information on your résumé that shows you to be especially interested in and qualified for the position. In other words, you use the letter of application to sell yourself as the best person for the job. You will probably write one to three short paragraphs for this purpose. The following paragraphs show examples from two different letters.

As you will see on the enclosed résumé, I will graduate from the University of Northern Idaho in June of this year with a Master of Business Administration degree and a specialty in financial services, so my training should qualify me for an entry-level position in your mortgage loan department. In addition, I have experience as a credit analyst with Smith Savings & Loan, a position I held during the past two summers.

During the years I have studied for my finance degree here at the University of Tempe, I have worked an average of 20 hours a week to pay approximately half my college and living expenses. At the same time, I have managed to maintain a cumulative GPA of 3.3 and have been active in a number of campus organizations, as you can see from my résumé. I believe this record shows that I am a conscientious worker with an ability to organize my time and achieve goals in a deadline-intensive environment.

The final paragraph should include a courteous closing and suggest a response from the reader or follow-up action you will take. You might suggest that you will call in a week or so to see whether the employer needs additional information. At the least, express enthusiasm for the position and a hope that you will hear from the employer soon:

I hope you will find my education and experience suitable for this position and that we can set up an interview soon to discuss the position further. I look forward to hearing from you.

Figure 12–2 shows a letter of application.

FIGURE 12–2 *Letter of Application.*

2134 Roxboro Road
Manassas, VA 22110
January 15, 1999

Ann Bradbury, CFO
STAR Solutions, Inc.
33 Hightower Building
Chantilly, VA 22102

Dear Ms. Bradbury:

It was a pleasure meeting you and Mr. Ellis last week at the Finance Club meeting here at George Mason University. As you suggested, I am sending you my résumé because you anticipate having an opening soon for which I would be qualified.

As my résumé shows, I will graduate from George Mason in May of this year with an MBA degree and a concentration in finance. I also have on-the-job experience as an intern with the Lockheed Martin Corporation here in Manassas. My work there last summer enabled me to participate in a number of cost and pricing analyses, as well as to get some practice in forecasting. I hope you will find that my education and experience make me a good candidate for a financial analyst position with STAR Solutions.

I would very much appreciate the opportunity to talk with you further about possible future employment. I look forward to hearing from you.

Sincerely,

Carla Bowen

Carla Bowen

Enclosure

WRITING A
THANK-YOU LETTER

With an impressive résumé and letter of application and good credentials to support them, as well as a little luck, you will probably have one or more interviews for jobs. After the interviews, write letters to the people

FIGURE 12–3 *Thank-You Letter*

2134 Roxboro Road
Manassas, VA 22110
April 23, 1998

Ann Bradbury, CFO
STAR Solutions, Inc.
33 Hightower Building
Chantilly, VA 22102

Dear Ms. Bradbury:

Thank you very much for meeting with me last week to discuss the possibility of my working for STAR Solutions after my graduation next month. I certainly enjoyed the opportunity to visit your office and meet the other members of the finance department. The lunch with June Oliver and Richard Wang was particularly pleasant and informative because they were able to share their experiences as first-year analysts.

I would very much welcome the opportunity to work as a financial analyst with your firm, so I hope that you will decide that my qualifications meet your needs. Please let me know if I can provide any additional information.

Thank you once again for your hospitality. I look forward to hearing from you.

Sincerely,

Carla Bowen

Carla Bowen

who met with you to thank them for their hospitality and to show enthusiasm for what you learned about the organization and the position for which you're applying.

This letter need not be long; two or three short paragraphs are usually long enough. Again, you need to address your readers by name and refer specifically to your meeting and to one or two of the topics you discussed. If you met any of the firm's other employees, it would be good to express pleasure at having that opportunity. End the letter with a courteous closing and express the hope that you will be hearing from the reader soon.

This letter, like the letter of application, should follow the guidelines for letters covered in Chapter 8. A sample thank-you letter is shown in Figure 12–3.

EXERCISES

Exercise 12–1

Imagine that you are an employer who receives the résumé shown in Figure 12–4. What is your reaction to the résumé? Would you give the applicant an interview? Why or why not?

Examine the résumé closely, noting the applicant's accomplishments and experience. Does this person indeed have credentials that might make him a good employee?

Rewrite this résumé so that the applicant's credentials show to good advantage. You may have to make up some details so that the résumé is complete.

Exercise 12–2

Draft your own résumé on a word processor. Then show it to a variety of your colleagues for helpful feedback. You might show it to several of your instructors as well as other finance students and, if possible, recent graduates who have been successful in finding a job.

Evaluate the suggestions you receive and revise your résumé so that it looks professional and shows your qualifications effectively.

Exercise 12–3

Imagine that you find the following advertisement in your hometown newspaper, the *Washington Post*. Prepare a letter of application for this position to accompany your résumé.

Associate
Pricing
Analyst

Excellent opportunity for a recent grad with a bachelor's degree and up to one year of experience in finance or related field to learn how pricing is

FIGURE 12–4 *Résumé to Accompany Exercise 12–1*

William H. Bonney

PRESENT ADDRESS
745 Main St.
Clovis, NM 85443
(506-512-6947)

PERMANENT ADDRESS
1634 Scaffold Lane
Fort Sumner, NM 87011
(505-867-9361)

EDUCATION

	GRAD. DATE	DEGREE MAJ. GPA	CUM. GPA
Eastern New Mexico University	6/97	3.4	3.5
Fort Sumner High School	6/91		3.9

MAJOR COURSES
Business Finance, Intermediate Finance, Financial Institutions and Markets, Investments, Case Studies in Finance

WORK EXPERIENCE	TITLE	FROM	TO
Telemarketing, Inc. Clovis, NM	Telemarketer	7/96	
Esops, Inc. Clovis, NM	Office/Customer svc.	6/95	10/95
Sam's Market Clovis, NM	Salesperson	11/94	1/95
Tulips Discount Stores Portales, NM	Clerk	6/94	9/94
Hamilton's Portales, NM	Cashier	5/92	9/93
Auto Stores, Inc. Fort Sumner, NM	Cashier	7/91	9/91

HONORS AND ACTIVITIES
Honors Program
Dean's List
Golden Key
Outstanding College Students of America
Phi Chi Theta Business Fraternity
Pat Garrett Scholarship
Marksmanship club

PERSONAL
Date of Birth- October 20, 1973; excellent health; prefer to work in the Santa Fe area.

done in the federal government procurement arena. Experience with federal government financial reporting, policies, procedures, and operations is a plus. Knowledge of Excel is preferred (Lotus OK) and good writing skills are required. Dynamic and demanding professional work environment requires someone with an ability to meet strict deadlines. Send resume to ICSI, ATTN: Luke S. Walker, 2700 Main, Fairfax, VA 22301.

ICSI

Intelligent Computer Systems, Inc.

Exercise 12–4

The letter of application you prepared for Exercise 12–3 was so effective and your résumé looked so impressive that ICSI invited you to come in for an office interview. At the interview, you met the company's president, George Owen, and several members of the finance department. You had lunch after the interview with Mary Wilson, a senior pricing analyst in the firm, as well as the controller. You learned that the company has been in business for nearly a decade but that it is now expanding its operations to participate in EC (Electronic Commerce) transactions with government agencies.

Write a thank-you letter to follow up on your interview.

13

Writing for Publication

As a finance professional, you may decide at some point in your career to write an article for publication. This might be a short article for publication in a newsletter, perhaps one published by the organization for which you work, or it might even be a longer article for publication in a professional journal, such as the *Financial Analyst's Journal, The Journal of Finance*, or *FM: The Journal of the Financial Management Association*. Many of the techniques already discussed in this book apply to writing for publication, but in this chapter we consider some additional pointers.

PLANNING YOUR ARTICLE

To plan your article, start by considering the publication for which you want to write and the topic you want to write about. Most likely, you'll be writing about your experience in practice, such as a better way to approach a financial issue or solve a financial problem. You may also write to express your opinion on a current finance or business issue, such as a position paper or essay on some controversial issue currently under discussion in the profession.

Whatever the topic you've chosen, target what you write to the editorial practices and readers of the publication to which you're submitting the article. Keep in mind that one of the best ways to ensure publication of an article is to write on a subject that is interesting and relevant to a wide range of the publication's readers.

One consideration is the type of writing typically published by the targeted publication. Do the editors prefer articles on scholarly research? *The Journal of Finance* is an example of this kind of publication. Other journals prefer practical articles. The *Financial Analysts' Journal* publishes practical articles on portfolio management, and *FPE* (*Financial Practice and Education*), as its title suggests, publishes articles of practical interest to financial practitioners and educators. Journals and newsletters published on the state or local levels might publish articles of general interest to financial professionals, but they also include articles of local interest.

Here are other questions to consider about the publication where you hope to publish your writing:

- Who are the readers of the publication? What are their interests and concerns? How much technical expertise on your topic are they likely to have?
- What format, organization, and length do the publication's editors prefer? You can learn this either from a statement of editorial policy or by studying articles already published.
- What style for documentation of sources does the publication use?
- What writing style do the editors prefer? Articles in professional journals may be written in a serious, scholarly style or a light, conversational tone. All publications prefer prose that is clear, readable, and concise.

RESEARCH

Once you have chosen a topic and a publication to target, it may be a good idea to find out what else has been written on the topic lately, especially if you are hoping to publish the article in a national or regional journal. You can search the Internet and visit a good library to find out this information. This research will help in several ways:

- You will find out what has been published recently on the topic so your article will not repeat what has already been done.
- You will find out what issues or approaches are of current interest in the profession.
- You may find references that you can use in your article to support your position. Alternatively, you may find positions taken by other people that you want to refute.

In addition to this background research to find out what has already been published on the topic, you may need to do some original research so that what you write is backed up by sound observations and reasoning. You may find it helpful to review Chapter 7 of this handbook, which discusses financial research in more detail.

DRAFTING
AND REVIEWING
THE ARTICLE

After you have planned the article and done any necessary research, you're ready to begin writing. Draft and revise your article according to the guidelines discussed throughout this book. When you feel reasonably satisfied with the article, ask colleagues to critique it. People who have successfully published may be particularly helpful.

For the final manuscript you will submit for publication, pay particular attention to a professional presentation, including an accurate and complete documentation of any sources you have used, prepared according to the guidelines of the journal to which you're sending the article. Professional appearance of the document pages is also important, and grammar and mechanics should be flawless.

SUBMITTING
THE ARTICLE

When you're finally ready to submit your article to the targeted publication, prepare a cover letter addressed to the editor by name. This letter should be concise and courteous, and it should mention the title of your article. You might also explain briefly why you think it would interest the publication's readers.

Double-check to make sure you comply with the submission requirements of the publication to which you are applying. For example, if the publication requirements state that your article must be written in Microsoft Word 97 and submitted on 3½-inch diskettes, then make sure you do so.

After all this preparation, your article should have a good chance of acceptance for publication. However, be prepared for the possibility that your article will be rejected by the first journal to which you send it.

If your article is rejected, turn it around and send it somewhere else. However, be sure to revise it to suit the readers and editorial policies of the new journal: type of articles published, interests and needs of the readers, length and style of writing, and style of documentation.

Writing for publication can be a rewarding component of your professional career, but like all the writing discussed in this book, it requires planning and attention to detail, including a concern for the readers.

EXERCISE

Obtain a recent issue of several professional publications. For each of these publications, answer the following questions:

1. What type of writing does this publication publish? Possibilities include academic research, practical finance applications, articles of organizational or local interest, or articles addressed to some special interest group.

2. Who writes the articles for these publications? They may be written by members of a sponsoring organization, professional writers, professors, or other finance people.

3. Analyze the specific articles published. Are they all the same length, format, and style? Some publications may publish a variety of articles, such as short notes and longer essays and articles.

4. What are standard editorial practices, such as article length and style of documentation?

14

Oral Presentations

Speaking before a group, like writing, is often an important part of a finance person's professional responsibilities, yet public speaking creates anxiety for many people. If you learn a few strategies for public speaking, however, and practice as often as possible, your fear of these situations will diminish. With guidance and practice comes mastery, and with mastery comes control.

In this chapter, you will find that effective oral presentations, like writing, result from a process: preparation, practice, and delivery. This chapter shows you how to prepare for speaking before a group and describes some techniques to use while speaking. We begin by discussing the first step in any important communication: analyzing the purpose of the presentation and the needs and interests of the audience.

PLANNING THE PRESENTATION: ANALYZING PURPOSE AND AUDIENCE

The first step in planning your presentation is to analyze its purpose. Perhaps you need to inform the listeners about the progress you've made on a project or propose that the decision makers in the group approve a new project. You may be convincing senior management to invest in a new system or explaining to coworkers how to implement the system already adopted. Remember that no matter what the primary purpose of your presentation, it has an important secondary purpose as well: your desire to impress your listeners as a competent professional.

As you analyze the purpose of the presentation, think also about the audience. How many people will you be speaking to? Will they be a fairly homogeneous group, or will you be speaking to people with different degrees of knowledge about your topic and different interests? An important consideration about the audience is which decision makers will be present. In planning your presentation, the needs and interests of these decision makers should be a primary concern.

Think in advance about the questions the audience will have about the topic, whether or not there will be a formal question-and-answer session as part of the presentation. By anticipating listeners' questions, you can explain your ideas in a convincing way. Anticipating questions and having the information ready to answer them also shows the audience that you are thoroughly prepared, credible, and professional.

Throughout the planning and preparation of the speech, think always about the audience: what they know about your topic, what they need to know, what their concerns and interests are, and what their attitudes may be toward your point of view and the information you'll present.

OTHER THINGS TO CONSIDER

In addition to analyzing your purpose and audience, you need to determine how much time you'll have for the presentation. In addition, find out how you will be speaking to your audience, whether formally from a podium or informally, perhaps from your seat in a conference setting.

Yet another consideration is whether to illustrate your speech with visual aids, such as charts or other graphic material. If you decide to use visual aids, consider the room where the presentation will be made. Will the space and facilities allow you to use the visual aids you prefer? A later section of this chapter discusses how to prepare effective visual aids. For now, the important point to remember is that you need to start planning visual aids early.

Finally, budget your time so you can complete the work needed to gather information, compose the speech, make notes, prepare visual aids, and practice the presentation. All of these steps take time, particularly if your topic requires much underlying research.

The key to handling all these tasks is to make a schedule with dates for the completion of each step. It's important to plan the work you have to do and budget your time.

GATHERING INFORMATION

The next step in preparing the presentation is to gather the necessary information. Be thorough in your research so that you can answer any questions the audience has. When you are thoroughly prepared, you will seem competent and professional, and your presentation will have an excellent chance of success.

Before you begin the research for your presentation, you may want to review chapter 2, which discusses how to generate ideas, and chapter 7, which covers finance research.

COMPOSING THE SPEECH

Once you've gathered the information you need, organize the material into an outline. Keeping in mind the purpose of the speech and the interests of your audience, identify the main points you want to make. *Your speech should contain no more than three to five main points.* These main points, with an introduction and conclusion, are the outline of your presentation. Let's look now at how to fill in that outline.

Introduction

The introduction should do two things: It should get the listeners' attention and preview for them the main points you will cover.

When you plan the opening sentences of the presentation, consider the listeners' point of view. Why should they listen to what you have to say? Will your speech be meaningful to them, perhaps helping them solve a problem or accomplish a goal? What do you and your listeners have in common that would make them interested in your presentation? What makes your topic particularly timely and relevant to your listeners? Questions such as these can help you compose the opening sentences of your presentation to get your audience's attention. Here are a few additional suggestions:

- Begin with an interesting story or a humorous example to introduce your topic.

  Once there were two financial analysts walking down the street. One saw a $10 bill lying on the sidewalk. "Oh, look," she said, "there's a $10 bill lying on the sidewalk."

  "Don't try to pick it up," said her colleague, who was a strong believer in the Efficient Market Hypothesis, "if it were really there someone would have picked it up already."[*]
- Cite a startling statistic.

[*]If you don't get this joke, spend some time reviewing the Efficient Market Hypothesis in any investments text.

Recent studies show that eight of the ten leading companies in this industry have never made a profit.

- Ask a rhetorical question—one that you don't expect your audience to answer but that will start them thinking about the topic.

    Do you know how long it would take to double your money if it's in an investment that is earning 10% interest annually?

These are just a few examples of ways to begin the presentation.

After your opening sentences, the next important part of the presentation is a preview of what the speech will cover. If you tell the audience what the main points will be, you'll help them remember what's important as you progress through your presentation.

Body of the Presentation

In the body of the presentation, you present again your main points and develop them in detail. Be specific and concrete: Use facts, examples, and, where appropriate, relevant statistics.

As you move from one main point to the next, you can help your listeners remember main ideas with two techniques: internal summaries of what you've already said and clear transitions that lead into the next main topic. For example, you might say something like this:

> So one advantage of this new system is that it would reduce the time needed to process customer accounts. [This is an internal summary. We know it's a summary because of the word *so*.] The second advantage is that the system would provide us with better records for our sales managers. [This sentence provides a transition into the next major section of the speech and identifies for the listeners the second main point.]

By providing internal summaries and obvious transitions, you can help your listeners remember main ideas as you give your presentation.

Conclusion

The last part of the formal presentation is the conclusion. Once again, you will help the listeners if you summarize the main ideas you want them to remember. Your presentation will be most effective, however, if you end with a forceful closing. Here are some suggestions:

- Ask your audience to do something. This call to action may be low key—a request that they consider your recommendation, for example. You may want to be more forceful and sometimes even dramatic if you think the topic warrants this approach and if this tone is suitable for your audience.
- Refer again to the opening sentences of your presentation. For example, if you used a story, example, or statistic, suggest how the ideas expressed in your speech relate to these concepts.

- Remind your audience of the benefits they will receive if they follow your recommendations.

For additional help in composing your speech, you will find it useful to review Chapter 3, which covers the principles of coherent organization.

MAKING THE NOTES

Once you have gathered your material and completed the outline, you are ready to put your notes in final form—the form from which you will actually speak. Notice that this section is *not* called "Writing Your Speech," and for a very good reason. Most experienced speakers find it unnecessary to write down every word they want to say. In fact, having a word-for-word manuscript of your speech could lead you to make two mistakes in your presentation: reading the speech or trying to memorize it. (More about these pitfalls later.)

The most helpful way to prepare notes is in outline form. You should already have this outline because you prepared it as you gathered information and organized your materials. Your job now is to put this outline into notes you can speak from. Here are a few pointers:

- Transfer the outline to note cards or standard-sized paper. Write in print that is large enough to see at a glance.
- Include main points, as well as supporting details and examples.
- Write out the opening sentences and the conclusion. (This is the exception to the advice not to write out the speech word-for-word.)
- Indicate in your notes where you will use your visual aids.
- As you review your notes, highlight or underline key phrases in a contrasting color of ink. When you make the presentation, these underlined phrases will remind you of the points you want to make.
- Number the notecards or pages and clip them together.

When we discuss practicing and delivering your presentation, you will see how notes prepared in this way will help you make a smooth presentation.

PREPARING
VISUAL AIDS

To appreciate how visual aids can contribute to an effective presentation, consider your audience's point of view.

When people read, they have a number of visual cues to help them identify and remember main ideas. They have titles and headings, paragraph breaks to signal a shift in topic, and often graphic illustrations. If they need to review something that has already been covered, they have only to turn back the page to see that material again.

Listeners to an oral presentation have none of these visual cues to help them follow the flow of thought, unless the speaker provides them with visual aids. A major advantage of visual aids is that they help listeners identify and remember main ideas. They offer another advantage as well, because well-constructed, attractive visual aids make the presentation more interesting.

Visual aids appeal to the audience by making the presentation easier to follow and more interesting. What are the best kinds of aids to use?

To some extent, your choices depend on where you'll be speaking. If you are making a classroom presentation, for example, you can prepare handouts, write on the chalkboard, prepare posters and charts, and probably use an overhead projector. In a work setting, you may also have access to more sophisticated equipment, such as videocassette players and projection equipment that can be run by computers.

You may decide to use more than one kind of visual aid. For example, handouts give your listeners something to take with them to reinforce what you've said, especially when you want to give them lengthy or detained information. You don't want them reading the handout instead of looking at you when you speak, so it may be a good idea to illustrate your presentation with posters or overhead transparencies and distribute the handouts after the presentation.

Let's look more closely at guidelines for preparing visual aids such as posters and overhead transparencies:

- Keep your aids simple. Use key words and phrases rather than sentences, and limit each aid to about ten lines.
- Be sure the writing is legible and large enough to be read from the back of the room. It's much better to prepare the aid using a software package, but if you must write by hand, write clearly in a dark or bright color so that the writing is easy to see.
- If possible, use bright colors to make your aids more attractive.
- Your aids should be neat and professional-looking. A computer with a graphics package will help you achieve a professional appearance. You might even consider having the aids prepared professionally.

You can include any information on your visual aid that will help your listeners understand and remember your message, but visual aids are particularly helpful in identifying your main points, summarizing your recommendations or conclusions, and providing a vivid illustration. You can also summarize statistical information in a table or graph. Yet another technique is to reproduce cartoons to amuse your listeners as you illustrate a point.

Once you have prepared your visual aids and notes, you are ready for the next important step in the preparation of the oral presentation: practice.

PRACTICING THE PRESENTATION

Practicing the presentation is essential for several reasons. For one thing, the more often you review the speech, the more familiar you become with it, so that when you speak before an audience you will appear knowledgeable and convincing. You will also feel more confident that you have mastered the ideas you want to present. When you practice, especially before other people, you also identify in advance any potential problems that could occur, such as a presentation that is too long or too short for the allotted time.

Here are some strategies that will make your practice time most useful:

- Practice the speech out loud. Pay attention to your voice, posture, and gestures.
- Time the presentation to make sure it is the appropriate length.
- Practice using the visual aids, including any equipment you will be using, such as an overhead projector.
- If possible, practice in the actual room you will be using for the presentation.
- Practice before a live audience, such as friends, family, or coworkers. Ask them to be critical of the content and delivery of the speech.
- If you have access to video equipment, ask someone to make a videotape of the presentation so that you can identify and correct any problems.

Finally, avoid this common pitfall:

Never read or try to memorize your speech!

The only exception to this guideline is that you may find it helpful to memorize the opening and closing sentences.

CHECKING THE ARRANGEMENTS

For some oral presentations, preparations will include arranging for a room and equipment. Even if someone else is responsible for these duties, it may be a good idea to check thoroughly. For example, be sure that the room will be unlocked in time for the early arrivals at the presentation and that equipment will be delivered and set up in working order. Also, check where the light dimmer switch is if you are going to need it during your presentation.

Check again on these arrangements a little while before the presentation begins. If there is some unforeseen problem, such as malfunctioning equipment, you'll have time to correct it.

APPEARANCE AND DRESS

A final consideration in the preparation for your presentation is appearance and dress. As in any professional situation, your grooming should be impeccable. The clothing you wear will depend to some extent on the situation, but professional styles and colors are almost always preferable. If you are in doubt, it's usually better to err on the side of conservatism.

In summary, thorough preparation for the presentation—your appearance, the arrangements, your visual aids, and the speech itself—will help you ensure good results when your speak before a group.

MAKING THE PRESENTATION

In the first portion of this chapter, we discussed the steps of preparing an oral presentation before you actually give it: planning, composing, and practice. This portion of the chapter looks at the qualities of effective delivery and strategies to help you become an accomplished public speaker.

The effect you should create on your audience is one of poise and confidence. With adequate practice and preparation, you are well on your way to reaching this goal. Let's look now at techniques of actual delivery that contribute to an effective presentation.

Eye Contact

One of the secrets of public speaking is eye contact between the speaker and the audience. When you look your listeners in the eye, you involve them in the topic and help ensure that they listen carefully.

Establish eye contact when you first stand before the audience: Stand straight, smile, and look around the room. Look directly at various people at different locations. This initial eye contact should probably last for a total of two or three seconds.

As you begin the presentation and progress through it, continue to maintain this eye contact. Hold the eye contact with each person for several seconds, perhaps the length of a complete phrase. Shift the contact from one side of the room to the other, front to back, and at various points in the middle. If your audience is small, you may be able to make eye contact with everyone in the room several times.

Regardless of the size of your audience, though, it's essential to establish eye contact with one important group of listeners: the decision makers. They will be judging the ideas you present and your effectiveness as a speaker. Good eye contact will help you keep their attention. You'll also seem confident and in control of the situation.

You may also find it helpful to look frequently at the listeners who seem most interested and supportive of what you are saying. You can recognize this group by their expressions of interest and attention, perhaps even nods and smiles. Their enthusiasm can give you extra energy and confidence.

When you think about the importance of maintaining good eye contact with the audience, it becomes obvious why you shouldn't read your speech and why you should be so familiar with your notes that you only glance at them from time to time.

Body Movement and Gestures

Poised, natural use of your body and gestures also contributes to an effective presentation. Stand still, with good posture, and look directly at the listeners. Don't move about, except to use your visual aids (for example, to point to something on a chart or to change a transparency on the overhead projector).

Natural, expressive use of your hands is an effective way to emphasize ideas and feelings. For this reason, it's better to place your notes on a table or podium so that your hands are free for gestures.

Voice

Three elements of your voice contribute to the effectiveness of a presentation: pitch, volume, and speed. Pitch is how high or low you speak. Most people's natural pitch is fine and requires no modification for public speaking. A few people need to pitch their voices a little lower than normal, especially if they are nervous when they speak.

Volume and speed may require more attention. The key to speaking at the correct volume is to speak loudly enough so that people in the back of the room can hear you. Be consistent; don't let your voice drop at the ends of sentences, for example, so that your audience misses the last words or must strain to hear you.

When you practice the presentation, pay particular attention to the speed at which you are speaking. You should speak slowly enough to enunciate each word clearly. Some speakers have a tendency to speak more rapidly when they are nervous. If you fall into this category, make a conscious effort to slow down.

MANAGING STAGE FRIGHT

Now that we've introduced the topic of nervousness, let's think for a minute about how to manage what for many speakers is the worst part of public speaking: stage fright. Notice that the heading for this section is "*Managing* Stage Fright," not "*Eliminating* Stage Fright." Even the most experienced, effective speakers usually have some stage fright; furthermore, they use this heightened emotion to help them make a more effective presentation. The emotion, if kept in control, can give you the extra charge to make an energetic, enthusiastic, and convincing presentation.

Too much stage fright is counterproductive. Let's look at some strategies you can use to manage stage fright before and during presentation.

Well in Advance

One advantage of thorough preparation and practice is that they help prevent stage fright. When you know you thoroughly understand the topic, and when you have thought in advance about the questions and interests of the listeners, you will *feel* prepared, and thus competent. A feeling of competence, in turn, gives you confidence in your ability to do a good job.

Practice before a live audience will also increase your confidence.

Just Before You Speak

Two tricks may be helpful in the last few minutes before you are scheduled to speak. The first is to use this time to go over your notes one last time, to be sure your main points, as well as your opening and closing sentences, are fresh in your mind. The second trick is this:

Don't think about how you're feeling!

If you think about being nervous, you'll only increase the feeling. Instead, think about something pleasant that is completely unrelated to your presentation. Perhaps you can think about something nice you will do later in the day.

During the Presentation

Most speakers find that their stage fright goes away after the first few minutes of their presentation. When you are speaking, look directly at the listeners with poise and confidence: They'll probably reflect these positive feelings back to you. Notice which of your listeners are most interested and receptive to what you're saying, and make frequent eye contact with these people. Their enthusiasm will add to your feelings of confidence and ensure that your presentation is effective.

SPECIAL CONSIDERATIONS IN FINANCIAL PRESENTATIONS

The standard techniques for presentations given in this chapter apply to financial presentations as well, of course, but there are a number of special considerations to bear in mind when you are presenting financial information. Most of the time the presentations that finance people give contain numbers, tabular data, and charts. The following points apply in this type of presentation:

- Make sure your numbers are consistent. If "Sales are expected to reach $7.25 million in 1999" appears on one slide, make sure your other slides don't contain some other number.*
- Make sure your numbers "add up." If your presentation includes a statement such as "Sales are expected to grow 20% from their 1998 level of $7 million, reaching $8.4 million in 1999," make sure that $7,000,000 × 1.20 does in fact equal $8,400,000 (which it does in this case).
- Make sure the audience can read the charts in your presentation. This applies to the size of charts as well as their design. For example, many members of the audience would have difficulty making out the slide in Figure 14–1. While the slide illustrates where the company's funds came from and where they went, the labels on the pie slices are too small to read. Also, there is a bit too much information on the slide to take in all at once. In this case, the presenter should probably separate the charts into two slides.
- Try to use computer-assisted presentations wherever possible. Presentations developed in graphics programs such as Microsoft PowerPoint, Corel Draw, or Lotus Freelance look very professional, and they could very well make the difference between your recommendations' being accepted or rejected. An example of a financial presentation created in MicroSoft Power-Point is shown in Figure 14–2. Although the presentation is reproduced here in black and white, you can imagine how the addition of color (accomplished automatically in PowerPoint) would bring the presentation to life.

FIGURE 14–1   *Example of a Poor Slide*

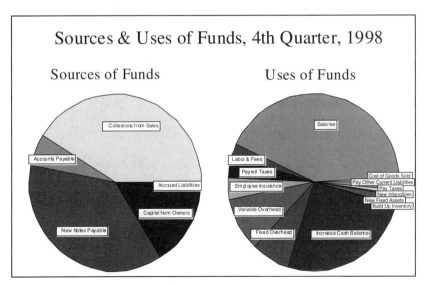

*It's easier to make this error than you might think. When a presentation is developed, it tends to be revised several times before a final version is produced. When numbers are changed during the revisions it is sometimes difficult to find all the places in the presentation where they appear. As a result, conflicting numbers end up in the final presentation.

FIGURE 14–2   *A Financial Presentation Created in Microsoft PowerPoint[1]*

GARDEN STATE CONTAINER CORPORATION

FINANCIAL ANALYSIS AND FORECASTING

Slide 1

Garden State Facts

- Main product line consists of boxes and other containers primarily for farm products
- 85% sales concentration in Northeast U.S
- First National Bank's analysis showed G.S financial position was bad and getting worse (1996-1997)

Slide 2

FIGURE 14–2 *A Financial Presentation Created in Microsoft Powerpoint (continued)*

Garden State Strengths

- Sales have remained strong compared to industry standards through 1997 due to price reductions, relaxed credit and favorable payment terms.

- Fixed asset turnover - Garden State is utilizing their P&E at an efficient rate relative to industry standards.

Slide 3

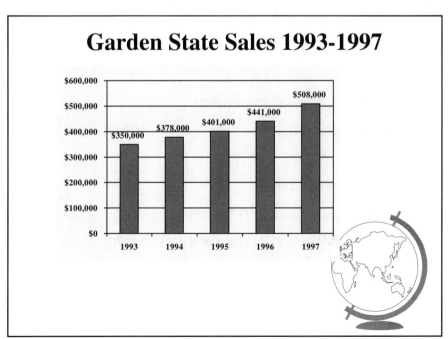

Garden State Sales 1993-1997

Slide 4

FIGURE 14–2   *A Financial Presentation Created in Microsoft Powerpoint (continued)*

Garden State Weaknesses

- Cash flow has dwindled due to:
  - recession / drought
  - Reduced product prices
  - Relaxed credit standards
- Limited sales regions
- Increased liabilities (ST bank loans)
- Narrow product line (one industry)

Slide 5

Garden State Weaknesses (Cont.)

- Poor I & R management
- Poor liquidity
- High interest expense in 1997
- Runaway costs
- Insufficient cash on hand
- Higher than average debt ratio upon entering 1997

Slide 6

FIGURE 14–2   *A Financial Presentation Created in Microsoft Powerpoint (continued)*

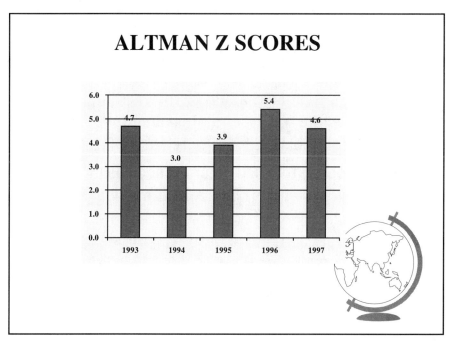

ALTMAN Z SCORES

Slide 7

Recommendations

- At this point in time bank should not grant requested $12 million for the following reasons:
  - A majority of the financial ratios are below industry averages
  - The trend analysis indicates a progressive downward direction

Slide 8

FIGURE 14–2 *A Financial Presentation Created in Microsoft Powerpoint (continued)*

Recommendations (Cont.)

- No excess funds should be invested in marketable securities at this point (1998 and 1999 cash balances are only 1.6% of sales)
- Do not use retained earnings and cash reserves to pay off all short-term debt.

Slide 9

Garden State Solutions

- Increase product lines.
- Increase geographic market.
- Expand target market (other industries).
- Employ JIT inventory system (improve management of inventory).

Slide 10

A FINAL WORD

Public speaking may always fill you with some apprehension. With practice, however, you will become much more sure of yourself and your ability to be an effective oral communicator. For that reason, it's a good idea to take advantage of every opportunity to practice your public speaking. The payoff will be greater professional success.

EXERCISES

Exercise 14–1

Select as a partner for this exercise one of your classmates. Imagine that you have been asked to introduce your classmate before a professional meeting of your peers. Interview your classmate, taking notes as you ask questions. Then review your notes for accuracy and organize them into an outline that you can use for a two- or three-minute introduction.

(Hint: Analyze the interests of your audience as the basis for the questions you ask in your interview.)

After you have completed one interview, you and your partner can switch roles so that you are interviewed for an introduction your partner will make.

Exercise 14–2

Select one of the following topics and prepare a five-minute presentation to give before your class:

- Career opportunities in finance
- Tips for studying finance
- Stereotypes about finance people
- The finance profession in the next decade
- The users of financial information

Exercise 14–3

Prepare an oral presentation of the report you wrote for Chapter 10. Assume the audience for the oral presentation is the same as that for the written report. If necessary, condense the material in the written report, prepare additional visual aids, or make any other changes needed for an effective oral presentation. Reminder: Do not read the report to the audience.

Your presentation should be about 20 minutes long.

Exercise 14–4

The more opportunities you have to speak before a group of people, the more confident you'll be of your abilities. With your instructor's approval, make these informal oral presentations:

1. Introduce the classmate you interviewed for Exercise 14–1.

2. Explain to the class how to work a finance problem that was assigned for homework.

Exercise 14–5

Present to your class the presentation you prepared for Exercise 14–2 or 14–3. After the presentation, ask your classmates and instructor to identify what you did well and to suggest ways you could improve.

Exercise 14–6

Have someone videotape a presentation you make before your class. Then review the tape to identify what you did well and what areas you need to improve.

Exercise 14–7

Learn to be a good listener. When classmates give oral presentations, listen politely and attentively. Then for each speaker, identify

- At least two strengths of the presentation
- Two suggestions for improvement

Write your evaluations on 3×5-inch cards, which you can give to the speakers at the end of class.

NOTES

1. Source: Unpublished student presentation by Chris Comstock and Jeffrey Richards, Webster University, Bolling AFB, Washington DC 1997. Presentation is based on case 36, "Garden State Container Corporation," in *Cases in Financial Mangement* by Eugene F. Brigham and Louis C. Gapenski, The Dryden Press, 1994.

Index

Page numbers set in *italic* represent figures.